Mikhail S. GORBACHEV
An Intimate Biography

By the Editors of TIME Magazine

With an Introduction by Strobe Talbott

Edited by Donald Morrison

A TIME BOOK

Distributed by New American Library

First Edition

Published by Time Incorporated
Time & Life Building
Rockefeller Center
1271 Avenue of the Americas
New York, New York 10020

Cover design: Robert Potter
Text design: H. Roberts
Composition services: Gary Deaton, Editorial Technology Group

Front cover photo: Raisa Gorbachev — Bryn Colton
Mikhail Gorbachev — SUTTON + SUTTON—J & R
Back cover photo: Gostelradio

Printed in the United States of America

10 9 8 7 6 5 4 3 2 1

ISBN Number 0-451-15700
Library of Congress Card Number 88-050093

Contents

Introduction

In the early afternoon of Dec. 8, 1987, Ronald Wilson Reagan stood at a lectern before a crackling fire in the State Dining Room of the White House to welcome Mikhail Sergeyevich Gorbachev to Washington. Television cameras carried the moment live around the nation and the world. In Moscow it was already evening. On Kalinin Prospect, the skyscraper-lined showcase thoroughfare of the Soviet capital, crowds of holiday shoppers were bundled against the sub-zero temperatures and the falling snow. As they made their way toward the Arbat metro station, many of them stopped and stared upward, transfixed by the flickering image of two familiar figures on a mammoth outdoor screen usually used to advertise Soviet films. Loudspeakers carried the voice-over translation as the President of the United States began to speak: "Ralph Waldo Emerson once wrote that there 'is properly no history, only biography.' He meant that it is not enough to talk about history as simply forces and factors."

Coincidentally, Gorbachev's speechwriters had found another Emerson quote for the occasion: "The reward of a thing well done is to have done it." The joint invocation of a 19th century transcendentalist thinker to set the tone for the state visit of a 20th—perhaps 21st—century Marxist to Washington was just another of the day's many incongruities. Here was one of the most striking odd couples of all time. The American host was a septuagenarian movie actor turned politician, an old-fashioned anti-Communist famous for denouncing the Soviet Union as an "evil empire" ruled by men who "reserve unto themselves the right to commit any crime, to lie, to cheat." Yet now the hammer-and-sickle flag of the U.S.S.R. was snapping in the breeze beside the Stars and Stripes along Pennsylvania Avenue. Standing next to Reagan, radiating confidence and youthful vigor, was a child of the Stalin era, an apparatchik turned reformer. (And nearby in the White House was Raisa Gorbachev, who—for a Soviet leader's wife—was uncommonly attractive and well informed.) Gorbachev had come to talk arms control with Reagan, but he ended up challenging the President for the world title of Great Communicator. The two men agreed at the outset of this, their third meeting, not only to eliminate two entire categories of nuclear weapons but also to call each other "Ron" and "Mikhail." That homey touch was hardly the main point, but it was not beside the point either: what happened was possible because *they* made it happen.

Thus in quoting Emerson's aphorism about the biographical underpinnings of history, Reagan chose a suitable motto for his meeting with Gorbachev that day and for the entire relationship between them—from their first encounter on neutral ground in Geneva two years earlier, to their second one, in Reykjavík, Iceland, a year after that, and most likely through their final meeting, which the two men announced they would hold in Moscow in 1988. Emerson's words might also serve as an epigraph for the pages that follow. Unlike

Reagan, who has been the object of some 200 volumes of political and psychological analysis, Gorbachev has been something of an enigma. Despite the Russian term that he has made a household word in the West, *glasnost* (openness), his own life has remained largely a closed book. Attempts to pry it open have inevitably been only partially successful. Recent volumes on Gorbachev, while often interesting and insightful, have tended more toward examinations of the Soviet political and social system than comprehensive accounts of Gorbachev's life.*

A major reason for that biographical imbalance is that Gorbachev emerged from almost total obscurity to power and prominence with relative suddenness, leaving little trail for Kremlinologists to follow. Not much about his origins, his early career and his private life has been published in the Soviet Union, and he has shied away from personal revelations in interviews and writings. He wants to avoid creating another "cult of personality," the euphemism for glorification of an all powerful leader. That phenomenon reached ridiculous heights under Joseph Stalin in Gorbachev's youth. Nikita Khrushchev was charged with excessive immodesty when he was overthrown in 1964, and similar accusations have been leveled at the late Leonid Brezhnev, presumably at Gorbachev's behest. Therefore, Gorbachev has reacted to incipient hagiography in the Soviet press by being protective of his private life. Subordinates take their cue from the boss. A high official mentioned to a group of my colleagues recently that he had known the General Secretary as a university student. "What was Gorbachev like in those days," the man was asked. He paused re-

---

*Books about Gorbachev include: Thomas Butson, *Mikhail Gorbachev*, Chelsea House, 1986; Mark Frankland, *The Sixth Continent: Mikhail Gorbachev and the Soviet Union*, Harper & Row, 1987; Marshall Goldman, *Gorbachev's Challenge*, Norton, 1987; Zhores A. Medvedev, *Gorbachev*, Norton, 1986; Richard Owen, *Comrade Chairman: Soviet Succession and the Rise of Gorbachev*, Arbor House, 1987; Christian Schmidt-Hauer, *Gorbachev: the Path to Power*, Salem House Publications, 1986; George Sullivan, *Mikhail Gorbachev*, Messner, 1988; Ilya Zmetsov, *Gorbachev: Between Past and Future*, Hero Books, 1987.

flectively, smiled and said, "I don't remember."

Gorbachev's official biography, which is not much more than a recitation of offices held and honors received, lacks even the most rudimentary personal information. For instance, it is not known for certain whether he has any siblings. Some Soviets say he has a brother who works in agriculture, but no one seems to know the man's name or age. Reports of a sister cannot be confirmed.

From a variety of sources, however, TIME has managed to fill in the blank spots in Gorbachev's story. The magazine's correspondents in the Soviet Union and beyond interviewed dozens of the General Secretary's colleagues, onetime school-mates, the handful of foreigners he has known and others who have encountered the former Stavropol farm boy on his journey to the Kremlin. Though my colleagues and I have been collecting information on Gorbachev for years, the project began in earnest in the autumn of 1987, when we started considering candidates for TIME's Man of the Year. Since 1927 that annual designation has gone to the newsmaker who has most influenced the year's events, for good or ill. Given Gorbachev's considerable accomplishments on the domestic and international fronts that year, the final choice was not difficult. What made Gorbachev a truly intriguing Man of the Year was that, despite his position as leader of one of the world's two most powerful countries, so little was known about him. Undeterred, we cast our net wide and came up with a prodigious amount of previously unpublished information, as well as the most comprehensive collection of official and family photographs of Gorbachev ever to appear in one place. After our 1987 Man of the Year issue appeared, however, we—and many readers—were still hungry to know more about him. So we cast our net wider still, went back to our sources and came up with even more facts and photos. The result is *Mikhail Gorbachev: An Intimate Biography,* which we believe to be the most detailed volume yet published about this extraordinary

Soviet leader.

The book is a first for TIME. For more than six decades the magazine's editors, writers, researchers and correspondents have concentrated their energies on putting out the weekly edition. Never before had TIME's research, reportorial and pictorial resources been focused on a book. The experience was instructive, satisfying and, we believe, successful. In the proper Emersonian spirit, we hope this volume restores some biographical parity to the superpower relationship.

Gorbachev was first mentioned in TIME in a short December 1979 World section article noting that this "relatively young unknown" Central Committee Secretary, then 48, had the combination of good luck, political dexterity and high-level protection to escape blame for that year's disastrous harvest. By 1983, when he was only slightly better known outside his country, U.S.-Soviet relations were heading into the most severe decline in two decades. That was the year a George Lucas science-fiction saga made it to the marquee of American foreign policy. In March 1983, Reagan delivered his "evil empire" speech to an audience of Christian Evangelicals in Florida and, two weeks later, unveiled "Star Wars," the Strategic Defense Initiative. The purpose of SDI, said the President, was to render nuclear weapons "impotent and obsolete." No one had any doubt whose weapons he had in mind.

That September the world was reminded that the Soviet Union had extensive, though less exotic strategic defenses of its own—and that they were on murderously hair-trigger alert. A Sukhoi-15 jet fighter attached to the Far East Air Defense Command shot down an off-course Korean airliner with 269 people on board. The same month, the Politburo released a statement in the name of General Secretary Yuri Andropov that seemed to write off the possibility of further business with the Reagan Administration. Meanwhile, a high-noon showdown was in progress over the prospective deployment of American intermediate-range missiles in Europe. By late November the weapons had arrived on schedule, and within days Soviet diplomats staged a walkout from arms-control negotiations in Geneva. But, in an era of nuclear weaponry, they could not turn and fire. They and their nations were doomed to what Khrushchev had called peaceful coexistence and Richard Nixon and Henry Kissinger had referred to as détente. A permanent state of cold war was impossible to sustain politically, just as a hot war would be militarily suicidal.

But the restoration of a degree of civility and constructive engagement required, on both sides, firm hands in the conduct of government and diplomacy. That crucial ingredient was missing on the Soviet side through much of 1983 and '84. The Kremlin leadership was, both literally and figuratively, on artificial life-support systems. Andropov was officially said to be suffering from a "cold," then a "severe cold." In fact he was dying of kidney disease. But the ruling élite of the Soviet Union has never been able to deal administratively with the encroachments of Comrade Death. No amount of warning and contingency planning can make the inevitable seem routine when the figure in declining health is the supreme leader. So it was with Lenin, Stalin and Brezhnev. In the Soviet Union, leadership transitions are, by definition, leadership crises. The most thoroughly managed of societies and political systems has never been able to manage successions in a way that avoids conveying a sense of potential upheaval both to the Soviet people and to the world. Top leaders never retire with honor. They either die on the job (as Lenin, Stalin and Brezhnev did), or they are thrown out and end up as pensioners and unpersons (as Khrushchev and his predecessor Georgi Malenkov did). Soviet leaders are unable to cope with the political implications of their own aging, infirmity and mortality for a reason that is simple and damning enough: since the 1917 Revolution, theirs has been a system based on the seizure, accumulation and consolidation of power; the Soviet state has no built-in mechanisms for the sharing or transferring of authority beyond the inner circle.

The conservative old men who ran the Soviet Union operated by two sets of rules—those they made by and for themselves, and those that were established and enforced by human mortality. With Andropov on his deathbed at the end of 1983, his comrades, who were mostly old and in many cases feeble men, found themselves in a dilemma that underscored both the irony of the Soviet Union's youthfulness as a state and the falsity of its claims to represent the wave of the future. The safe choice would be for the Old Guard to pick someone from its own ranks, perpetuating the gerontocracy and protecting its power, even though that would mean going through the same trauma again, sooner rather than later. Choosing a younger successor would carry a higher degree of uncertainty, of unpredictability. Ostensibly the custodians of a revolutionary tradition, Soviet leaders have tended to be among the most conservative politicians on earth. They hate uncertainty and unpredictability. For them to yield to the next generation might reinvigorate the leadership, but it would just as surely hasten their own political demise.

When Andropov died in February 1984, some handicappers in the West were betting that Gorbachev had a good shot at succeeding him. A few, however, put their money on Konstantin Chernenko—and, of course, won. But the old men in the Kremlin had bet against the actuarial tables—and, once again, lost. Chernenko, a decrepit Brezhnev yes-man, died of a heart attack in March 1985. Andropov had lasted 15 months, Chernenko only 13.

The Politburo now found itself suffering a morbid embarrassment. Red Square was turning into a giant funeral parlor. Radio Moscow found it could not play slow music by Tchaikovsky for fear of sparking rumors that another somber announcement was imminent. If there is anything that the rulers of the Soviet Union hate more than unpredictability and uncertainty, it is the knowledge that they are the object of scorn, that they are considered weak and fading. So this time the old men swallowed hard and looked to their junior member. Now they were betting on Gorbachev as someone who could instill pride and energy at home and compete effectively with Ronald Reagan for the hearts and minds of international public opinion.

Nominating Gorbachev in a speech to the Central Committee, the notoriously dour Foreign Minister, Andrei Gromyko, delivered an unusual and highly revealing endorsement: "This man has a nice smile, but he has teeth of iron." Gorbachev was 54. At last, the Soviet Union had a leader younger than itself. If he lived as long as Brezhnev, he would still be in charge in the year 2006. But was he destined to be remembered for his smile or for his teeth?

Gorbachev's appearance on the front pages of the world the following week spawned a joke in Moscow. Mikhail Sergeyevich, it was said, had not known he had a port-wine birthmark on his forehead until he saw his picture in the papers. Why? Because in all his photographs in the Soviet press, the blemish had been airbrushed out.

Gorbachev wasted no time in setting a tone of can-do urgency. He declared a crackdown on alcoholism. As if to underscore the contrast with his aged and often invisible predecessors, he traveled widely, exchanging his trilby for a hard hat to inspect factories, and showing off his stylish and outspoken wife Raisa abroad. He moved quickly to consolidate his personal power. His principal competitor for the top job, Leningrad Boss Grigori Romanov, suffered the double indignity of sudden retirement and, it was widely rumored, commitment to a treatment center for alcoholics. Remarkably soon there was talk of a Gorbachev era. It was premature, but it conveyed the sense among citizens and observers of the Soviet Union that he was more than just the supreme leader of a vast, heavily armed country: he also represented the potential for dramatic change.

In domestic policy, Gorbachev made preliminary moves toward streamlining the bloated bureaucracy and eradicating corruption. Some of his own aides said that he was "radicalized" by the inertia he encountered and the frustration he experienced. He wanted to transform the country from a musclebound but backward empire into a modern state able to hold its own in the global marketplace of goods and ideas. The U.S.S.R., said Gorbachev, must become a "real superpower." Implicit in that phrase was a stunning confession: take away its 3.7 million men under arms and its 25,000-odd nuclear weapons and the Soviet Union would be a Third World country. There would be no Second World. A note of alarm, even shame, and a growing tone of restlessness could be detected in the way he talked about the society and economy over which he presided. A new specter haunted the land of Marx and Lenin, the specter of apostasy imposed from above. Gorbachev began to speak not just of reform but of revolution, quoting Lenin's definition of a revolutionary situation as one in which the people on top are unable—and the people below are unwilling—to continue in the old ways. This was tough talk, exhilarating to those who shared Gorbachev's aspirations and impatience, frightening to those millions with a vested interest in the status quo. On the eve of his second summit meeting with Reagan, at Reykjavík in October 1986, a number of sophisticated Central Committee spokesmen and court intellectuals conducted a press conference at which they said that the Gorbachev reforms faced "resistance at all levels"—including, presumably, at the highest level, the Politburo. The performance was interpreted as a veiled but still stunning appeal to liberal Western opinion makers to help Gorbachev and his allies at home win the day against his own conservative opponents.

In foreign policy, Gorbachev knew that the Soviet Union needed a respite—a *peredyshka,* or breathing spell—from all-out competition with the West. He sought a relaxation of tensions (the dictionary definition of détente) so that he could devote energy and resources to his domestic reforms. That was why he was so determined to engage Ronald Reagan, the most anti-Soviet of American Presidents, in personal diplomacy. Gorbachev needed to persuade international public opinion that he was one of history's good guys.

He did this partly in the way he turned his attention to the critical area of Soviet-American arms control, stagnated since the collapse of talks in late 1983. The Soviet Union had neither the diplomatic nor the military means to counter the continuing American missile deployments in Western Europe. Immediately on assuming command, Gorbachev ordered that the ministries of Foreign Affairs and Defense, as well as the General Staff of the armed forces, give him an explanation of how the impasse had arisen. The request was an implicit criticism of his predecessors and many of his subordinates. Both in standing up to his Western foes in the military competition and sitting down with them at the negotiating table, Gorbachev was determined to put a new premium on ingenuity and agility. The Soviet Union had developed a reputation for saying *nyet* automatically, stubbornly and counterproductively. The Americans had grown used to a Soviet adversary who seemed most comfortable sitting on a block of ice, scowling and shaking his head in response to U.S. initiatives. Gorbachev began to experiment with the diplomacy of *da*.

American experts had often said that their side came to the table as though arms control were poker, with the U.S. as the dealer, while the Soviet Union played it as plodding, defensive chess, from the black side of the board. Gorbachev changed all that. He showed an ability to combine the tactics of the two games in a way that was sometimes masterly, sometimes maddening, sometimes both. The Kremlin started making diplomatic and arms-control proposals faster than the Reagan Administration could reject them. In terms of poker,

Gorbachev shuffled the deck, dealt himself new cards, upped the ante, bluffed and called. In terms of chess, he played white, and he did so with the aggressive, unorthodox, intuitive style of the new Soviet champion, Gary Kasparov.

In the area of intermediate-range nuclear forces (INF), Gorbachev dodged and weaved his way toward eventual acceptance of the so-called zero option—the elimination of an entire class of Soviet missiles in exchange for the withdrawal and destruction of the American missiles that had been deployed in Europe since 1983. Reagan had originally proposed the zero option in 1981 and congratulated himself when it formed the centerpiece of the Washington summit in December 1987. But Gorbachev could claim vindication too. It was a long-standing imperative of Soviet foreign and defense policy to prevent NATO from having land-based ballistic missiles around the periphery of the U.S.S.R. Gorbachev's predecessors had allowed U.S. missiles to arrive in Europe; he got them out.

He showed similar adroitness and persistence in strategic arms control. The Soviet goal was to use the prospect of deep reductions in offensive weaponry as an inducement for the U.S. to accept restrictions on SDI. When Gorbachev came into office, he inherited a demand that the U.S. cancel Star Wars in its entirety, including research. That position was unreasonable and non-negotiable, a classic example of old thinking and old methods. Many American scientists and military experts were skeptical about the technical feasibility of the President's dream of a comprehensive, impregnable, space-based shield against ballistic missiles. Yet most of them also felt that the U.S. must continue to experiment with defensive technologies in case SDI worked, in case there were indeed a god that might be released from the machine to lessen if not eradicate the reliance on mutual assured destruction as the basis of deterrence. Gorbachev used the occasion of an August 1985 interview in TIME to signal an important shift in the Soviet position on Star

Wars. "Research in fundamental science ... concerning space," he said, "is going on, and it will continue." It was a tacit acknowledgment that an eventual strategic arms-control deal must permit some research and development on SDI—and a tacit admission that there was a similar program on the Soviet side.

The editors and correspondents who conducted that two-hour session with the General Secretary were struck by his commanding presence, his ability to convey both toughness and likability, authority and alertness. He surprised them too with a penchant for religious turns of phrase, such as "Surely God on high has not refused to give us enough wisdom to find ways to bring us an improvement" in relations. The reference was apparently surprising to Soviet editors as well. In reprinting the interview, they secularized the sentence by substituting "history" for "God." Less than a year later, in July 1986, Gorbachev put on a similar bravura performance for another American visitor, Richard Nixon. In a confidential memorandum to Reagan, the former President offered this assessment of Gorbachev: "Unlike Khrushchev, he has no inferiority complex. He is totally confident, in command, and secure. Gorbachev is as tough as Brezhnev but better educated, more skillful, more subtle ... Brezhnev used a meat-ax in his negotiations. Gorbachev uses a stiletto. But beneath the velvet glove he always wears there is a steel fist."

All these attributes were much in evidence three months later, in October 1986, when the Soviet leader met Reagan in Reykjavík. Demonstrating boldness and dexterity that were stunning even by his own standards, Gorbachev surprised the American delegation by bringing a proposal for the so-called grand compromise in arms control—the zero option in INF, deep cuts in offensive strategic missiles and confinement of Star Wars to laboratory research. During a weekend of whirlwind negotiating, considerable progress was made on offensive arms, but a final deal fell apart over what Reagan said was Gorbachev's effort to "kill" SDI. Almost immediately, Gorbachev began adjusting his position on SDI further. He was advised that the Soviet side could soften its demands without jeopardizing its goals and interests. That advice came from Soviet scientists, whom Gorbachev, more than any of his predecessors, has included in his inner circle, and from sophisticated political experts, such as Anatoli Dobrynin, the longtime Ambassador to Washington whom Gorbachev put in charge of foreign policy for the Central Committee. Those experts could see that a skeptical, cost-conscious U.S. Congress was likely to impose enough limits on SDI to satisfy Soviet requirements.

Meanwhile, Gorbachev has proved himself a master of low-risk, high-payoff gestures, doing things that in other societies would be considered only normal and civilized. He let the Nobel Peace Prize–winning physicist Andrei Sakharov return to Moscow from internal exile, earning cautious, qualified support of many dissident intellectuals, including Sakharov himself. Gorbachev talked about the dangers of the nuclear and geopolitical competition, about the need for "sufficiency" rather than superiority, and the importance of "interdependence" and "mutual security." This last phrase was pitched to resonate pleasingly in the ears of the West. Traditionally, the Soviet Union has in effect defined its security at the expense of other nations'. Soviet leaders have made clear, by their actions and often by their words as well, that they would not feel entirely secure until everyone else on earth felt entirely insecure. Whether the men in the Kremlin were paranoiacs or expansionists—whether their international behavior was driven by fear or by a master plan for world conquest—was almost beside the point. The effect was the same. There was nothing more offensive than a Russian bear on the defensive. Along came Gorbachev, talking a very different game. In keeping with his insistence that "new thinking" should animate Soviet policy, he stood on its head the country's traditional definition of security. He said that the Soviet Union could not be truly secure unless other nations, notably including the U.S., also felt secure. He explained that in an era of nuclear overkill, when peace depends on a stable balance of terror, it is crucial for each superpower to avoid military deployments that seem intended to make its adversary's deterrent vulnerable to a preemptive first strike.

This reassuring rhetoric was intriguingly—or, skeptics would say, suspiciously—similar to what liberal Western strategists had accepted as conventional wisdom for decades. In part for that reason, Gorbachev's "new thinking" was an immensely successful public relations theme. In the spring and summer of 1987, some European opinion polls found that the man in the Kremlin was more popular than the one in the White House.

Gorbachev even managed to work his way into the American presidential campaign of 1988—not as the Dark Lord of the Evil Empire but as a kind of Communist Kennedy figure, someone whom the Americans had better be able to match. In varying degrees and ways, all the Democratic contenders tried to work the Gorbachev challenge into their campaigns. Stumping through the South, where he hoped to emerge as a regional favorite son, Senator Albert Gore Jr. of Tennessee kept saying, "We need a new, vigorous generation of leadership in this country to deal with the new, vigorous leader in the Kremlin. I'm the one who can deal with Gorbachev—who can stand up to him where that is necessary, who can sit down with him when that is possible, who can test the sincerity of his intentions where they suit our interests."

The Gorbachev phenomenon even contributed to the single most bizarre development of the year in American politics: Gary Hart's pre-Christmas surprise announcement that he was putting monkey business behind him and re-entering the presidential race. Hart was still brooding over a televised debate on Dec. 1 among the other candidates when Gorbachev came to Washington a week later. According to an aide, Hart concluded that the other aspirants just weren't up to the job. "I can lead this country," the candidate said. "I can deal with this man. I have to try."

During the late summer and fall of 1987, Gorbachev became an object of mystery and concern. The resistance he and his partisans had often talked about seemed to turn active. In August, for reasons that were never entirely explained, he delayed his departure to southern Russia for his vacation, then failed to return to Moscow on schedule. There were rumors and Kremlinological auguries that his opponents were moving against him. Comrades on the Politburo, known to be skeptical about Gorbachev's reforms, seemed suddenly emboldened. Newspapers and journals that were associated with some of Gorbachev's rivals suddenly put their own gloss on *glasnost*— they grumbled with cautions and criticisms that seemed directed against Gorbachev's policies and slogans, including *glasnost* itself. Stories circulated first in Moscow, then in the West, to the effect that Gorbachev faced a major backlash. Some versions included intriguing details about how he had received delegations of worried well-wishers who urged him, for his own sake and that of his program, to go slow. The tales could not be confirmed, but some were not authoritatively denied either. The General Secretary was away from Moscow for 52 days. He was officially said to be taking some extra time to finish his book, *Perestroika*, published in the fall of 1987 by Harper and Row. But the signs of trouble continued after he returned to Moscow. The 70th anniversary celebration of the Bolshevik Revolution was approaching in early November. Gorbachev and his supporters let it be known in advance that they wanted to use the occasion to accelerate the reforms, setting ambitious goals for the future and facing up to some of the uglier truths of the Stalinist past.

But Gorbachev apparently suffered a significant setback at a Central Committee meeting in October. Ironically, the precipitating event was a speech by Boris Yeltsin, the Moscow party chief, who was among the most vigorous of Gorbachev's allies. For example, it was Yeltsin who had, over the objections of more orthodox custodians and policemen of culture, permitted unofficial, dissident, even religious artists to display and sell their works at an outdoor market every weekend. At the Central Committee meeting in October, Yeltsin delivered an impassioned attack on opponents of reform, including Yegor Ligachev, presumed to be the No. 2 man in the leadership and the chief skeptic about the pace of Gorbachev's reform.

The outburst was deeply embarrassing to Gorbachev. He ended up delivering an anniversary speech that was less sweeping in its condemnation of the past and less visionary about the future than many had expected. Gorbachev quickly demonstrated his political deftness—and his toughness. He sacrificed Yeltsin virtually on the spot, denouncing him as a hothead who had violated the "norms" of party behavior. In the wake of the uproar, Gorbachev managed to appear, at least for the time being, as a moderate, resisting pressure from two camps: the "conservatives" who opposed his reforms and the "adventurists" like Yeltsin who wanted to go too far too fast. Yeltsin was briefly hospitalized and then demoted—although, perhaps significantly, not purged altogether.

In the midst of this crisis, on Oct. 23, George Shultz arrived in Moscow to set a date for Gorbachev's visit to Washington. The Soviet leader was preoccupied by his troubles within the Politburo and possibly worried about what moves his comrades might be planning next. In addition, the U.S. was still reeling from Black Monday, the selling panic that had hit world stock markets only four days earlier. Gorbachev's foreign policy advisers reportedly told him he might be able to up the ante for a summit, exploiting Reagan's own presumed political vulnerabilities in the wake of the crash. Indeed, Gorbachev told Shultz he wanted more American concessions on the Strategic Defense Initiative before he would come to Washington. The Reagan Administration hung tough, and once again Gorbachev adjusted quickly, agreeing to the summit after all.

Gorbachev's status as a media hero and popular celebrity was confirmed during the Washington summit. Traveling between the White House and the Soviet embassy, he stopped his motorcade at the corner of Connecticut Avenue and L Street. No one was more astonished than the bodyguards from the Secret Service. They did their best to make their horror look like vigilance as Gorbachev leaped from his limousine and waded into the crowd. "Keep your hands out of your pockets!" they barked at the surprised and delighted pedestrians. There was no need for the order. All hands were outstretched to touch the General Secretary as he exuded good will, guaranteeing himself an extra few minutes of the best possible exposure on both local and national TV news.

A local radio station dedicated a forecast of unseasonably mild and sunny weather, followed by Paul Simon's upbeat *Graceland,* to "our Russian friends." My son's second-grade classmates at the Maret School in northwest Washington brought home what were intended to be flattering drawings, birthmark and all, of the man from Moscow. At a number of shops and sidewalk stalls downtown, T shirts proclaiming GORBACHEV TOUR '87 outsold Washington Redskins paraphernalia. That would be extraordinary enough by itself, since the federal city is chronically delirious about its home team and generally jaded about big-shot foreign visitors. Moreover, the Redskins had just clinched a spot in the National Football League playoffs in January. Yet for a few days at least, the 'Skins had to yield pride of place at the souvenir stands to a Communist leader who, as President Reagan later noted, probably did not even know who Joe DiMaggio was, not to mention Wide Receiver Ricky Sanders or Defensive Tackle Dave Butz. Yet Gorbachev, who was nothing if not a quick study, found out exactly who Joe DiMaggio was when his name showed up on the guest list for the White House state dinner, and he cheerfully agreed to autograph a baseball for the New York Yankees star. It was yet another gesture by the visitor sure to please the home-team crowd.

Evidence of the impact lingered after Gorbachev left town. One postsummit poll, conducted by *U.S. News & World Report*, showed that those Americans surveyed still considered their President more "committed to freedom," but that they perceived the General Secretary to be smarter. Throughout Western Europe, the Washington summit only solidified Gorbachev's standing. In Great Britain the Sunday *Telegraph* and the Gallup organization found him No. 1 on the most admired list, ahead of Bob Geldof, the Irish rock singer and antihunger campaigner, and Terry Waite, the Church of England negotiator held hostage in Lebanon. President Reagan did not even make the list. Sensing the trend, a pair of San Francisco businessmen quickly launched their own version of *perestroika* (restructuring). They had lost money trying to cash in on the sudden burst of Olliemania earlier in the year with 1-ft.-tall likenesses of Lieut. Colonel North, so they quickly converted their remaining inventory to Gorby dolls by replacing the heads and adding some padding. And they replaced the Marine uniform not with the baggy pants and ill-fitting jacket that used to be the trademark of commissars but with a stylishly tailored business suit in keeping with the new look of Soviet officials.

The hoopla was not music to all ears. Commentators warned that treating Gorbachev as a celebrity was fraught with many dangers—of unrealistic expectations, of inevitable disillusionment, of self-delusion, of deceit and perhaps treachery from this sweet-smiling, steel-toothed flimflam man and his entourage of sharpies. Stephen Sestanovich, a former Administration Kremlinologist, diagnosed this latest strain of Potomac fever as "glasnostalgia," and some disgruntled conservatives warned that the capital was going through an unseemly bout of "Gorbasms."

Yet behind Gorbachev's appealing façade was an even more appealing idea. He was not just a new kind of Soviet leader; he seemed to want to preside over a new kind of Soviet Union. Of that there was little question. But there was a very big question indeed about a) what exactly he wanted to do, b) whether he would succeed, and c) whether freethinking citizens of the world, both within the U.S.S.R. and abroad, should wish him success. Did he simply want to make the Soviet Union more efficient as a totalitarian state and therefore more formidable as an enemy of democratic values and Western interests? Or did he, in some sense, want to establish a more humane relationship between the regime and the individual, thus laying the basis for the evolution of the Soviet Union into a nation-state with which other countries would find it easier to share the planet?

There was reason to wish him well. The essence of Gorbachev's economic reforms is decentralization—less planning and direction from the top down, more responsibility for local authorities and the managers of enterprises. Karl Marx himself taught that economic relations are the basis of political ones. Economic decentralization would almost certainly be accompanied by a measure of political decentralization, and that in turn could mean a loosening of the totalitarian grip of the state on the life of the individual. Americans have always objected to the oppressive, often repressive relationship between the state and the individual in the U.S.S.R. Beyond geopolitics and conflicting great-power interests, the bottom line of U.S.-Soviet hostility is ideological. In Gorbachev, the Soviet Union suddenly had a leader who seemed bent on at least tinkering with ideology and its application in real life in a way that could, over time, ameliorate what has always been most offensive about the other superpower.

There was also reason for concern and show-me skepticism—about Gorbachev's own intentions, about the willingness of his comrades to let him have his way, and about the responsiveness of the system to reform in general, particularly to the paradox of decentralization ordered by the central authorities. Gorbachev's televised farewell press conference in Washington after the December 1987 summit offered a sobering glimpse into his management style back home. For the millions of Americans watching, it was like having a guest pass to a Moscow party meeting, and it was not a pretty sight. He harangued his audience of journalists, exuding smugness and arrogance. It was a reminder that for all the new look and new talk and even new thinking, this was still very much a Soviet politician, not a Jeffersonian democrat. He protested too much against what he tried to dismiss as the morbid and mischievous interest of the Western press in Kremlin machinations. The more he denied that he faced meaningful opposition, the more apparent it was that he did.

Domestic opposition should be expected. More often than not, the legacy of Russian and Soviet reformers has been reaction. Thaws have turned to chills. The substance of Gorbachev's rhetoric remains to be tested—in Afghanistan, Nicaragua, the Persian Gulf, Southeast Asia and Europe. His enlightened (yet highly derivative) thoughts on sufficiency and mutual security still need to be translated into arms-control agreements that will strengthen the nuclear peace. Gromyko used to say there is a big difference between words and deeds. Yet in a country where one can still be sent to the Gulag for saying the wrong thing, words *are* deeds. In a closed, hidebound dictatorship, Gorbachev's slogans of openness, restructuring, democratization, new thinking and mutual security are either particularly cynical or stunningly significant.

They could also be inflammatory close to home. Gorbachev's popularity in Eastern Europe seems already to be backfiring against the satellite regimes in the region, and therefore against Soviet control. The year 1987 saw Gorbachev become a popular hero in Czechoslovakia. Waving his picture became a way for citizens of that sad and defeated country to express their resentment against the regime that the Soviet Union itself had imposed with tanks in 1968. One of the most extraordinary images of 1987 came in June at the Berlin Wall. A group of East German youths had gathered in hopes of hearing a rock concert on the other side, when armed police moved in. The youths took up a chant: "Gorbachev! Gorbachev!" In effect, they were invoking his new thinking to mitigate the brutality of the old order. The tactic did not work. The police cracked heads and dispersed the crowd. The moment did not augur well, either, for the more free-spirited citizens of the Soviet bloc or for Gorbachev himself. It demonstrated that, too often, Soviet power still comes from the barrel of a gun or the business end of a truncheon.

Marxists have long relished pointing out the "contradictions" in other political systems. Now Gorbachev was forcing them to face up to some excruciating contradictions in their own. Whether, and how, he can resolve them is one of the most important questions of the decade, perhaps even of the era. And, for the Soviet Union, it may indeed turn out to be the Gorbachev era. For the answers to those questions, we obviously have to wait. But as we wait, and watch, and formulate our own new thinking for dealing with this new man in the Kremlin, there has been another question that might—with hard digging—yield some more immediate answers: Who is he? Where did he come from? What were the biographical roots of his determination to make history? Those were the queries we posed, and tried to answer, in our Man of the Year cover story. Those are also the questions that we are trying to answer at greater length, in greater depth and, we hope, with similar success in this book.

—Strobe Talbott

1

Growing Up

The village of Privolnoye is spread out amid gently rolling steppe lands in the Stavropol territory of southern Russia. Today it is a hardworking agricultural settlement with a population of about 3,000, the center of the Sverdlov collective farm in Krasnogvardeisky district. The homesteads are scattered on rich farmland that stretches as far as the eye can see. In the foreshortened days of late fall, the scene is a patchwork of mellow colors: undulating strips of thick black earth, fallow meadows of parched brown grass, and fields that are splotched with the emerald green shoots of winter wheat. The winters are hard, though not so brutal as in other parts of the Russian republic, and by March the winds are starting to carry warm hints of new beginnings to Privolnoye. In this quiet, pleasantly pastoral hamlet, Mikhail Gorbachev was born on March 2, 1931.

By Soviet standards, Privolnoye today is "modern." There are no quaint streets of gingerbread houses, no onion-domed churches with the winter sun flashing off the gold. A row of shops, a new supermarket and a columned palace of culture surround that quintessentially Soviet emblem of the sacred: a war memorial with its eternal flame and inscribed stone slabs. Among the names are seven Gorbachevs, relatives of the Soviet leader. The Gorbachev family home is located on a side street a short distance from the center of the village. Foreigners and reporters have so far been kept scrupulously away from the dwelling, perhaps as much to discourage a Gorbachev personality cult as to preserve the Soviet tradition of obsessive secrecy about the personal origins of the country's leaders. The house is a one-story brick structure, indistinguishable from its neighbors, with three rooms and a small kitchen. A well-kept garden plot surrounds the house, which is set back and fenced off from the road. Gorbachev's mother Maria Panteleyevna, in her late 70s, was still living there in 1988 on her pension of 36 rubles ($60) a month, tending her private plot, keeping chickens and a cow.

The appearance of long-settled tranquillity in this part of the Soviet Union's wheat granary is deceiving. The village was settled only in the late 18th century, when the growing Russian empire began to push south into the Caucasus. For most of Russian history, the area between the Black and Caspian Seas was the domain of diverse and often warring ethnic groups, none of them owing any allegiance to the Czar in Moscow or St. Petersburg. Under Catherine the Great (1762-1796), the growing military power of Russia was directed against both the Ottoman Turks in the Crimea and the warlike Muslim tribes of the Caucasus region. The city of Stavropol, from which Stavropol Krai takes its name, was established in 1777 by Catherine's favorite village builder, Grigori Potemkin. During a stately tour of newly conquered territories in southern Russia organized by Potemkin, squalid, or even nonexistent villages were made to appear as attractive settlements by placing painted façades of them along Catherine's route—hence the term "Potemkin village."

Stavropol, which means "city of the cross" in Greek, was from the beginning intended by Catherine to be a fortress of Russian power opposed to the Ottomans and an outpost of the Christian faith established in an area previously dominated by Islam. Today the territory comprises about 3 million people in a smorgasbord of dozens of separate ethnic and national groups, ranging from the numerically dominant Russians to Ukrainians, Jews, Byelorussians and tough mountain tribes like the Ossetians and the Kabardians. Though Stavropol is located in the southernmost part of the Russian Socialist Federated Soviet Republic, one of the 15 constituent republics of the Soviet Union, it is considered a *krai* (territory) rather than the more common administrative term *oblast* (region) because the Karachay-Cherkess autonomous region is located within its boundaries. Sensitive to preserve at least the appearances of respect for ethnic minorities, the Soviets have demonstrated a generally consistent policy, where possible, of incorporating distinct ethnic groups within their own recognizable administrative boundaries. Still, in the Caucasus region, national and ethnic tensions have always been latent, and they burst out in force during the brief Nazi occupation of the area in World War II.

For ethnic Russians, though, the territory has in the past had something of the frontier connotations instinctively evoked in the minds of foreigners when they think about the American West. The Caucasus featured prominently in the writings of 19th century Russian romantic writers. More important, the fabulous riches of the region's ebony black soil drew wave after wave of Russian immigrants from the Don and Volga regions and from the more populous areas of European and central Russia. The Russian peasants who began to settle there from the late 18th century onward were different from their compatriots in the rest of the country: they were not serfs. The early groups of cossacks moving south were joined in the second half of the 19th century by another wave of immigrants, Russian peasants who had been freed from the estates of the nobility by the Emancipation Act of 1861 (by a remarkable historical coincidence, only two years before the emancipation of slaves in the U.S.). Privolnoye, in fact, means "free," the very name being an acknowledgment of the difference between Gorbachev's ancestors and the land-bound serfs who populated the great estates in the rest of the country.

Gorbachev's forebears were from this enterprising yeoman stock of Russian peasants who were prepared to take their chances on the rich soil, with the ever-present danger of drought. Privolnoye is some 100 miles from Stavropol City, near the northwestern border of the territory, and nearly 1,000 miles from Moscow. Gorbachev's grandparents, who had a major role in his upbringing during World War II, were born in the last quarter of the 19th century, after the emancipation of the serfs but before the dramatic czarist-era agrarian reforms introduced by Prime Minister Stolypin in 1906. Those reforms did more to transform the Russian countryside than the emancipation of the serfs had done in 1861, for they legalized independent land ownership by the peasants within village communities, as well as the consolidation of strips of previously communally owned land uneconomically separated from one another. This led to the creation of an independent farming class, some of whose members, through diligence and talent, became successful and wealthy. Before 1914, when World War I broke up for good the economic and social progress of the final years of Czardom, Russian grain production was so bountiful that the country was exporting large quantities of wheat to Western Europe. Encouraging entrepreneurial skills in agriculture, though, produced an inevitable economic shaking out of the countryside as a whole. Some peasants became indigent, while others grew prosperous and influential. The successful ones, forming perhaps 5% of that 96% of the peasantry who were independent small holders, were later branded by Stalin as kulaks (rich peasants) and were the targets of probably the most vicious of Stalin's efforts at revolutionary social engineering in the 1930s.

The Krasnogvardeisky district of Stavropol Krai, in which Privolnoye is located, had a particularly turbulent history in the first quarter of the 20th century. The name, which means "Red Guard," is testimony to the violence of the fighting during the Russian civil war of 1918-1921 that swept over the region. The Red, i.e. Communist, armies and their "white" anti-Bolshevik opponents struggled fiercely for control of the territory, which, with a total land area of 31,000 sq. mi., is approximately the size of South Carolina. Finally, by February 1920, the Red forces had retaken the entire territory.

Little is known of the role of Gorbachev's grandparents in these great events, but by examining their circumstances and the events of the day, it is possible to paint a reasonably complete picture of the world into which Mikhail was born. It is almost certain, for instance, that the Gorbachevs supported the Bolsheviks. Not only was grandfather Andrei a party member, he also took a leading role on the government side in the collectivization of Soviet agriculture in the late 1920s and early 1930s. He was elected chairman of the Khleborob (bread producer) collective farm just before Gorbachev's birth. Gorbachev's father Sergei Andreyevich, born in 1909, was too young to have understood the turmoil of the civil war. But he became a young supporter of the new order of things during Stalin's terrifying assault upon the Russian countryside from 1929 to 1931.

One of the most remarkable aspects of Gorbachev's rise to power is the simple chronological fact that he is the first Soviet leader in seven decades of Communist rule to have been born after the Bolshevik Revolution of 1917. In this respect, he shares a demographic trait with 14 of 15 Soviet citizens alive today. Moreover, the period of Gorbachev's birth was the most brutal and violent period of the entire panorama of the Soviet experience. Before the late 1920s, the Soviet Union seemed poised to move in a number of possible directions. It could have continued the relatively moderate economic and social policies of the period of the New Economic Plan (N.E.P.), inaugurated by Lenin in 1921 basically to pull the country from the brink of total collapse. By the same token, the Soviet Union might have found a modus vivendi between the desire of the Communist Party to extend social experimentation into all aspects of society—including the solidly conservative peasantry—and the reluctance of the country as a whole to be dragooned further into the terra incognita of futuristic social engineering. Conceivably, with proper checks and balances against the assumption of total political power, the Soviet Communist Party might have evolved into something far less intimidating than what it did in fact become.

This window of opportunity had disappeared by the beginning of the 1930s. Once Stalin had launched his country along the course of collectivization, however, and into the party despotism needed to enforce it, the pathway of development for the country was destined for decades to be determined by the possibilities and limits of national coercion. Gorbachev was born at that point when Stalinist terror seemed irreversible. The wrenching decision to collectivize the agriculture of the entire country, made in 1929 and carried on through the early 1930s, forced Soviet society to see itself fundamentally as an extension of the political imagination of an all-powerful individual, Joseph Stalin. When Stalin died, no single successor stepped into his shoes, but the party attempted to appropriate the emblems of Stalin's style of rule: the aura of infallibility, of omniscience and of implacable hostility to criticism or opposition. In some ways, the Soviet Union of today is more the heir to a historical drama acted out at the time of Gorbachev's birth than to the initial seizure of power by the Bolsheviks in 1917.

The watershed of 1929-1931 also changed the international character of the Soviet Union. Through the unprecedented focus of Stalin on investment in heavy industry, the country by the end of the decade of the 1930s emerged as the greatest industrial power in Europe and the second largest, after the U.S., in the world. Industrial output in 1931 was 21% greater than that in the year before, an economic jump probably unmatched by any country since the Industrial Revolution in England in the late 18th century. As Gorbachev himself has asserted, Soviet economic power in 1941 spelled the difference between defeat and survival when Hitler's well-trained armies poured across the country's ill-defended borders. Despite the might of the Nazi military machine, Soviet tank production in 1941 already exceeded that of Nazi Germany. It is doubtful that the Soviets could have withstood the German onslaught in Operation Barbarossa, Hitler's code name for the invasion of the Soviet Union, without the raw industrial might constructed during the previous traumatic decade.

The backdrop to the collectivization drive was a slow buildup of Stalin's hold on the party apparatus. For two years before Gorbachev was born, the first Soviet "show trials" had been under way in Moscow. Stalin, who had plotted to consolidate power in his hands upon Lenin's death in 1924, had ruled until 1927 as part of a shifting and uneasy triumvirate that included Leon Trotsky and Nikolai Bukharin. Seemingly uncertain about his own policy preferences for national development, he successfully played off the left of the party, which wanted rapid and forced collectivization, against the right, which supported a continuation of most aspects of Lenin's N.E.P. But in 1927, there was a major political shift in the Soviet Union. Stalin outmaneuvered his rival, Trotsky, forcing this brilliant but abrasive man into permanent exile. Two years later, he changed tack, manipulating the left of the party to get rid of Bukharin, who, though as committed a Marxist-Leninist as Stalin, represented a far more gradualist approach to economic change in the country.

The political maneuvering was accomplished in an atmosphere of growing domestic witch-hunts, the prototypes of the terrifying tribunals that dominated the Soviet Union during the great purges of 1936-1938. On the day Gorbachev was born, *Pravda* was discussing the latest developments in a series of trials of Mensheviks—Communists who had disagreed with Lenin on revolutionary tactics before and during the October Revolution—for alleged "wrecking and sabotage." As was to be the pattern in almost every one of the show trials of the 1930s, the evidence was either invented or extracted through torture, and in some cases both. In April 1929, at the 16th Congress of the Communist Party, a resolution had been passed calling for a general purge of the party. In the same month, there was a new offensive against the Russian Orthodox Church: hundreds of churches were destroyed and the bells of those that survived were removed so that their ringing "would not disturb the workers." On Stalin's 50th birthday, Dec. 21, sycophantic editorials appeared in the Soviet press, proclaiming, among other things, that Stalin ever since 1917 had been the "great leader" of the entire Soviet people.

In November, Stalin announced that there would be a "second revolution" in the country to finish the major tasks that had not yet been accomplished by the 1917 uprising. Reversing his previous position of opposition to dramatic economic changes in the countryside, Stalin declared that the Soviet Union, having recovered from the ravages of the civil war and the famine that followed, needed a new surge in the direction of socialism. Speaking to a conference on agrarian affairs in December, Stalin declared that the N.E.P., introduced by Lenin in 1921, was over. "What does this mean?" he asked rhetorically. Then he answered: "It means that, after a policy that consisted in limiting the exploitative tendencies of the kulaks, we have switched to a policy of eliminating the kulaks as a class."

Stalin's "new revolution" amounted to an ambitious

five-year plan for industrialization that would be financed by the total collectivization of the Soviet peasantry. That group, sullen and generally anti-Bolshevik, had hitherto been unresponsive to the Stalinist vision of an egalitarian, heavily industrialized society. More strenuously opposed to any proposal for change in rural property relations were the kulaks, who had grown rich in the wake of the Stolypin reforms before World War I. The kulaks constituted a major political obstacle to the total consolidation of Soviet power in the country.

To enforce collectivization across the Soviet Union, between 1929 and 1931, Red Army detachments and frontier troops of the NKVD (the forerunner organization of the KGB), rounded up peasants, expropriated their livestock and herded them into the just formed *kolkhozes* (collective farms). Millions of peasants were arrested and sent to camps, and millions more were shot or starved to death. In innumerable cases, the division between kulaks and ordinary peasants who happened to own livestock was largely fictional: a kulak could be anyone who owned two cows or a nice house. Many other peasants who did not fit the arbitrary economic definition of a kulak were rounded up anyway because they were deemed unsympathetic to what was happening around them. Entire communities were targeted for expropriation and arrest. By 1933 there were 800,000 peasants being held in "places of confinement," meaning transit points, prior to their removal to the camps of the Gulag or to execution. Those in the Gulag already numbered several million.

Many peasants were wiped out in futile efforts to resist the well-equipped NKVD or Red Army units. Millions of others struck against expropriation of their property by slaughtering their livestock rather than permitting it to fall into the hands of the Communists. As a result, food production in the Soviet Union plunged dramatically in the early 1930s. In 1928 there were 33.5 million horses in the Soviet Union. By 1932 the number had dropped to 19.6 million. During the same period, the number of pigs declined from 26 million to 11.6 million, sheep and goats from 146 million to 52.1 million, and cattle from 70.5 million to 40.7 million. Stalin in 1945 reportedly admitted that nearly 10 million kulaks had been "annihilated," though it is not clear precisely what he meant by that. Some Western scholars believe the total number of kulaks killed was much smaller. In any case, it is likely that 5 million to 7 million people died in the man-made famine in southern Russia that followed the collectivization. Living standards throughout the Soviet Union dropped by one-third between 1928 and 1933.

In the northern Caucasus early in 1931, at the time and the place where Gorbachev was born, the slaughter and the mayhem were especially fierce. A total of 86.4% of rural households in the area—which was called the North Caucasus until the early 1930s, when it became known as Stavropol Krai—had been collectivized. The deaths of kulaks and other peasants who resisted the expropriation of their property, their livestock and their produce had already reached the scores of thousands. Prominent Soviet literary supporters of Stalin like the writer Maxim Gorky entered into the spirit of the era. "We are opposed by everything that has outlived the time set for it by history," Gorky wrote in the government newspaper *Izvestia* in November 1930, "and this gives us the right to consider ourselves again in a state of civil war. The conclusion naturally follows that if the enemy does not surrender, he must be destroyed."

But the "enemy," which meant in practice any peasant who disagreed with being collectivized, was not usually given the chance even of surrendering. Stalin had decided on liquidation rather than coercion of the kulaks, so "destroyed" they were. Naturally, some peasants fought back effectively, murdering a small number of Communist Party members and sympathizers whenever they could. But such desperate acts of resistance only sharpened Stalin's appetite for further punitive measures. At a Politburo meeting in Moscow in 1930, General Frinovsky, commander of the frontier forces of the NKVD, reported that the rivers of the northern Caucasus were carrying thousands of bodies to the sea.

Possibly because of the long traditions of peasant freedom in the region, the general resistance and the subsequent slaughter in the territory where Gorbachev was born was especially grim. In October 1932, Stalin created a special commission, presided over by one of his top aides, Politburo Member Lazar Kaganovich, to deal with the unrest in the North Caucasus. Commission members included longtime Political Survivor Anastas Mikoyan, who became Moscow's best-known foreign trade official, Genrickh Yagoda, who was to head the NKVD, and Mikhail Suslov, who went on to be the Kremlin's chief ideologist and, eventually, a Gorbachev mentor.

The Kaganovich commission had extraordinary powers to investigate and arrest peasants, and it showed no mercy to those it suspected of opposition to collectivization. Gorbachev Biographer Zhores Medvedev, a former Soviet citizen with longtime family connections in the Stavropol area, writes, "Almost every family lost relatives, friends, or neighbors during this period, and Privolnoye was no exception . . . In the early 1930s, terror and lawlessness ruled the rural life of the North Caucasus."

The North Caucasus party chief at the time of Gorbachev's birth was Boris Sheboldaev. In November 1932 he was demanding the arrest and deportation of whole villages because of the resistance of only some of the villages' peasants. "The really conscientious individual peasants," Sheboldaev declared, "must answer for the condition of their neighbors." Sheboldaev was himself engulfed in a fresh wave of purges in 1937 and was shot. But that would have been little consolation to scores of thousands of stricken families in the territory. In some villages, because of malnutrition or in the course of raids by the government forces, all the children below two years old died. A Soviet writer, A.B. Kosterin, cited by Medvedev, visited the area around Privolnoye in 1933 and 1934, when Gorbachev was an infant. Everywhere Kosterin traveled he saw houses with boarded-up windows, empty barnyards and abandoned farm equipment in the fields. The mortality of children seemed to be particularly high. "On the deserted road to Stavropol," Kosterin wrote, "I met a peasant with a knapsack. We stopped, greeted each other, had a smoke. I asked him, 'Where are you tramping comrade?' "

"To prison," the man replied. The local constable was unable to accompany him, he explained, so he was escorting himself. Given the famine and repression rampant in the area, prison may not have seemed such a bad alternative.

There is no doubt that Gorbachev, even as a small boy, would have seen and heard many of the terrible things that were taking place in the countryside around him. If he was too young to comprehend fully the events as they occurred, stories of what had happened, quietly related to him later among close friends or family members, would have made it clear. In fact, shortly after Stalin died in 1953, Gorbachev confided to friends at Moscow State University that one of his family's close relatives, a "middle peasant," had been unjustly arrested and, presumably, killed during the collectivization drive. Middle peasants were those who had land of their own to farm, and perhaps a cow or two, but not enough land to be able to hire other peasants to help work it for them. They were rounded up by the millions along with kulaks, from whom there was little to distinguish them.

Gorbachev has said nothing in detail about this unfortunate relative, but he clearly retains a lingering sense of grievance at the injustice committed more than 50 years ago. In the General Secretary's speech commemorating the 70th Anniversary of the October Revolution in November 1987, he referred with a special tone of regret to the sufferings of the middle peasants. By the time that collectivization started, he said, the middle peasants had become a "staunch and dependable ally of the working class, an ally on a new basis, becoming convinced in practical terms that life was increasingly taking a turn for the better." If more consideration had been given to this group, Gorbachev went on, "there would not have been all those excesses that occurred in carrying out collectivization."

But on the altogether more fundamental issue of whether Stalin was morally justified, for the sake of enforced rapid industrialization, in liquidating millions of kulaks, Gorbachev in the same speech was as unrelenting as every previous leader of the Soviet Union. The policy of fighting the kulaks was "basically correct," he insisted, even if it was often interpreted "so broadly that it swept in a considerable part of the middle peasantry too." Gorbachev added somberly, "Such is the reality of history." As for the overall role of collectivization in "consolidating socialism in the countryside," Gorbachev asserted, "it was in the final analysis a transformation of fundamental importance." This position is even strengthened in his 1987 book *Perestroika*. "Collectivization was a great historic act," the Soviet leader writes, "the most important social change since 1917. Yes, it proceeded painfully, not without serious excesses and blunders in methods and pace. But further progress for our country would have been impossible without it." Some Western scholars would disagree with that assertion. Historians of the Soviet Union Mikhail Heller and Alexander Nekrich, for instance, observe in their 1986 book *Utopia in Power*, "The entire subsequent history of the Soviet Union demonstrates that collectivization left the economy with a gaping wound that never healed."

Neither Gorbachev nor any other Soviet leader in the near future is likely to repudiate Stalin's collectivization altogether. The Communist Party has simply too much complicity in the events to be able to deal with them easily. There are other, more intimate reasons why it would be difficult for Gorbachev personally to disavow collectivization. Both his grandfather Andrei and his father Sergei were keen supporters of the policy and played an important productive role setting up the *kolkhoz* at Privolnoye. Gorbachev's physical survival as a small boy at a time of desperate famine probably owed something to the pro-government attitude of his family. Sergei was a combine-harvester driver at one of the machine tractor stations established by Stalin as a way of ensuring more accurate reporting of agricultural statistics—and of exercising additional political control over the peasants. Both Andrei and Sergei were party members and thus frontline advocates of party policy as collectivization rolled over the countryside. At a time of food scarcity throughout the country, the authorities would have done their best to ensure that peasants loyal to the regime had at least adequate supplies of the necessities of life.

Gorbachev enrolled at the Privolnoye village school for his primary education, joining an entire generation of young peasants who were receiving formal instruction for the first time. He would have been taught the same basic literature and mathematics subjects as millions of other Soviet children in the 1930s, along with adulatory details about Joseph Stalin and the all wise Communist Party over which the "great leader" benignly presided. As the country became engulfed in the paranoia of espionage, "wrecking," "sabotage" and other alleged "counterrevolutionary" activities during the great purges of 1936-1938, even schoolchildren would not have escaped the national obsession with rooting out enemies of the people in their midst. As a country youth exposed to the grim reality of rural life, he may have noted the glaring differences between Stalinist rhetoric and everyday reality at an earlier stage than urban children would have.

Gorbachev did not spend all his school years in Privolnoye. For his secondary education, he moved to another school in a small town nine miles from his home, traveling at least part of the distance every day on foot. For reasons that the Soviets do not make clear, but were probably a consequence of the brief Nazi occupation of Stavropol territory, Gorbachev at the beginning of his fifth year of schooling had to stay home for three months because his mother was too poor to buy shoes for him. His father, writing urgently from the front to Maria Panteleyevna, Gorbachev's mother, gave an instant command to sell whatever was necessary to buy shoes. "Misha must go to school," he reportedly said. The young Gorbachev, according to this somewhat hagiographic Soviet version, then quickly caught up with his comrades and eventually won a prize for scholarly achievement.

The Soviets are understandably coy about a brief period of Gorbachev's childhood that must have influenced him dramatically. This was the five months from Aug. 5, 1942, to Jan. 21, 1943, when the German army occupied Stavropol city and most of the North Caucasus. The move into the Caucasus was part of a two-pronged effort under the command of Field Marshal Siegmund Wilhelm List to move through Stalingrad toward the Caspian Sea and the oil fields of Baku. After an easy initial advance, the German columns rolled into Stavropol so swiftly that they almost caught the convoys of NKVD troops, under Suslov's control, as the Soviets hastily exited the city with whatever documents and machinery the Communist authorities could remove at short notice. Within days, people queued in front of city kiosks to buy copies of *Stavropolskye Vedomosti* (Stavropol *News*), the Russian-language occupation newspaper that the Germans set about publishing as soon as they arrived in the city.

One of the first headlines in the paper was CHRIST IS RISEN. The phrase was intended as a signal to the Russian civilian population that, in contrast with the Soviet authorities, the Nazis would encourage the fullest expressions of Christian worship within the areas under their control. Churches were reopened, priests permitted to resume their offices and Christian celebrations openly encouraged. There was even something of a revival of Orthodox belief and practice under German rule. Capitalizing further on the general unpopularity of Soviet atheistic campaigns, the Germans replaced the Marxist-Leninist parts of school curricula with religious instruction.

The German occupation in Stavropol, as everywhere else in the Soviet Union, had its dark side. One of the first brutal moves was the rounding up and execution by German SS units of some 660 mental patients in Stavropol city hospitals. According to the Soviets, by the time the Wehrmacht had been pushed out of the city in a bitter winter blizzard in January 1943, the civilian death toll in Privolnoye and the surrounding area was 10,000.

By contrast, the Germans evidently scored significant political and propaganda successes among some of the ethnic groups of the North Caucasus, who saw themselves as beset by a double burden of enforced russification and enforced Soviet rule. Though Nazi doctrine lumped all "non-Aryan" peoples in the same despised pot, German military and political tactics saw considerable merit in exploiting ethnic tensions within the Soviet Union. Shortly before the 1942 offensive in the Caucasus got under way, Field Marshal List issued instructions to his troops to respect local customs. The ethnic-minority cooperative farms in the North Caucasus were permitted to disband, in contrast with German policy elsewhere under the occupation, which simply used the collective farms as supply bases for the Wehrmacht. Hitler in particular had been persuaded that the Kuban cossacks of North Caucasus were somehow descended from the Ostrogoths, a Teutonic tribe, and so he permitted them not only to form their own administrative district in October 1942, with 160,000 inhabitants, but to return to private land ownership. Many of the area's cossacks, whose numbers had been decimated during the 1930s, joined the German army outright as independent units and retreated with the Nazi forces when the Soviet counterpush moved the Germans back out of the Caucasus.

Though undercut in the long run by the latent brutality of the Nazi occupation, German policies of respecting the minorities, along with minority recollection of the brutalities inflicted upon them in the recent past, made overall Soviet resistance problematic. Only six partisan groups were able to operate in the entire area during German rule because of the absence of strong pro-Soviet sentiments among much of the population.

The disaffection of the ethnic minorities enraged Stalin. Not long after the Germans had been pushed decisively back from the Caucasus, he ordered reprisals against ethnic communities he felt had compromised with the German invaders or even actively assisted them. Toward the end of 1943, with the strong support of Suslov, who had returned to Stavropol with the reconquering Soviet troops, Stalin ordered the deportation of entire ethnic communities to different parts of the Soviet Union. Approximately 1 million people were rounded up, packed into unheated cattle cars and sent off to the camps of the frozen north and Siberia. The Kalmucks, Chechen Ingush, Kabardians, Balkars, Crimean Tatars and Volga Germans suffered wholesale deportation in this way. Not until 1956 and Khrushchev's secret speech denouncing Stalin were they permitted to begin to return to their original homes. Even today, the Crimean Tatars and Volga Germans remain locked out of their native regions, victims of a policy set in motion 44 years ago.

Under the system of ten-year schooling introduced throughout the Soviet Union during the 1930s, Gorbachev would have completed at most four grades of primary school by the time of the occupation. It is unlikely that German troops would have moved into a village as small as Privolnoye, nor is Gorbachev thought to have been evacuated to a more remote area, as were many other Soviet children during the war. But he could scarcely have avoided hearing of the activities of German units, and he must have seen them from time to time even in the remoteness of Privolnoye village. Soviet sources are strangely silent about Gorbachev's whereabouts during the five-month period of German rule, virtually confirming the young boy's continuing presence in an area occupied by them.

The war must have been emotionally difficult for him for other reasons. His father had been mobilized along with all other able-bodied men as soon as hostilities broke out, and spent four years away at the front. At one point, according to Gorbachev, Sergei fought in the Carpathians. Gorbachev's mother may have been away part of the time, too, for the boy evidently spent a considerable amount of time with his grandparents and came to know them well. Despite grandfather Andrei's party membership, the two elder Gorbachevs seem to have maintained strong Christian beliefs. Mikhail told an audience in England in 1984 that his grandparents had actually kept icons in their home, but had been forced by a general fear of the authorities to hide them behind portraits of Lenin and Stalin. His grandparents also took the young boy to church, but Gorbachev says that after the first visit he did not feel the need to return. Sergei, who died in Privolnoye in 1976, is not known to have had any particular feelings about religion. Gorbachev's mother, by contrast, is said to have remained an Orthodox believer to this day, attending church not far from her Privolnoye home.

Is Gorbachev sympathetic to Christianity? Since becoming General Secretary of the Communist Party, Gorbachev has certainly shown no particular favoritism toward Russia's Christians—Orthodox, Catholic or Protestant. In fact, he has spoken out on at least one occasion on the need to combat manifestations of religious sentiment. Yet the Soviet leader has also not demonstrated the sort of vituperative antireligious rhetoric that some of his predecessors, notably Nikita Khrushchev, have shown from time to time.

Whatever Gorbachev's own views of religion, the lessons

of German tolerance for it were not lost even on Stalin as the grim struggle against the Nazi occupation went into its third year. Despite initial German efforts to win over the civilian population, nothing in the long run could conceal from the people they occupied the fundamental evil behind the Nazi ideology that had led to war in the first place. The reality of the Third Reich quickly sunk in as the SS Einsatz groups rampaged through the rear areas of the occupation, seeking out Jews, Communists and anyone considered a dangerous adversary of Hitler's deranged beliefs. In the Stavropol territory as a whole, goodwill toward the Germans appears to have lasted longer, during a short occupation, than in other areas. Overall, though, the unmistakable contempt that the Nazis felt toward the Slavic peoples in general led inevitably to a resurgence of traditional Russian patriotism. At this point, even the Communist Party, as principal organizer of resistance to the conquerors, benefited from a sense of attachment to the Russian land and to Russian history that had far more to do with traditional, non-Communist Russian culture than to the ideology of Marx and Lenin.

Grasping the importance of this tradition, with its images of heroic Christian leaders of old Russia fighting the Turkish or Mongol invaders, Stalin in 1942 relaxed the regime's opposition to such "feudal" symbols of national pride, declaring Alexander Nevsky, the 13th century Russian conqueror of the Teutonic knights, to be a national hero. More important, in September 1943, Stalin ordered churches reopened and encouraged the beleaguered clergy to resume their traditional roles as emblems of traditional Russian identity. This recognition of the lingering power of tradition may also have persuaded the Kremlin not to order the name of the city of Stavropol changed once Soviet forces had resumed control. In 1935, as part of Stalin's growing personality cult, Stavropol had been renamed Voroshilovsk, after Kliment Voroshilov, the Defense Minister. The Nazis, in a popular move, restored the name of

Stavropol. Not wishing to antagonize the city's proud inhabitants, Moscow then permitted the German restoration of the original name to stand.

For Gorbachev, the key personal event when hostilities came to an end in Europe in May 1945 must have been the return of his father. Sergei Gorbachev had by all accounts fought bravely at the Carpathian front and, along with millions of demobilized Soviet troops, came back to his native region to pick up the pieces of his interrupted life. He resumed the job of combine harvester driver that he had held at the very beginning of collectivization, spending long hours in the field with his son Mikhail. For young Gorbachev, it must have been a rewarding time of companionship as the years of childhood slipped into youth and early adulthood.

By 1945 the eager and earnest young man had already experienced hardship, turmoil and the rigors of a full-length day of adult work. Under emergency wartime conditions, Soviet school children had been mobilized by the Soviets during the war for emergency harvest work. With millions of Soviet men fighting or working in arduous factory jobs for military production, only the women, the children and the older folk were left to bear the brunt of agricultural labor to feed the nation. As soon as children were strong enough physically, they were required to perform adult jobs. At the age of 14, Gorbachev could already drive a combine harvester. It was not, as it might have been on any farm in the West, something one did for fun. More often, Gorbachev had to perform the tedious but essential task of working in tandem with his father as the driver's assistant.

It was a back-breaking and grimy job. The assistant had to follow behind the tractor and gather up the sheaves. In summer the blazing southern sun pushed temperatures into the 90s, baking the black soil into a hard-caked crust, which broke up into fine dust as the tracks of the harvester rode over it. There was no protective cabin for the driver, and after a mere

ten minutes of the work, both he and his assistant would be engulfed in clouds of chaff and dust that made breathing difficult. The men's sweating skin, meanwhile, would soon become
caked in grime and particles of straw and grit. In winter, when
Gorbachev sometimes performed the job of the driver, the
freezing wind off the steppe would clutch at any part of flesh
not sufficiently covered. To ward off frostbite, Gorbachev
would wrap himself in bales of straw as he drove across the
cold brittle fields.

For all the hardships, there is little doubt Gorbachev derived personal satisfaction from this hard toil after school
hours and in the summer vacation period. He also appears to
have embraced fully the Communist Party view of World War
II—"the Great Patriotic War," as the conflict is universally
known in the Soviet Union—and its aftermath. This idealized
definition of the world had elements of truth, especially in the
context of the just completed war. Yet its main purpose was to
set forth a clear-cut world view with an optimistic outlook on
the future, as well as an all-embracing explanation of the hor-
rors of the past conflict and the continuing hardships of the
postwar era. According to the official view of domestic and international life in the late 1940s, a benevolent, near omni-
scient Soviet leader, Joseph Stalin, had calmly led his people
through a purgatory of invasion and suffering onward to final
victory over the enemy; heroic and self-sacrificing party members had been first in defense of their country and in postwar
reconstruction; and the Soviet Union was the sole outpost of
hope for mankind in a world imperiled by "imperialist war-
mongers"—especially the U.S., archenemy of all that was
good and progressive—and the hyenas of international monopoly capitalism. Stalin was painted in terms of the world
leader of "progressive" (i.e., pro-Communist) humanity
against an evil cabal of revenge-seeking imperialist states
(namely, the U.S., Western Europe and their allies elsewhere
in the world).

Gorbachev almost certainly accepted at face value most of this lore, maintaining a skepticism only for those aspects of detailed regime propaganda about Soviet rural life that he knew from personal experience were patently false. Not long after he became eligible at the age of 14, he joined the Komsomol, the Young Communist League. The young man was already demonstrating social and intellectual gifts: an ability to make his points forcefully and articulately before an audience, an excellent memory for detail, a single-minded enthusiasm for tasks in hand and, by no means least, an ability to impress his superiors with his solicitude and evident loyalty to them.

At the same time, as 1949 gave way to 1950, Gorbachev was drawing to the end of his formal secondary education. The disruption of the war had delayed his graduation by a year, and he was thus 19 before he completed his high school courses. He was highly intelligent, though not brilliant, diligent at his studies but no mere grind, and interested almost in too many subjects for his own good. He was not even sure what subject he was best at. He loved literature and committed to memory the poetry of Pushkin and Lermontov that generations of Russian children have enjoyed listening to and reciting. In 1986 he told an interviewer for *L'Unita,* the Italian Communist newspaper, "To this day, I can recite by heart poetry that I learned at school." But his generalist rather than specialist intelligence even then seemed to have given him cause for self-doubt. "I've always considered it a weakness on my part," he told the same interviewer, "to have been interested in numerous questions in several different areas. I cannot even say for which subjects I felt a special interest in school." Scholastically, Gorbachev did very well, but he was not at the top of his high school graduating class: he was awarded the silver medal rather than the gold medal for outstanding student. (His wife Raisa, at a different school in a different city, won the gold medal.)

Had Gorbachev needed to rest on his academic laurels to

secure a career away from the provinciality of Stavropol, he might never have made it to Moscow. Places in higher education were at a premium after World War II, with hundreds of thousands of returning soldiers competing for the college education they had been denied by the war. At the same time, there were plenty of youths in Moscow, Leningrad and other major cities whose parental background (party membership or professional education and attainment) made them more attractive candidates than Gorbachev for coveted slots in the major universities. Fortunately for Gorbachev, he had shown excellence in two other areas of life: political work as a member of the Komsomol and physical work on the collective farm during the long summers of rural toil. The Komsomol became Gorbachev's springboard to prominence not just at Moscow State University, but at the beginning of his rapid rise up the bureaucratic ladder on returning to Stavropol in 1955.

For the majority of youths in the Soviet Union, joining the Young Pioneers in primary school and then the Komsomol at age 14 or later has since the Bolshevik Revolution been something of a rite of passage. Komsomol membership is so widespread that it confers no special privileges in itself. Yet it is an indispensable qualification for subsequent Communist Party membership, or indeed for any professional career with the promise of advancement to a position of responsibility. Komsomol activities range from obligatory attendance at weekly political lectures to community improvement projects, to vacation trips that are sheer fun. Young, earnest and energetic, Gorbachev must have showed enthusiasm for all aspects of membership, including those that most young people considered tedious chores: assisting party workers in dealing with day-to-day neighborhood municipal matters, for example, or taking part in education and propaganda presentations at schools and factories.

Gorbachev has never publicly discussed his early Komsomol work in Privolnoye, or indicated how he managed to attract the attention of Komsomol officials in Stavropol. Yet he obviously impressed important Communist Party functionaries with a display of leadership qualities that set him apart from average Komsomol members. Probably it was his general enthusiasm for all kinds of labor, inside and outside the Komsomol, that won him the award, at the remarkably young age of 18, of the Order of the Red Banner of Labor. The honor was usually reserved for senior workers with a lifetime of experience and loyal hard work behind them. Gorbachev appears to have earned it primarily because of particular diligence he demonstrated during the gathering of the successful Stavropol Krai harvest of 1949. This, along with the incipient organizational and political skills he demonstrated in his Komsomol activities, was sufficient to put him in the category, in 1950, of exceptional rural youths admitted to the largest institution of Soviet higher education, Moscow State University.

In September 1950, Gorbachev said goodbye to his parents and friends and boarded the train for the nearly 1,000-mile ride from Stavropol to Moscow to take up his studies. Any youth from the countryside of southern Russia would have been thrilled at the opportunity of journeying to the Soviet capital for a university course. Along the way, though, Gorbachev had a sobering vision: a stark, frightening understanding of how much destruction the Soviet Union had undergone during World War II. Privolnoye apparently had sustained little physical damage from the war, and Stavropol had suffered relatively little despite months and years of bombing, as well as attack and counterattack by Soviet and German forces alike. Yet the itinerary of Gorbachev's train ride to the Soviet capital read like a roster of heroic Soviet battles against the Germans during World War II. Stalingrad, Rostov, Kharkov, Orel, Kursk and Voronezh sat astride the major railroad line from southern Russia. Recalling in 1986 the shock of that first journey to Moscow in 1950, Gorbachev told an interviewer, "I went to study at Moscow State University, and I traveled through Stalingrad, which had been destroyed, through Voronezh, which had been destroyed [and] Rostov was destroyed. Nothing but ruins everywhere. I traveled as a student and saw it all. The whole country was in ruins."

For an ambitious young man traveling to the capital city of his nation for the first time, that ride was certainly a shocking introduction to the realities of Soviet life after World War II. Gorbachev, though, probably saw it also as a sober personal reminder to take his studies with the utmost seriousness. Already interested in the political process and the world around him, he arrived in Moscow zealously determined to excel, his motivation a blend of patriotism and personal ambition. At 19, Gorbachev was young, fresh, idealistic. Few young men or women of the same age in other countries would have been as well-tempered by harsh experience to take on the tough challenges of adult life.

2

University Years

When the long and sobering train journey from Stavropol to Moscow came to an end for Gorbachev at Moscow's Kursk Railway Station in September 1950, the young man knew well enough what new challenge he faced in the Soviet capital. He arrived with one suitcase, one overcoat, a cossack-style fur hat, one pair of everyday trousers, a bare minimum of personal belongings and the expectations of his family, his village and the Stavropol Krai's Krasnogvardeisky district Komsomol authorities. It is not known whether anyone met him at the station or whether he had any contacts in the capital. Though he bore the prestigious Red Banner of Labor and an extraordinary amount of self-confidence for someone his age, Gorbachev at 19 must have grasped quickly that only his wits and hard work would keep him at Moscow State University and provide him with a starting point for any worthwhile career afterward.

He had been admitted to the law faculty (faculty in the

European sense of a university department) of Moscow university, and it had evidently not been his first choice. In the interview with Italy's *L'Unita* mentioned earlier, when Gorbachev had hinted at being interested in a great diversity of topics, the Soviet leader frankly admitted that law was not what he had originally wanted to study. "I entered the law faculty," he said, "but at the outset I wanted to enter the physics faculty." He had felt an equal interest in mathematics, history and literature, he said. His assignment to study law may simply have been the result of not quite adequate grades in mathematics and science. In these areas, after all, he would have faced tough competition from returning military veterans and academic achievers from around the country.

There were other reasons why Gorbachev might have been unhappy at being assigned to study law. The profession had extremely low prestige in the Soviet Union. The very notion of law under both Marxist-Leninist doctrine and actual Soviet practice during the Stalin years was far degraded from the two-millenniums-old tradition of jurisprudence in the West. The function of Soviet lawyers, for the most part, was to provide briskly argued rationalizations for the Soviet state to crush its opponents. The gargantuan purges and show trials of the 1930s had made a mockery of due process, principally because overwhelming emphasis was placed on the confessions of the accused. With the sophisticated methods of torture routinely practiced in Lubyanka and other notorious Moscow prisons, victims of the Stalinist juridical machine could be made to confess things that it was physically impossible for them to have done. This in fact happened several times and was one of the factors that eventually led to the discrediting of the Stalin purges. Ordinarily, a simple method sufficed to induce confession of virtually any transgression: the deprivation of sleep continuously for several days. This particular form of severe pressure, which did not leave any marks on the body, was known in the Soviet Union as *konveyer* (conveyor, as in conveyor belt).

The emphasis on confession and the practice of placing all evidentiary burdens on the accused were made notorious by the principal producer and stage manager of the Moscow show trials, General Prosecutor Andrei Vyshinsky. One by one, during the nightmare purges of the 1930s, former associates of Lenin and Stalin were rounded up, tortured and made to confess fantastic "counterrevolutionary" crimes involving alleged espionage with the Japanese, the British or some other foreign or émigré group. By the time Gorbachev entered law school, Vyshinsky had moved on to be, briefly, Foreign Minister and then Soviet representative to the United Nations. His shadow still hung over Soviet law, however, dominating the official view of the profession, the textbooks and the day-to-day activities of lawyers. The vast majority of law graduates went into the procuracy, the Soviet administrative apparatus for conducting prosecutions, or the "organs," the still current euphemism for the security services (the KGB in its present form was established only in 1954, after power was taken from the Ministry of Internal Affairs, which was previously responsible for security and intelligence). Neither the procuracy nor the organs, though each offered a comfortable and exciting life, was an attractive career prospect to students with a larger than average measure of self-respect.

The poor reputation of law as an academic subject was reflected in the small number of young people studying it in the Soviet Union in the 1950s: only 45,000 out of a total student population of 1.2 million. By 1958-59, that number had declined to 36,000 despite a doubling of the total number of students and despite the considerable social relaxation that took place in the Soviet Union after destalinization. Vratislav Pechota, an expert on Soviet law at Columbia University who studied law at Kiev and Leningrad universities at approximately the same time that Gorbachev was in Moscow, observes, "Law was not the favorite discipline because the role of law was not very significant at this time."

Despite law's poor reputation, Gorbachev entered Moscow State University and serendipitously stumbled into the one academic area most conducive to refining his strongly emerging political interests. Though he never practiced law, he put to good advantage the rigorous intellectual training that Moscow university provided its students even in the dark Stalinist days of the early 1950s. It is an interesting parallel that both Gorbachev and the founder of the Soviet state Vladimir Lenin, whom Gorbachev reveres as a source of spiritual and intellectual inspiration, were the only Soviet leaders to have acquired university degrees, and that the degrees of both men were in law.

In the early 1950s, the law faculty was housed not in what is now the central location of Moscow State University, the 34-story Stalinesque skyscraper in the Lenin Hills on the outskirts of Moscow. Instead, it was a pleasant, prerevolutionary colonnaded building on Karl Marx Prospect in the center of the capital, across from the old czarist stables. Gorbachev commuted there from his dormitory in the Sokolniki district of northeastern Moscow six days a week for long hours of lectures, seminars, library research and study, no doubt marveling in his first few weeks at the gleaming marble columns and crystal chandeliers of the Moscow subway. The impressive and immensely ambitious public works project had been pushed ahead by Stalin in the 1930s at enormous cost as a sort of foretaste of what Communism would be like.

The majority of Gorbachev's fellow students in the law faculty were veterans of World War II, men in their mid- or even late 20s who had fought with the Soviet armies across their own country, Eastern Europe and into the heart of Germany. Some had undoubtedly taken part in the Soviet Union's brief end-of-war offensive against Japan in 1945. A smaller group had matriculated straight out of secondary schools in Moscow, Leningrad and other large Soviet cities. These were usually the children of relatively privileged parents, loyal professionals who had somehow survived and prospered by Soviet standards through the various campaigns Stalin launched against the Soviet intelligentsia in the 1930s, '40s and '50s. A third and even smaller category of Soviet students to which Gorbachev belonged was made up of exceptionally talented or politically sound students from the Soviet provinces. Gorbachev probably would have lacked the parental influence to gain admission to the most prestigious of the country's higher educational institutions, the Moscow State Institute of International Relations, where many of the nation's future leaders were being trained in the intricacies of diplomacy and international law. In any event, there is no evidence that he aspired to anything grander than Moscow State University.

There was another, even tinier category of students at the university in the early 1950s never previously seen in the Soviet Union. These were handpicked foreigners from the newly Communist-ruled, Soviet-dominated countries of Eastern Europe—the fraternal socialist bloc countries, to use the Soviet term. The new arrivals from Czechoslovakia, East Germany, Bulgaria, Albania and even China added an exotic note to the student body, which was otherwise totally isolated from the rest of the world by censorship, radio jamming and police surveillance. The foreign students fitted in with the Soviet goal of "instilling internationalism" in Soviet youth, reminding them, in effect, of the Soviet Union's role and duties as leader of the world socialist bloc in the struggle against Western imperialism.

The foreigners had for the most part been selected to study in Moscow because of their strong Communist convictions and the belief of the regimes that sent them that they would represent the new, pro-Soviet leadership élite once they had returned to their own countries. They were carefully watched by both their own embassies and the Soviet security authorities, lest their more cosmopolitan and in many cases

Western background and experience inadvertently contaminate their Soviet fellow students.

One of the foreigners who entered the law faculty at Moscow university the same fall as Gorbachev was Zdeněk Mlynář, a young Czech who was an ardent Communist and intensely interested in politics. Mlynář was to pursue a successful career in the Czech Communist Party, rising to membership on the Central Committee, until the advent of the Prague Spring liberalization in 1968. He then became increasingly disenchanted with his party's rigid, Stalinist method of rule and threw in his lot with the reformers who eventually brought Alexander Dubček to power that year. When Soviet tanks crushed the Czech reform movement in late summer, Mlynář lost all his official positions and ended up quietly tending a butterfly collection at a Prague research institute. He emigrated to Austria in 1977 and now directs a research institute in Vienna.

Mlynář and Gorbachev were assigned to the same seminar study group under a program that sought to provide greater student-teacher involvement and gave the professors a better opportunity to monitor the progress of the law students. Though it was, in Mlynář's words, "by sheer accident" that the two were in the same group, they became close friends, studying together, preparing for examinations together and traveling around Moscow in each other's company. While students, they even married women who were themselves close friends. Most important of all, though, Gorbachev confided in Mlynář his personal views on politics, economics and life in general, to a degree that was unusual between a Soviet citizen and a foreigner at the time, even a foreigner from a fraternal socialist bloc country. Most of what is known about Gorbachev's political ideas as a university student come from Mlynář's recollection of conversations with him.

The course was five years long and far more intense than most comparable academic programs in the West, either then or now. Lectures or seminars began before 9 a.m. and continued until 3 p.m., six days a week, throughout the academic year. Attendance was monitored, and an absence without adequate excuse could result in the suspension of a financial stipend or even, in serious cases, expulsion from the university. On the other hand, a consistently good academic and conduct record could gain a student badly needed financial assistance. Gorbachev received a Stalin Scholarship after he arrived in Moscow, which helped him cover basic living necessities.

A heavy proportion of the law program was pure Marxism-Leninism, just as every humanities course in the Soviet Union today has obligatory instruction in Soviet ideology. Gorbachev attended lectures and seminars on dialectics, historical materialism, political economy and the works of Marx, Engels, Lenin and Stalin. Since Marxist-Leninist ideology was the central theoretical justification for the structure of the Soviet state and hence the role of Soviet law, it was more central in law studies than any other field except philosophy. Law students not only read extensively in Marxism-Leninism but also were required to have a precise understanding of the texts, as though interpreting the scriptures of a religious faith.

Many of the law students undoubtedly paid lip service to the founders of the Marxist faith they were obliged to study, learning enough merely to keep up their grades. Even upon those, though, the impact of the ceaseless exposure to the didactic works of the founders of Marxism-Leninism was virtually lifelong, as some who experienced it have testified. Fridrikh Neznansky, a Soviet émigré who received his Moscow university law degree the year before Gorbachev and had many contacts with the Soviet leader, puts it this way: "Marxism-Leninism creates an atmosphere, an understanding, a comprehension of Soviet ideology and of the definite limits of what the system permits and doesn't permit."

For Gorbachev, though, and indeed for Mlynář, the topic was intellectually challenging. Gorbachev had entered Moscow State University a convinced Communist, and at several points during his university career he had ample opportunity to reaffirm his basic ideological commitment. The educational experience of delving into Marxian and Leninist argumentation provided him with a theoretical or, as Gorbachev puts it today, a "spiritual" core to his beliefs, on which he appears to have drawn ever since. To unlettered Westerners, for whom Marxism-Leninism is so much mumbo jumbo used to justify any pragmatically adopted decision, this may be hard to comprehend. Gorbachev studied Lenin to appreciate his gifts not just as a theoretician but as a master political tactician, a man who knew when to advance and when to retreat, yet who never lost sight of his ultimate goal, which was not just the achievement of Communist power in Russia but its extension throughout the world. Neznansky recalls Gorbachev speaking with admiration for Lenin's decision to make a disadvantageous peace with the Germans at Brest-Litovsk in 1918 during World War I. Lenin's justification of this policy to his skeptical Bolshevik comrades, as Gorbachev understood well, was that once having consolidated the revolution at home the Soviets would be in a stronger position to see it spread to the outside world.

Yet Gorbachev also admired Lenin for his relatively humane treatment of his Menshevik rival Julius Martov, who opposed Lenin both before and after the October Revolution in 1917. It was a dangerous sentiment for Gorbachev to confide, even to a friend. The official history of the U.S.S.R. as studied at Moscow State University in 1952 prescribed that anyone opposing the party line dictated from above was advocating "anti-party deviation," a crime that could lead to a long time in the Gulag or even death. Such people, in the frenzied Stalinist paranoia of the day, were hideous criminals whose very names needed to be excised from the history books. Recalls Mlynář: "It was at that time that Gorbachev said to me, 'Nevertheless, Lenin did not arrest Martov but let him emigrate from the country.' " For Mlynář, Gorbachev's boldness in expressing distinctly heretical views was demonstration that his Russian friend was not an opportunist.

Besides demanding thorough knowledge of the classics of Marxism-Leninism, though, the law course was comprehensive in its coverage of both Soviet and prerevolutionary law and of several subjects essential to an understanding of the role of law in the world at large. The more than 40 separate courses included a broad section on legal topics and a wide-ranging curriculum in general humanities subjects. The Soviet law section included textbooks like *A Course on Soviet Criminal Law* by Professors A.A. Piontovsky and V.D. Menshagin. The work described the show trials of the 1930s, predictably, as examples of true "socialist legality." The term enemy of the people was still current, and there was no self-consciousness about lumping political and criminal offenses in the same container. Still, according to Neznansky, not all of the professors, even in the courses confined to Soviet legal topics, were followers of the line of Vyshinsky, for whom confession remained the touchstone of guilt or innocence. Some, though careful never to express a heterodox political opinion, quietly maintained standards of professionalism in the definition and discussion of criminal codes.

Where Gorbachev must have benefited most from his law course was the large segment of the curriculum devoted to broad legal and humanities topics. There were lectures and seminars in Roman law, the history of law, international law, civil law and employment law. Students discussed the Code of Hammurabi, Machiavelli's *History of Florence,* the works of Thomas Aquinas, Hobbes, Hegel and Rousseau, and even the U.S. Constitution. At one point, studying Roman law, the future leader of the Soviet Union spent a semester wrestling with the intricacies of Latin. The professors for many of these topics were survivors of pre-Bolshevik times, scholars who had kept out of politics altogether and managed to endure wars, purges and other hazards of Soviet life in the quiet pursuit of learning and teaching. Many of them were first-rate scholars and excellent teachers.

The two-year course on the history of political ideas, requiring four lecture hours and four tutorial hours a week, was, in Mlynář's view, one of the intellectual highlights of the Moscow university law program. Conducted by Professor Stepan Fyodorovich Kechekyan, the course exposed students, however formally and cautiously, to an intellectual and political world created before and existing beyond the confines of Stalinist thought. Kechekyan had received his training before the Bolshevik Revolution, and managed to convey to the students the power of a mind unfettered by the dogmatic certitudes of late-Stalinist dialectics. Recalls Mlynář of this remarkable teacher: "He was very popular. I remember that Gorbachev was impressed by those other [political] ideas."

As he acquired a breadth of knowledge in many different areas of politics and philosophy, Gorbachev was also experiencing, like countless undergraduates before and after him, some of the epiphanies of intellectual discovery. "I remember a conversation with Gorbachev about Hegel," Mlynář adds. "Professor Kechekyan said that Hegel had reined in his horses before the Brandenburg Gate [a metaphor for Hegel's understanding of the relationship of philosophy to political power]. Gorbachev observed to me that this turn of phrase showed the quality of the professor. I was surprised that Gorbachev, a student from a small rural village, had this need for quality of such a type." Gorbachev, Mlynář says, was also struck by an aphorism of Hegel's: "Truth is always concrete." Writing a month after Gorbachev's accession to power in 1985 in L'Unita, Mlynář recalled, "Unlike us, he did not use this in the precise sense of Hegel's philosophy. He liked to repeat it whenever a teacher or student waffled on about general principles, ignoring the issue of how much they had in common with real life. Unlike many Soviet students, he did not see Marxist theory as a collection of axioms to be committed to memory. Instead, it had the value of an instrument for understanding the world and a credo which not even 30 years on can have dissolved into political pragmatism."

What is not clear is how much Gorbachev really learned about the outside world and about foreign, particularly Western, systems of law and politics from the courses he took and the writings he studied. According to Alexander Stromas, a Lithuanian who studied at Moscow university at a time that overlapped with Gorbachev's, the general education on writings before Marx was good, because works by people whom Marx himself had studied were not censored in the Soviet Union. Mlynář says that he thinks the U.S. Constitution was presented in a positive light, even though professors felt obliged to assert that the document's glowing words were violated across the board in the reality of American life. There was a total ban on importing or possessing within the Soviet Union any contemporary foreign newspaper or books unless they were approved by the authorities, which in most cases meant that the works were supportive of the Soviet view of the world. But Lev Yudovich, who also studied law at Moscow State University and was in a class two years ahead of Gorbachev and Mlynář, says that the ban on potentially heterodox materials also extended to Soviet books or Bolshevik writings from the prerevolutionary period and the 1920s. He says it was often impossible to obtain works in this category from the library. Ironically, Yudovich notes, students could not even get their hands on copies of *Iskra* (The Spark), the Bolshevik newspaper founded by Lenin in 1900.

The overall political climate in Moscow, in any case, was extremely hostile to most of the outside world. The idolatry of Joseph Stalin, who by 1950 had been the unchallenged leader of the Soviet Union for 23 years, was at its apogee. In addition to the East European states that had fallen one by one under Soviet political control after World War II, China in 1949 had joined the Soviet-led "socialist camp," bringing Communist rule to one-third of the world's population. The Korean War broke out in June of the year Gorbachev arrived in Moscow and seemed, with the initial defeats of U.S. and U.N. forces, to mark the beginning of a major erosion of American global power. Outwardly, political unity and ideological unanimity characterized the socialist world from Berlin to Shanghai, from Arkhangelsk to Canton. Over it all presided Stalin, a political demigod of immense authority, possessing in 1950 probably the greatest political power of any person in modern history. Perhaps no year brought the notion of a monolithic world-Communist system closer to reality than 1950, even though, in retrospect, the appearance of unity masked serious internal problems later to emerge dramatically in the Sino-Soviet split.

Stalin was everywhere. Paintings, busts, statues and photographs of him confronted Soviet citizens—along with Hungarians, Poles, Chinese and North Koreans, among others—at every turn. His words adorned porticoes, school halls, factory entrances and collective-farm auditoriums across ten countries. To the inhabitants of the Soviet Union, on a daily basis, he was "Father of the Peoples," "Wise and Intelligent Chief of the Soviet People," "Coryphaeus of the Sciences," the "Greatest Genius of All Times and Peoples." Most important, in the relentless drumbeat of propaganda idolizing him, Stalin was represented as the leader of progressive humanity in a titanic struggle with the evil forces of Western imperialism, of which the leader, and the embodiment of total evil, was the U.S.

The anti-Americanism was of a virulence that today, in the world of post-détente diplomatese, is hard to grasp. But it was real enough, and no one who was a student in the Soviet Union at the same time as Gorbachev can forget it. One contemporary was Arkady Shevchenko, former Under Secretary General of the U.N. and a Soviet citizen who defected to the U.S. in 1978. Shevchenko was studying at Moscow's prestigious Institute of International Relations, and was graduated in 1954, the year before Gorbachev completed his Moscow State University degree. "America was the Great Satan," Shevchenko remembers, using in irony a phrase introduced by the Ayatullah Khomeini of Iran in a later epoch. "Most of the students accepted the extreme view of the U.S. as the country most responsible for the problems of the world. The image was absolutely terrible and left an indelible imprint on me." Shevchenko, who became a career Soviet diplomat, says it was not until years later, after he actually visited the U.S., that he was able to escape the negative indoctrination about the U.S. he had received in Moscow during his student years.

Vratislav Pechota has similar memories. "The atmosphere was tense," he says. "Freedom of life was extremely limited. The Korean War seemed to be the culmination of the cold war." Fellow Law Student Neznansky adds, "Day in and day out, we who were in school were constantly reminded that we were on the eve of war, and this time the enemy would be the United States. Children in school and students in college were being told that Soviet man stood higher than Western man, that the difficulties we faced were all temporary, but that we had to bear them in order to be ready for the coming conflict." Gorbachev has not put on record his impression of the U.S. while at Moscow State University, but it is likely that the early message he heard about the U.S. as a society that was both wicked and failing struck a responsive chord in his mind. Westerners with whom Gorbachev has talked since he began to attract attention outside his country in the early 1980s report hearing a consistent thread of sentiments strongly critical of life in the U.S. and at times frankly contemptuous of America. Mlynář, while not denying the impact of such Stalinist indoctrination in the 1950s, explains it in the overall context both of the Stalinism of the day and of Gorbachev's subsequently expressed sympathy for reform. "He like everyone else at the time was a Stalinist," says Mlynář. "In order to be a true reforming Communist you have to have been be a true Stalinist."

The long hours of lectures and seminars, not to mention the time needed to study, left little opportunity for reflection upon the mass of information to which the students were exposed every day. Most of them had time for almost nothing else during the six-day week of six-hour lectures except spending the requisite time at the law faculty and the library, and returning by metro to the student dormitory in northeastern Moscow.

That was not much to return to. The Stromynka Student Hostel still stands today, a drab, light-salmon-colored quadrangular edifice at the point where Stromynka Street ends and Sailors' Bridge crosses the Yauza River in the city's Sokolniki district. The building no longer has any connection with Moscow State University but is the headquarters for the external study program of the All-Union Institute for Machine Building. The plain, modern window frames on the upper two floors of the structure, which is roofed with sheet metal, betray a later addition to what was once an older building of neoclassical style. Much older, in fact. The original structure dates from the time of Peter the Great (1672-1725), when it was a military barracks. Two upper stories were added later, and by 1950 the "student village," as it was called, was a teeming warren of 10,000 students.

Conditions were primitive in the extreme. Male and female students inhabited the building together, though in sex-segregated rooms, with as many as 15 people and no fewer than six sharing a room. On each floor were a kitchen, a washroom and communal toilets, but no facilities whatever for bathing. Gorbachev and the other students would typically head for the public bathhouses twice a month to get properly clean. The rooms were spartan and undecorated, and personal belongings had to be stored in suitcases the students kept under their beds. The residence was noisy, cold and oppressively

unprivate, and its zoolike conditions were only slightly miti-
gated by the fact that men and women lived on the same
floors. The dormitory had a "culture club" on the main floor,
where movies, lectures and other activities were held almost
every evening. Gorbachev and Mlynář, occupying another
room across the hall from each other would rise around 8 a.m.,
grab a piece of bread and a cup of tea, then walk to the nearby
Sokolniki Park metro station for the ride to the law faculty.

Money was always tight. The monthly stipend of 200 to
300 rubles barely covered the essentials of living, including
food, and there was nothing left to buy clothes, not to mention
luxuries that are taken for granted by students in the West today. One Soviet who was a fellow student of Gorbachev's says
he remembers the Soviet leader wearing the same pair of pants
every day year in and year out, even after Gorbachev acciden-
tally tore a slight hole in them. Even tea was expensive: students who could not afford to pay for it in the hostel resorted to
"student tea," a euphemism for a mixture of hot water and
sugar. The only square meal of the day for most students was
taken in the cafeteria at the law faculty when the lectures were
over. The cafeteria held about 150 people, Mlynář recalls, and
it was invariably crowded. The food was barely eatable. "It
was a monotonous kind of food," he says. "Things like kasha
(a kind of buckwheat gruel). It was awful." The few treats
most students could ever afford were occasional visits to the
movies or the theater—then, as now in the Soviet Union, tickets were not expensive—or, far more rarely, a shared bottle of
vodka. On Sundays, if they were not studying, students would
try to explore Moscow or look up friends in other institutions
of learning. Most of the time, though, life was an unending
grind, punctuated only by summer vacations and military
training. Like all university students in the Soviet Union, Gorbachev was exempt from the military draft, though he had to
endure reserve officer training.

Ironically, the most popular diversion of all for Soviet

students in the early 1950s, when war with the West seemed never far beyond the horizon, was American films. In one of those marvelous cultural titrations engineered by war, the victorious Soviet armies returning from Berlin had brought home among the booty thousands of old movie reels found in Nazi archives and in movie theaters in the ruined German cities. Marlene Dietrich, Errol Flynn—who knows? perhaps even Ronald Reagan—flickered through the sparse lives of earnest Soviet students in the last days of Stalin, suggesting a universe beyond the harsh confines of censors and propagandists. Audiences were never told who the producer, director or actors were, much less which country the movie came from. Sometimes the titles were not shown at all. Recalls Vratislav Pechota: "They just said, 'This is a foreign movie.' "

The hands-down favorite was always the same: Johnny Weissmuller playing Tarzan. The series was shown frequently at the Stromynka Student Hostel, invariably to an enthusiastic audience. After the showing, the corridors of the dormitory would resound to the jungle-like whoops of would-be Soviet Tarzans. For a few moments afterward, perhaps there would be time for "student tea" and a piece of Russian black bread, or whatever other scrap of food anyone had. Then the great teeming dormitory slowly settled down for the night as the students tucked themselves deep inside their blankets.

The suffocating lack of privacy, the overcrowding and the constant academic and political pressure must have been potent ingredients in the smoldering daily contacts between men and women on the same floor. Sexual liaisons out of marriage were politically and socially risky in the stern atmosphere of Stalinist morality, and for students without friends or relatives with apartments in the city, the logistics of such trysts would have been a nearly insuperable deterrent. As a result, to fight off desperate loneliness and sexual frustration, student marriages were common, even within the dormitory, and with the knowledge that it might be months before husband and wife could live together on a regular basis. Mlynář, far from his home and family, entered into a passionate but short-lived marriage with another Czech student, marrying and divorcing her within the five-year period of his studies. The marriage, however, had one interesting historical consequence. Sharing the same dormitory room as Mlynář's wife was a well-educated philosophy student named Raisa Maximovna Titorenko.

Raisa was a popular student, intelligent and pretty, and Mlynář says that Gorbachev practically had to fight his way through crowds of admirers to get to know her. She was a year younger than Gorbachev, the daughter of a railroad engineer, but a woman evidently at home with the cultural amenities of Moscow. They met during a class in ballroom dancing, where Gorbachev had gone to make friendly fun of a fellow student, Vladimir Lieberman, who was a serious practitioner of the waltz. Lieberman was eight years older than Gorbachev, and though a student, had been a colonel in the Soviet army. He was also Jewish, which caused some problems later in his law studies. Gorbachev, who had a pleasant-looking face and a fine head of dark hair while in his 20s, was immediately drawn to Raisa. She was, after all, bright, independent and attractive. She was also more cultured than he was, a fact that did not seem to threaten him—and his self-confidence perhaps made Gorbachev more appealing to her.

As they got to know each other, Raisa took Gorbachev to plays and concerts. Nadezhda Mikhaleva, a fellow student of Gorbachev's, remembers both of them well. "Raisa was very smart, as well as being very pretty," Mikhaleva told Robert Scheer of the Los Angeles *Times* late in 1987 at a reunion of former Moscow State University students, "and she's still both. So why shouldn't she play a leading role?" For her part, Raisa was evidently won over by what Mlynář calls Gorbachev's "lack of vulgarity," his willingness to treat her as a partner in interests and career. This contrasted starkly with the somewhat chauvinistic and boorish attitude toward female company of many Soviet men both then and now.

Apart from visits to cultural events, there was precious little to do on dates at the Stromynka complex. Dormitory roommates, however, did contrive ways to permit one another to spend private time with friends of the opposite sex. On the wall of Gorbachev's room was a timetable that gave each student at least one hour a week there for himself. By agreement, the others would have to find somewhere else to go. To preserve appearances, those periods of privacy were described on the timetable as "cleaning hours." How much Gorbachev and Raisa availed themselves of these rare hours, no one knows. Early in 1954, though, they decided to marry.

It was a simple, probably typical student wedding, with few frills and an absolute minimum of expense. As required by Soviet law, the actual ceremony was almost certainly a brief affair before duly appointed Soviet officials who performed several marriages each day. After the formalities, about 30 of the couple's friends celebrated modestly in a corner of the eating hall at the dormitory. There was no honeymoon. The wedding night was spent in Gorbachev's room, all of the other roommates having agreed to find somewhere else to sleep. "Everybody had to disappear," says Mlynář. They did—for one night. The following day, Raisa went back to her own room, and Gorbachev's roommates returned to his. Not until several months later, by one account, after completion of the residential quarters for married students in the new Moscow university skyscraper in the Lenin Hills, were the two able to live together as man and wife.

Gorbachev's self-confidence, intelligence, maturity and broad range of intellectual interests impressed many other students who knew him. He did not abstain from alcohol, which would have been an extraordinary eccentricity, but he drank only sparingly. According to Lieberman, one of the most striking of Gorbachev's characteristics was the combination of dedicated Communist convictions and a dislike of bureaucratic formality. He was, Lieberman told an interviewer, "on the verge of nonconformity." On one occasion, Gorbachev became irritated when an instructor insisted on reading aloud in class page after page of a new work by Stalin instead of analyzing or discussing it. Gorbachev and Lieberman wrote an anonymous note to the lecturer, dryly reminding him that everyone in the class could read. When the instructor found it, he was so angry he read the note aloud before the class and denounced the author as antisocialist. Gorbachev calmly rose to acknowledge his authorship, pointed out his own Communist convictions and his leading role as a Komsomol member, and insisted that he merely disliked the instructor's pedantic manner of presenting Stalin's work. Though later criticized by officials for this act of impertinence, Gorbachev was not otherwise disciplined. The lecturer was replaced.

Mlynář and others recall Gorbachev as tending to mix with students older than himself, often with veterans of World War II like Lieberman, yet not given to flaunting his own political achievements, which he could have done if he had worn to classes his Red Banner of Labor emblem. The award, with its connotation of political excellence, might have won him favor from instructors, but in Mlynář's view, to have done so would have been out of character with Gorbachev's desire to do things on his own. The future Soviet leader, Mlynář has written, "was an open-minded person, and his intelligence never led him into arrogance. He knew how to listen and was willing to do so to others. He was honest and goodwilled. He had acquired a natural rather than a formal authority, while maintaining his pride. He was reformist by nature." Yet Mlynář acknowledges a complexity to Gorbachev's nature that goes beyond these fine but easily discerned attributes. He has, the Czech agrees, "various layers of personality. What belongs to his character and what is very positive is that he has self-assurance. This could also be a danger because he is such a self-made man and could overestimate his qualities. It was clear that neither of us would pursue a legal career."

Alexander Stromas, who did not know Gorbachev well, and who was graduated three years before Gorbachev, nonetheless describes him as a determined, self-contained and tidy person. "He was a very, very thorough man. He was quite disciplined. He got a good degree." Stromas says he had reason to be grateful to Gorbachev for using his political influence as a Komsomol activist to get Stromas out of unspecified political trouble at the university. Neznansky, who is otherwise somewhat critical of Gorbachev, recalls that Gorbachev also helped him after a choice postgraduation assignment he had won was transferred to another student with political connections. Gorbachev protested the case, says Neznansky, and succeeded in having the injustice reversed. On another occasion recalled by Neznansky, Gorbachev put himself on the line during a period of military training that all students were obliged to fulfill as part of their studies. When a brutal sergeant major forced the students to do exhausting drills without a rest after an eight-mile run, Gorbachev protested to an officer and had the order rescinded.

In another incident recalled by Mlynář, Gorbachev revealed an openness about secret-police practices that could be considered unusual. During the summer of 1951, at the end of the first academic year, Gorbachev returned to Privolnoye to work on the harvest, and Mlynář went back to Prague. From there, he innocently sent a postcard to Gorbachev. When the card arrived, though, it caused havoc among security officials of the Ministry of Internal Affairs, which was in charge of police work throughout the Soviet Union. Anything received from abroad was an object of suspicion, even if from a "fraternal socialist" country, and the recipient became the subject of an investigation. Gorbachev told Mlynář later that the local police chief had delivered the card to him in person, presumably in order to investigate the potential security risk in his midst. Obviously, Gorbachev was able to explain away the incident, and both men laughed at the drama ensuing from such an innocent gesture.

Some former Soviet citizens have expressed surprise at Gorbachev's candor with Mlynář, interpreting it as more likely to have been a deliberate effort to draw the Czech out than an expression of his own views. They reason that Gorbachev would probably have been required to write reports on Mlynář, who was after all a foreigner, for the secret police, and that it would have been unusual for a Soviet citizen to be so forthright in his views with a foreigner for any other reason. While Gorbachev may have written such reports on Mlynář for the secret police, there were obviously two quite distinct sides to the young Soviet in his student years. One side, which he evidently displayed to very few people—among them, Mlynář—displayed a frank skepticism about some specific aspects of Soviet internal policy under Stalin. Soviet fellow students of Gorbachev's have confirmed that fairly frank political debates did occur in those days, albeit within small circles of trusted friends. The other side of Gorbachev, which was quite different, was his official side, characterized by the external brusqueness of a Komsomol leader conscious of making a good impression on Communist Party officials observing his conduct. Impressions of Gorbachev among those who knew him at Moscow State University vary entirely according to whether they were privy to his intimate, intellectual nature, or whether they merely saw his more officious Komsomol front.

According to the recollections of Mlynář, which are supported in tone if not in detail by other former students still in the Soviet Union and generally supportive of the regime there, Gorbachev was genuinely irritated by the more foolish aspects of Soviet internal propaganda. This was particularly the case when his own experience as a youth on a collective farm contradicted the falsehoods about Soviet rural life generated daily in the Soviet press. Once, Gorbachev and Mlynář watched together the Stalinist-era propaganda movie *Cossacks of the Ku-*

ban. In some respects the movie was as good an example of Soviet disinformation as Leni Riefenstahl's *Triumph of the Will* was a classic of Nazi propaganda. The theme of *Cossacks* is the collectivization of the 1930s, and scene after scene shows smiling peasants gathered around tables sagging under the weight of delicious-looking food. Gorbachev, who was intimate with the North Caucasus region depicted in the film and with the undernourished reality of life there, commented sardonically, "It's not like that at all."

In another episode recounted by Mlynář, Gorbachev's remembrances of grim experiences in the countryside rose up in him when he and his fellow students took up the subject of *kolkhoz* law, a part of the overall field of Soviet law. "When we were studying collective-farm law," said Mlynář, "Gorbachev explained to me how insignificant collective-farm legislation was in day-to-day life and how important, on the other hand, was brute force, which alone secured working discipline on the collective farms."

This was a daring thing for any Soviet citizen to have said, especially to a foreigner. But it is probable that Gorbachev felt willing to trust Mlynář precisely because Mlynář, being a foreigner, was himself vulnerable. And the Czech, with his more European-oriented view of the world, had introduced Gorbachev—at some risk to himself—to facts and notions about the outside world of which any mention inside the Soviet Union was forbidden. There is another point about the friendship that must have been a vital ingredient in the ease with which both men confided their views to each other: both were dedicated Communists. They believed unquestioningly that socialism—that is, as Soviet ideology still interprets it, a state in which all means of production are in the hands of the state, and the state itself is guided by a Communist Party with a monopoly of political power—was the world path of the future and the only possible form of society for the U.S.S.R. Finally, unlike many fellow students, who merely went through the motions of political involvement, both Gorbachev and Mlynář were intensely interested in politics. They believed that politics could make a difference in people's lives, and despite everything they were not cynical about Soviet society.

Mlynář recalls, "Our political discussions were very open. He was one of the few who talked about politics. The others were just not interested. I knew that he was a convinced ideological Communist and that we shared the conviction that Communism was the way of the future. He was never cynical. He was reformist by nature." At one point Mlynář wrote a paper for their student seminar in which he said the state should be the watchdog of economic life rather than the organizer of every aspect of it. "I said that the state had to distribute rewards to those who deserved them," says Mlynář. "There was a long discussion, and Gorbachev said, 'Yes, you are right that rewards should be according to performance, but in reality it is quite different.' He said then that socialist justice should consist in socialist distribution of rewards that correspond to the quality and quantity of labor."

The intellectual discussions, which must have been exciting for both Mlynář and Gorbachev, were only one side of Gorbachev's Moscow university years. For all his interest in theory, Gorbachev was demonstrating at a very early age the skills of a talented politician. One of the courses in the law faculty was practice in courtroom rhetoric. The course gave students an opportunity to learn the arts of oral persuasion by trying them in a risk-free environment and receiving excellent professional critiques. To this day Gorbachev has demonstrated the fruits of this training. Though he can be long-winded and at times quite dogmatic, he is the most effective public speaker of any Soviet leader since Lenin.

The main feature of Gorbachev's political life at Moscow university was not, however, rhetoric; it was his enthusiastic and successful career in the university Komsomol. He had arrived in Moscow with an outstanding reference from the

Komsomol committee of the Krasnogvardeisky district of Stavropol Krai. It is highly probable, in fact, that the Komsomol recommendation he received from Stavropol played a major role in securing him a place at Moscow university. The most detailed authority on Gorbachev's Komsomol career at Moscow university is Fridrikh Neznansky, who did political and community-service work in the same Moscow Komsomol district as Gorbachev (Krasnaya Presnya), worked part-time in the same collective farm outside Moscow during occasional school-year periods, and was a fellow cadet at the Gorokhovetsky army camp near Kovrov, some 150 miles east of Moscow. Perhaps because Gorbachev's Komsomol career is a much less appealing side of the young man's career as a student in Moscow, Mlynář is almost silent on the subject. Neznansky, who emigrated from the Soviet Union legally in 1978, is more forthcoming.

Gorbachev was evidently cautious in the Komsomol during his first academic year in Moscow. In 1951, though, he was elected *komsorg kursa,* a job whose Russian title is an acronym for Komsomol organizer for the course, but could be paraphrased to Komsomol organizer for the class. During his university years, in fact, Gorbachev rose to be one of eleven members of the Komsomol committee for the law faculty, responsible, among other things, for educational affairs. Finally, from 1952 to 1954, he became Komsomol organizer for the law faculty as a whole. According to Neznansky, Gorbachev's elevation to the initial *komsorg* job was accomplished in a somewhat unscrupulous manner, with Gorbachev replacing the existing *komsorg* reportedly after getting the man drunk the night before a Komsomol meeting and then denouncing his behavior as unworthy of a Communist youth activist. Other fellow students of Gorbachev's either do not recall or will not discuss this incident. They do, however, remember the young man from the provinces as unusually officious, and even strident, in his performance of the Komsomol duties.

There are, in fact, conflicting recollections of Gorbachev as *komsorg*. Even Neznansky acknowledges that Gorbachev used his political clout to help Neznansky in the final stages of his law course, when he was preparing for his first job assignment outside the university. Stromas also credits Gorbachev with getting him out of political trouble, and Lieberman, a Jew, asserts that Gorbachev did not dissociate himself from the anti-Semitic paranoia that gripped the Soviet Union in early 1953, during the last months of Stalin's life. Yet Gorbachev appears to have been an unusually strict disciplinarian. Once, Neznansky recalls, when several students were late for a compulsory Komsomol meeting because they had attended a concert, other Komsomol organizers merely asked those present not to be late again. Gorbachev, however, reprimanded his group in formal and grating terms.

More disturbing, Gorbachev was evidently zealous in seeking the expulsion from the Komsomol, and in some cases from Moscow university, of students with relatives who were prisoners in the labor camps or were in some kind of politically bad odor. Lev Yudovich says he can remember the "steely voice of the Komsomol secretary of the law faculty, Gorbachev, demanding expulsion from the Komsomol for the slightest offenses, from telling political anecdotes to shirking being sent to a *kolkhoz.*" Yudovich, who was graduated two years before Gorbachev from the law faculty, says that he and his friends were wary of Gorbachev because of the young man's ideological zeal. Yudovich says he remembers seeing Gorbachev in the lobby of the law faculty not long after Gorbachev had begun his first year. Gorbachev was wearing a dark blue military-style coat and a cossack-fur hat. "Be careful of him," said a friend, nodding toward Gorbachev. Yudovich says Gorbachev had a reputation for being politically officious and self-serving. He adds, "Some of us regarded him as a two-faced person. He was very good in his relations with his fellow students. He wanted to help some of them, but when he took the

floor to speak, he didn't speak out. He just uttered slogans."
Neznansky says that while Gorbachev was not personally arrogant and did not use his Komsomol position to secure material or other privileges, his zeal in towing the party line in public made him unpopular with some students.

Thus emerges a picture of the young Gorbachev as something of a Goody Two-Shoes, punctilious in performing his
Komsomol duties and even in keeping his room clean. One of
the lesser honors he shared during his university career was a
prize for having the tidiest quarters. That may have owed less
to Gorbachev's efforts than to the fact that the room leader
was reportedly a former army sergeant major. Gorbachev's
Komsomol duties consisted largely of carrying out political
and administrative chores at the agitpunkt, or propaganda
center, of the Krasnaya Presnya party district in Moscow.
Komsomol activists had to help get people living in the district
to vote in the formal elections, at which attendance was obligatory and seldom went below 99.9%, or had to attend to residents' problems with their apartment roofs or plumbing. In
keeping with the complex layers of his personality, Gorbachev
may have genuinely enjoyed helping ordinary Muscovites
with the problems of daily life; at the same time he was reap-
ing the rewards of conspicuous political zeal. Neznansky, however, says that Gorbachev's chief concern was not so much the
welfare of the Kransaya Presnya constituents as the reputation for excellence of his particular Komsomol unit.

In 1951, the year he began his *komsorg* career, Gorbachev also became a candidate-member of the Communist Party of the Soviet Union. After the requisite one-year probation-
ary period, during which Gorbachev attended party meetings
but could not take part in the decision-making process, the
young man was formally enrolled in the ranks of the party.
This occurred shortly before the final party congress of the
Stalin years, the 19th, in a political atmosphere of intense hostility toward the West and toward putative enemies of the par-

ty within the country. By all accounts, Gorbachev embraced the official line, at party and Komsomol meetings, with the appearance—and no doubt the reality—of great personal conviction. But it is this very quality that raises questions about one aspect of Gorbachev's Komsomol role at Moscow State University in 1953, namely his conduct during the infamous "Doctors' Plot" episode in the twilight months of Stalin's life.

It would be hard to exaggerate the degree of political paranoia that smothered most of normal life in the Soviet Union in the last few months and years of Stalin's life. The Soviet Union had just acquired the hydrogen bomb, and international tensions were at a dangerous level. The Korean War was still raging, although the military situation was at a stalemate. Stalin's foreign policy setbacks in Europe—the collapse of the blockade of Berlin after the airlift of 1948-49, the failure to overthrow President Tito in Yugoslavia and the formation in 1949 of the North Atlantic Treaty Organization—had only intensified the Soviet leader's determination to impose his political will throughout the Continent. Secret Czechoslovak Communist Party documents made public during the Prague Spring in 1968 indicate that Stalin from 1952 onward was considering a military invasion of Western Europe.

Internally, the Soviet Union was in the grip of yet another purge of the intelligentsia and a witch-hunt for intellectuals who did not follow the party line in culture and art. It was the time of the so-called Zhdanovshchina, a period of suffocating orthodoxy in both cultural expression and scientific research, named after Andrei Zhdanov, a Politburo member who was Stalin's instrument for enforcing the leader's will in those areas. Though Zhdanov died in 1949, the assault on presumed foes of the Soviet state throughout the arts and sciences continued until Stalin's death in March 1953. The campaign began to take a particularly vicious turn in 1949, when the regime started referring to its internal enemies as "rootless, stateless cosmopolitans." At this point the thrust was unmistakably anti-Semitic, since so many outstanding Soviet intellectuals were of Jewish origin. Stalin and his ideological minions then went even further: a trend began in the Soviet press to identify virtually all important inventions of the modern era as Russian.

Many Jewish scholars and professors were purged from academic and professional positions during the 1949-53 period. But it was not until January 1953 that the campaign against "cosmopolitanism" began to reach terrifying proportions. In a last gasp effort to do away with an entire stratum of underlings whom he no longer trusted, Stalin began planning one final purge of the party and society. His principal target was Lavrenti Beria, the head of the secret police, whom Stalin himself was beginning to fear. But the device he selected to introduce the purge was a fictitious scheme against the entire Politburo that became known as the Doctors' Plot. Succinctly put, the allegation was that senior Kremlin doctors, many of whom were Jewish, had secretly been trying to poison Moscow's top leadership for years. Although the charges were false, some credibility was achieved after a few actual Kremlin physicians, who happened to be Jewish, did indeed confess to everything. The confessions were, of course, forced. The ultimate stage of the Doctors' Plot, in Stalin's plans, would have involved the arrests of thousands of Jews across the Soviet Union and the deportation of most of the Soviet Jewish population to a remote location in Siberia.

By late January 1953 the rooting out of "cosmopolitanism" and "Zionism" was gathering steam throughout Soviet society. Meetings at the Komsomol, labor union, factory, *kolkhoz* and other levels were being held to seek out and purge the alleged followers of the "doctors" wherever they could be found in Soviet public life. At Moscow State University and in several institutes of higher learning in the Soviet capital, Jewish professors were being denounced and forced out of their jobs. Says Dmitri Simes, a Soviet émigré who is now a scholar at Washington's Carnegie Endowment for International Peace: "I know from my parents that a real anti-Semitic pogrom was taking place. My father's closest friend and confidant was arrested and executed then." Michel Tatu, France's top Sovietologist and the author of a thoroughly researched biography of Gorbachev published in France in 1987, says that Gorbachev "had to howl with the wolves like everyone else." Tatu adds, "It is highly probable that the little Komsomol chief had to make his own contribution to the speeches against 'cosmopolitanism,' the 'Judases of medicine,' and 'corrupt liberalism.' "

Mlynář, who was close to Gorbachev through this period, does not deny that Gorbachev joined in all the ugly anti-Semitic rhetoric, but he insists that Gorbachev was not specifically responsible for the suffering of any individual at the university. "I know that Gorbachev was not involved in any affair that had tragic consequences," he asserts carefully. Stromas, who has attested to Gorbachev's streak of decency in protecting him during his own political difficulties, simply says, "I am sure that if Gorbachev had been asked to play a role in that [anti-Semitic campaign], he would have done so without any hesitation."

Finally, and quite providentially, the man behind the Doctors' Plot died on March 5, 1953. For many Soviet citizens, and not just Jews, awaiting with anguish the next murderous onslaught of Stalin's paranoia, the news of the leader's demise was greeted with profound relief. Nonetheless, for millions of ordinary Soviets who thought of Stalin in quasi-mythical terms as the infallible "Father of the Peoples," the savior of the nation who had led them to victory over the Germans in World War II, the loss was utterly traumatic. On the fourth and final day of Stalin's lying in state, thousands of Muscovites, frantic with grief and hysteria, stampeded in Moscow's streets close to where the body was on display.

Other startling things happened: the Doctors' Plot died

as suddenly as it had started, saving the Soviet Jewish community from a new wave of barbarism. Portraits of Beria, who
had been feared as much as Stalin, suddenly and mysteriously
disappeared from public places in June. It was later revealed
that the secret-police chief had been arrested and shot by a Politburo terrified that he might become the new Soviet dictator.
Within two years, even more dramatic changes had taken
place. One of the first signs of the post-Stalin thaw was the
slow and painful rehabilitation of victims of Stalin's political
terror. Literally millions of inhabitants of the Gulag—whose
population at Stalin's death was estimated to be about 8 million—were absolved of the charges of "counterrevolutionary
crimes" and started shuffling back into view in Soviet cities.
Suddenly, Soviet citizens began to realize that a legal system
they had been led to believe was the most humane and just in
the world was in fact a disgrace. For young people brought up
on the supposedly infallible verities of Stalinism, the revelations were shattering. Comments Soviet Historian Roy Medvedev, who has, despite official disapproval, meticulously
chronicled Stalinism: "It is easy to deal with these incidents
now as facts of history, but they were colossal events of personal importance to anyone living then who believed in Communist ideals, particularly for someone who wanted to be a lawyer. It was a shattering blow to previously held notions of
justice."

Neznansky says that Gorbachev dramatically changed
his views of Stalin, at least for public consumption, after Stalin's death. While he had always refrained from general discussions of Stalin during the Soviet leader's lifetime, no doubt
because he wished to avoid the charge of hypocrisy, Gorbachev, says Neznansky, became outspoken about him after
March 1953. For the first time, Gorbachev began talking of
the injustices done to the "middle peasants" during the 1930s
collectivization, mentioning a relative who had been unjustly
arrested. Stalin's own record, Gorbachev now began to say,

had been "half white and half black." According to Nez-nansky, Gorbachev began to acknowledge that Stalin had made mistakes in domestic policy, especially in agriculture, and that the total isolation in which he had kept the Soviet Union had also been wrong.

In fact, the suddenness of Gorbachev's change of attitude toward Stalin was obviously more apparent than real. As Mlynář makes clear, in private conversations without mentioning Stalin's name, the young man from Stavropol had all along harbored plenty of reservations about Soviet life under the dictator. However, since Gorbachev was required as a *komsorg* to extol the Soviet leader publicly, he obviously shared whatever doubts he had with only a few people, those he trusted utterly. Ironically, as Mlynář admits, the men with whom Gorbachev was closest had themselves started out as dedicated Stalinists.

The official Soviet biography says that Gorbachev was *komsorg* from 1952 until he was graduated in 1955. While this is technically correct, Neznansky claims that Gorbachev's Komsomol career at Moscow university experienced a set-back in 1954 after the merger of the Moscow Law Institute, a separate school, with the law faculty of Moscow State University. The merger, Neznansky says, led to the combining of the two Komsomol organizations of each institution. To preside over the joint organization, according to Neznansky, a position of Komsomol secretary was created, and there followed stiff competition between the institute's Komsomol activists and those of the law faculty. Naturally, the Moscow State University law faculty Komsomol backed Gorbachev for the position, but he faced opposition from the institute's *komsorg*, a certain Kondratenko, whose support lay largely in the World War II veterans both at his institute and at the university. Gorbachev, Neznansky asserts, was outmaneuvered by Kondratenko for the job, and thus lost what might have been a fine opportunity for pursuing a political career through the Moscow Komsomol apparatus.

As his graduation drew closer in 1955, Gorbachev must have known that there would be no comfortable job for him in Moscow and that he was obliged to return to Stavropol. He had already decided not to pursue a career in law, probably in part because he did not wish to have a career which was inextricably entangled with the security agencies. He was, in any event, much more interested in politics and the way that power changes nations and individual lives. It is also likely that, having assisted him into Moscow State University in the first place, the Komsomol authorities of Stavropol Krai had placed upon him the obligation to return to his roots and find employment there for at least a time.

The decision, if indeed there were alternatives, cannot have been easy. Raisa was comfortable and well adapted to urban living, particularly in the capital city of the Soviet Union, where cultural life was far richer than anything that could be found in the Soviet provinces. Gorbachev had done well: he was graduated from the law faculty with distinction, approximately the equivalent of a degree cum laude. He had demonstrated to the satisfaction of himself and others a self-confidence in public situations, in making his own way in life and in commanding the respect of his peers. That in itself would have been remarkable enough for a boy from a poor provincial background. More important, though, Gorbachev had discovered the joys of political life, of cajoling, persuading, arguing and planning. He had scratched in his mind a still incomplete notion of what the Soviet Union might be like with the "right" policies, and perhaps even what the world might be like. He needed to begin the long, arduous and, in the Soviet Union, sometimes dangerous process of moving up the ladder of the political apparatus to the point where he could begin to wield the power necessary to bring that notion to reality. As the train pulled out of Moscow's Kursk Railway Station in the summer of 1955, Gorbachev, with Raisa and their luggage beside him, must surely have had misgivings at leaving behind the city that had been his home for five difficult and often exciting years. He was not to return permanently until 23 years later. Meanwhile, his talents and energies were to find a new focus—the sleepy provincial capital of Stavropol, some 1,000 miles away.

3

Stavropol Years

Braving brisk gusts of wind, a handful of Stavropol residents take a shortcut across Lenin Square, a broad, paved plaza stretching from the spartan, five-story headquarters of the regional Communist Party committee to the city's oval sports stadium. Few glance at the monumental statue of Lenin, one hand clutching his coat lapel and eyes staring fixedly into the future from atop a granite pedestal by the entrance to the party building. Nor do the passersby pay much attention to an enormous sign above the gates of the athletic field: STAVROPOLITANS: RESOLUTELY BRING THE COURSE SET AT THE 27TH PARTY CONGRESS INTO LIFE. They hurry to the more sheltered, treelined shopping precincts, where the modernistic Central Department Store, abbreviated TsUM, towers above quaint two-story buildings painted in pastel colors with white trim.

The propaganda claims of *glasnost* and *perestroika* are relegated to second place during shopping hours in this south

Russian city, which sits astride the 45th parallel on a high-lying stretch of land between the snowcapped peaks of the Caucasus and the steppe country to the north. Most of its 300,000-plus inhabitants are preoccupied with a host of more mundane problems. Some may be heading to the wide-screen Ekran Theater just down from Lenin Square to pick up tickets for a showing of the Japanese movie *The Seven Samurai.* (Coming soon: *Dandy with the Nickname Crocodile,* better known as the Australian film *Crocodile Dundee.)* Others may be intent on checking the prices of meat at cooperative stores, grumbling under their breath that the subsidized products at state-run butchershops now go mainly to invalids and war veterans. A few may be tempted to stop on their way to the modern, enclosed market hall and splurge on a bouquet of white chrysanthemums, sold at inflated prices by peasant flower sellers.

The scene could be set in any of a hundred provincial cities across the Soviet Union, except that this regional capital can claim a major distinction. It is Gorbachev country, the place where he got his start as a politician. But the list of prominent officials with roots in Stavropol does not stop there. Another Soviet party leader, Yuri Andropov, was born in the railway station town of Nagutskaya in Stavropol Krai. In addition, Mikhail Suslov, the dour Politburo ideologist, held the job of Stavropol Krai party chief from 1939 to 1944. Another official who rose to prominence from that post was Fyodor Kulakov, who was a Kremlin agricultural expert in the 1960s and '70s and would play a critical role in pushing the young Gorbachev forward before Kulakov's own career came to a sudden end in 1978. Because of this unusual intersection of so many political power lines in an outlying region of Russia, Kremlinologists often speak of the "Stavropol connection."

If hearts beat faster now at the mention of Gorbachev's name in Stavropol, the locals do their best not to show it. At most they may venture an affectionate jibe, well into a restaurant meal, about what "Misha" Gorbachev, the "mineral water" General Secretary, would think of their enjoying a carafe of vodka. At the office of the regional Communist Party newspaper, *Stavropolskaya Pravda,* a commemorative album with pictures of distinguished visitors contains just a simple black-and-white photograph of Gorbachev as Stavropol Krai party boss during one of his meetings with local editors. After he was elected to the Communist Party's highest post in March 1985, the only change made in the scrapbook caption was to paste a paper strip with his new title over the old one. Street-corner posters with red letters on white spread the Kremlin's new political message: MAXIMIZING DEMOCRACY IS NOT JUST A SLOGAN BUT THE ESSENCE OF PERESTROIKA. Banners with similar texts in other towns refer to Gorbachev by name, but in his home region the Soviet leader's thoughts are more modestly attributed to the "materials" from party plenums. Stavropol is not a place for building personality cults.

During a local political career spanning more than two decades, Gorbachev made a slow and at times unspectacular journey from a modest position with the local Komsomol organization to the region's top job, chief of the Stavropol Krai party organization, before leaving for Moscow in 1978. If the young provincial political activist had his sights set on a position in the Kremlin during his Stavropol years, he was careful not to show it. Unlike an ambitious Governor of an American state, who can throw his hat into the presidential ring simply by announcing to the press that he wants the Oval Office job, those men who climb to the pinnacle of power in the Soviet Union typically display a skill at concealment, knowing when to speak out and when to hold their tongues. Gorbachev was no exception. Those Stavropolitans who encountered the future General Secretary during his years in their midst admit that his emergence later as an innovative reformer and major world leader caught them by surprise. As a Stavropol journalist said, "Gorbachev was an exemplary regional party secretary who stood out because of his broader knowledge. He was clearly someone above the provincial level. But we never expected that a new era would begin with him."

When they arrived from Moscow in the summer of 1955 after five heady years at Moscow State University, Gorbachev, then 24, and his wife Raisa must have found adjusting to life in Stavropol somewhat difficult. Vladimir Maximov, a Soviet writer now living in Paris who worked on the local Komsomol newspaper in the mid-1950s, remembers the territorial capital, which then had a population of only about 120,000, as little more than an "overgrown agricultural village whose life centered entirely on a single street." Karl Marx Prospect still has a pleasant, sloping park and shabbily elegant 19th century mansions with curlicued ironwork around their doorways. The street recalls those long past days when Stavropol played host to such Russian literary luminaries as the poets Alexander Pushkin and Mikhail Lermontov and Novelist Leo Tolstoy. Yet Karl Marx Prospect could hardly be mentioned in the same breath with Gorky Street, Kuznetsky Most or any of the other imposing boulevards that the Gorbachevs had left behind in the Soviet capital.

If Gorbachev had any misgivings about his new assignment, working in one of the departments of the Stavropol city Komsomol, he apparently did not let it show. He tackled the propaganda work and political education programs that are the bread and butter of this youth arm of the Communist Party with such dispatch that he was promoted to the position of first secretary in the city organization only a year later, in 1956. Considering the turmoil and confusion in the offices of state procurators around the country that followed the arrest and execution of former Secret Police Chief Lavrenti Beria in 1953, and the subsequent breakdown of Stalin's fearsome terror machine of prisons and labor camps, Gorbachev may have considered himself fortunate to be out of the legal profession. But there were more revelations to come, and those would shatter whatever political illusions Gorbachev still might have held about Stalin and put his Communist convictions to the test. On the morning of Feb. 25, 1956, Nikita Khrushchev delivered a secret speech, "On the Cult of Personality and Its Consequences," to the 20th Communist Party Congress. The speech was an event of such historical import that its repercussions can still be felt in the Soviet Union more than three decades later.

According to Historian Roy Medvedev's account, Khrushchev, working from a text that he had not submitted in advance for the approval of his comrades in the party Presidium, took advantage of the moment between the election of a new Central Committee and the formal announcement of its membership to expose the crimes of Stalin. While the carefully screened audience in the Great Hall of the Kremlin followed his words in rapt horror, the First Secretary presented a chilling exposé of the great wave of terror, torture, mass arrest and imprisonment—a purge that had reached into the highest ranks of the Kremlin's ruling élite and stripped the 1934 Central Committee of two-thirds of its members. Khrushchev also dared to besmirch Stalin's hallowed war record, blaming him for the string of defeats in 1941 that allowed Hitler's invading forces to advance almost to the gates of Moscow.

Khrushchev's secret speech proved to be anything but secret. It was soon being read around the globe in an English translation made available by an obliging U.S. State Department. Whatever opposition the Stalinist Old Guard might have raised to releasing the text of the report on the "cult of personality" within the Soviet Union apparently crumbled when angry supporters of the dead dictator took to the streets in his home republic of Georgia to mark the third anniversary of his death. One month after the Feb. 25 address, the complete text was circulated in a special printing to regional and city party officials. They, in turn, arranged gatherings across the country at which Khrushchev's denunciations were read in full. The debate was often stormy and emotional, as anger

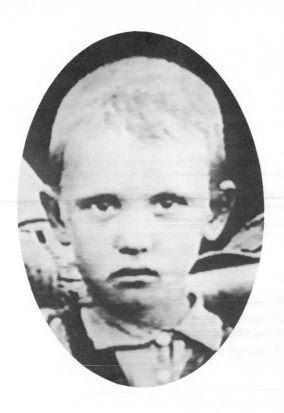

At age four, "Misha" Gorbachev already had the penetrating gaze that would be one of his hallmarks as a politician. There was much for the boy to see. Growing up in Privolnoye during the 1930s, he could not help experiencing the privation and repression that accompanied Stalin's forced collectivization of agriculture. He also endured the Nazi occupation of the Stavropol region during World War II—and had a brief encounter with religion. His grandparents, who kept icons hidden behind portraits of Lenin and Stalin, once took him to church. But, as he said later, he felt no need to make a return visit.   *Gostelradio*

With his grandparents in Privolnoye, circa 1935.   *Gostelradio*

His father Sergei
Andreyevich Gorbachev,
late 1940s.
Gostelradio

His mother Maria
Panteleyevna Gorbachev,
circa 1987.
Gostelradio

Mikhail at age 19.
Gostelradio

As a student at Moscow State University, early 1950s.   *Gostelradio*

САВКИН С.Ф. ВОЛОБУЕВА САФРОНО
...В.М. ГОРБАЧЕВ М.С. ТАПИЛИН

The house on Dzerzhinsky Street, Stavropol, where the rising provincial party official lived with his wife Raisa until 1978.
Rudi Frey—TIME

Mikhail and Raisa around the time of their wedding, 1954.
Gostelradio

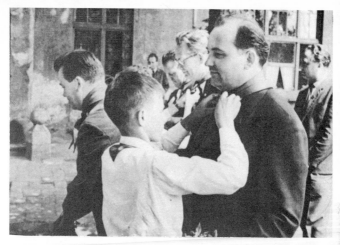

During a 1966 visit to East Germany, he receives a kerchief from a Young Pioneer.   *ADN—Zentralbild*

Family portrait, probably taken in the 1970s. From left: Maria Panteleyevna, Daughter Irina, Mikhail, Raisa, Son-in-Law Anatoli. *Richardson + Steirman*

Mikhail and Raisa on vacation in the Soviet Union, circa 1986.
Richardson + Steirman

that had accumulated over the years was finally vented. But Historian Medvedev recalls that sometimes there was almost no discussion of the text. Many Communist Party workers who had been loyal followers of Stalin left in silence with their heads bowed, undoubtedly too stunned and ashamed to risk looking anyone else in the eye. As a young Komsomol activist in Stavropol, Gorbachev must have found himself hard pressed to explain the stunning turn of events to workers and students within the Communist youth organization.

What had been a trickle of returning prisoners from the Gulag soon became a flood as special commissions were set up in the camps to review the cases of millions who had been arbitrarily arrested during Stalin's reign of terror. The entire nation experienced an extraordinary new sense of freedom. The title of Soviet Writer Ilya Ehrenburg's novel *The Thaw* provided perhaps the defining image for the era of change following Stalin's death, and Novelist Vladimir Dudintsev signaled the new quest for personal values in his book *Not by Bread Alone*. As the rigid artistic canons of the Stalinist period melted, critics debated the topic of "sincerity in literature" in the pages of Moscow's literary journals. Overnight a new generation of poets appeared on the scene—Andrei Voznesensky, Yevgeni Yevtushenko, Bulat Okudzhava—who would lend their lyric voices three decades later in support of Gorbachev's policy of openness. The new buoyant mood infected all of Moscow in the summer of 1957, when the Soviet capital opened its long-closed doors to the world to welcome foreign visitors participating in the Sixth International Youth Festival.

Even provincial Stavropol was swept by the currents of change from the capital. Emigré Writer Maximov remembers encountering Gorbachev, then the Stavropol city first secretary, in the editorial office of the local Komsomol newspaper, where the young official would come to discuss the exciting developments in Moscow. According to Maximov, Gorbachev was always careful to toe the party line but welcomed the transformation in Soviet political life. Though he would later earn a reputation as an ardent campaigner for sobriety, Gorbachev was not averse to sharing a drink or two with friends in the heat of the discussion. "He would sit down with us in a casual manner," Maximov later recalled. "We would uncork a bottle of wine and usually talk politics. Khrushchev's report on the crimes of the Stalinist era had recently appeared. The entire country was still reeling from the shock, in the mistaken expectation that a dawn of democracy might appear."

If that first glimmer of light proved premature, the experiences of the thaw years left an indelible imprint on the political thinking of Gorbachev and his contemporaries, who still sometimes refer to themselves as "the children of the 20th Congress." Gorbachev has occasionally made reference to this watershed party conclave while promoting his own policy of *perestroika*. During a meeting with party activists in the Moscow region agriculture belt in August 1987, Gorbachev made a personal aside about the Khrushchev years that was edited out of the account of the meeting when it appeared in the Communist party daily, *Pravda*. Looking out over the attentive audience, he noted that, with few exceptions, they were all of his generation, political activists who had begun their careers at the time of the 20th Party Congress. "We have experienced it all and we know the pluses and minuses, the gains and the losses," he said, his voice ringing with emotion. "Let's renew ourselves!" For the moment, he seemed transformed into a Russian revivalist preacher.

Even in his Komsomol days, the young Gorbachev displayed something of a reformer's zeal, as if he could right the wrongs of the past by his own personal dedication to the cause. He was not like other youth league activists, who carried out their educational visits to work sites in a perfunctory manner. When local journalists not long ago asked the construction crew at an irrigation project in the Stavropol territory if they could remember any of the names of the Komsomol members who had come to encourage them in token propaganda meetings, the name Gorbachev stuck in their minds. They remembered a certain Misha who appeared at the canal site and spent the entire day with them. When Khrushchev launched a campaign in July 1958 "On Strengthening the Link Between School and Life," as his memo to the Central Committee phrased it, he found an ardent supporter in Gorbachev. Undoubtedly remembering his own years divided between the classroom and the grain fields of Privolnoye, the Komsomol leader helped organize work-study programs for schoolchildren, called "Stavropol instructional brigades," that soon served as a model for the entire country.

Gorbachev's apparent skill at promoting party policies at the Stavropol city level won him an appointment to the propaganda department of the Stavropol Krai Komsomol in 1958. He soon advanced to territorial second secretary and then, in 1960, to the post of first secretary and a seat on the Stavropol Krai party committee. While attending meetings at party headquarters, Gorbachev encountered Fyodor Kulakov, an ambitious agronomist who had recently suffered a political setback and been shipped out from the Ministry of Grain Produce in Moscow to become chief of the Stavropol Krai party organization. Kulakov had been Komsomol first secretary in the Penza region and may have felt a special bond to the young Stavropol Komsomol leader who had graduated from Moscow State University. In any event, it was a friendship that would help Gorbachev's political career.

The Communist youth league activist from Privolnoye was also learning a few lessons about the use and abuse of influence, a tool that would serve him well in his advance through the Soviet bureaucracy. Vladimir Maximov tells how Gorbachev was once approached by a Stavropol poet who asked the Komsomol leader if he would not mind using his connections to get the writer a Volga car. Gorbachev agreed to pull a few strings, and the poet was able to buy his auto. But he promptly sold it on the black market and came back to ask his well-connected friend for another one. "Gorbachev did not usually lose his temper," says Maximov, "but on that occasion he started shouting and threw the poet out of the office, ordering him never to show his face there again."

Emigré Fridrikh Neznansky also noticed a steely, hard-edged side to his old law school companion while working as a criminal investigator in the Stavropol region in 1956. As head of the city Communist youth league, Gorbachev was in a position to advise city officials on whether errant party activists should be subject to criminal prosecution. Though Gorbachev raised no objections to the arrest of a Komsomol member who had been accused of rape, the Stavropol city first secretary took a different view when Neznansky sought to press charges against a Komsomol secretary who had used his office to pilfer dues. Gorbachev received him in a "democratic" way, Neznansky recalls, but objected to any arrest on the grounds that it would damage the prestige of the Communist youth league. His decision was upheld by city party leaders.

If Khrushchev's campaign to dismantle the myth of Stalin had already sent shock waves rumbling through the party establishment, his proposals to abolish abuses of party privilege and revamp the bureaucracy prodded the Old Guard into open revolt. At a special meeting of the leadership in June 1957, Communist Party Presidium Members Vyacheslav Molotov, Georgi Malenkov and Lazar Kaganovich tried to remove the First Secretary from his post. The coup was foiled when Khrushchev went over the heads of the Presidium and rallied support at an extraordinary Central Committee session. Khrushchev had his revenge by forcing this so-called antiparty group of unreconstructed Stalinists out of the Presidium. The way was cleared to strike a second blow against Stalin's grim legacy at the 22nd Party Congress, in October 1961. Among the delegates was the first secretary of the Stavropol Krai Komsomol, Mikhail Gorbachev.

The meeting went even further than the 20th Congress in denouncing the crimes of Stalin and widened the circle of blame to include Khrushchev's foes in the antiparty group. Gorbachev must have winced when the attack turned to former General Prosecutor Andrei Vyshinsky, the guiding intelligence behind Stalin-era justice, whose thinking had permeated the education of an entire generation of Soviet lawyers. With the ardor of true iconoclasts, the 5,000 delegates in the Kremlin's Great Hall set about shattering the last vestiges of the personality cult. The heroic city of Stalingrad was rechristened Volgograd, and thousands of cities, towns, villages, schools, factories, streets and squares were stripped of the dictator's name. The real moment of drama came when a resolution was passed to remove the body of Stalin from the mausoleum in Red Square where it had rested beside Lenin's. But Poet Yevgeni Yevtushenko expressed the fears of many Soviet intellectuals that the exorcism of Stalin had not gone far enough. In his poem *The Heirs of Stalin,* he pleaded with the Kremlin to "double, treble the guards over that gravestone slab, so that Stalin should not rise and with Stalin—the past."

Because of Khrushchev's lingering suspicion of the old Stalinist flank of the party, Gorbachev and his contemporaries were told that they were the future hope of the nation. The Soviet Premier's penchant for shuffling and tinkering with party and government organizations opened the way for many university graduates and holders of higher degrees to move into positions of relative importance within the party establishment. In March 1962 Khrushchev unveiled another such scheme to set up new administrative organizations for agriculture that would rank above existing district party and government committees. The title of the new organizations—territorial agricultural production units—was cumbersome, and so was their functioning. The units oversaw the operation of as many as 25 to 30 collective and state farms in an area that sometimes encompassed two or three of the old administrative districts. The result in many cases was bureaucratic chaos. But for Gorbachev, the time had come to make the jump from the Komsomol to the party apparatus, and he accepted the post of party organizer in one of the 16 units that had been carved out of the Stavropol Krai.

For his new job Gorbachev needed theoretical training to go along with what he had learned working with his hands in the fields of Privolnoye, so he enrolled in correspondence courses at the Stavropol Agricultural Institute. Before the year was out, he had been promoted to the party organizational department of the Stavropol Krai committee, a key posting that allowed him to influence the promotion or demotion of party workers in the *nomenklatura*, a list of positions controlled by the party. Khrushchev's obsessive concern with boosting agricultural yields and his constant meddling in matters as arcane as crop rotation did not make life easy for party workers in this south Russian breadbasket. Sometimes they faced dubious directives to plow fallow fields, at other times they endured unrealistic schemes designed to surpass the U.S. in the production of meat and dairy products. When Khrushchev authorized a price hike of about 30% for meat and butter products in June 1962 as a way of encouraging increased production, discontent with the Soviet leader's brand of reforms broke into the open in the north Caucasus. In Novocherkassk, a city in the neighboring Rostov region, Soviet soldiers opened fire on a mob marching toward city hall.

Khrushchev was planning to launch yet another scheme to dismantle and reorganize Soviet agriculture in the autumn of 1964, but it was never realized. He was ousted on Oct. 14 from the posts of party First Secretary and Premier, accused of everything from treating the ruling Presidium with contempt to bestowing inappropriate honors on the leaders of Third World client states. Leonid Brezhnev was appointed the new party First Secretary, and Alexei Kosygin assumed the post of Premier, as head of the Council of Ministers. The ruling *troika* was completed in 1965 when Nikolai Podgorny became President—or, more formally, Chairman of the Presidium of the Supreme Soviet. According to Historian Medvedev, there is evidence that the party putsch had been planned in the Stavropol territory a month before Khrushchev's downfall, when select Presidium and Central Committee members gathered at the invitation of local Party Boss Kulakov for several days of "hunting and fishing" near Manych Lakes. It is unlikely that Gorbachev, who was still working in the Stavropol Krai's party-organization department, played any part in the plan. Kulakov's rise into the ruling élite was confirmed at the party plenum in November 1964, when he was placed in charge of the agricultural department of the Central Committee.

Gorbachev was also moving up the local bureaucracy in Stavropol and was appointed first secretary of the city Communist Party committee in September 1966. He moved into offices in the old governor's mansion at 94 Karl Marx Prospect, a three-story red brick building, trimmed in stone, whose entryway is watched by four monumental caryatids draped in Grecian robes. The guardians of the New Order, Marx and Lenin, keep watch from pedestals in a park across the street. No matter how elegantly bourgeois the Stavropol city party headquarters might appear, it could not have more impeccable revolutionary credentials. A plaque near the main entrance informs all passersby that the building was the headquarters in 1918 of the first Council of the People's Commissars, the local branch of the ministerial structure, in Stavropol territory.

As de facto mayor of the city, Gorbachev was expected not only to make sure that the buses ran on time but also to monitor the latest urban policy pronouncements from Moscow and try to carry them out. Even at this period in his career, Gorbachev already displayed a penchant for finding unorthodox solutions to problems. He decided that Stavropol needed a permanent circus to meet the growing demand for entertainment from an increasingly youthful population. He took his request to Moscow, only to have the door slammed in his face. A city the size of Stavropol, Gorbachev was told, did not need—and could not financially support—its own circus. Undeterred, Gorbachev gathered funding from a variety of organizations and institutions and launched a cooperative venture to build Stavropol a circus. He proved the Moscow *nyet*-sayers wrong. The concrete, flying-saucer-like "big top," which he helped nudge toward completion with frequent visits to the construction site, now stands on Karl Marx Prospect.

In the late spring of 1966, while Gorbachev was still assigned to the territorial party-organization department, he was finally granted a glimpse of the outside world. He made an eleven-day trip to the German Democratic Republic to "study the experiences" of the East German comrades. The congenial visitor from Stavropol inspected stalls at a pig-breeding farm, looked over the student honor board at the Hoyerswerda Polytechnical School, accepted bouquets from kindergarten children and found time to exchange toasts with his East German hosts and go rafting in the forest streams of Spreewald. The future world statesman and summiteer also visited the chambers in the Cecilienhof Palace in Potsdam where President Harry Truman had prepared for his meetings in 1945 with Stalin.

Gorbachev's first look at the capitalist world also came in 1966, when he traveled to France as part of a Soviet delegation. The group's expenses were covered by Jean-Baptiste Doumeng, a leftist French businessman sometimes called the "red millionaire." When French Sovietologist Michel Tatu in 1985 asked Gorbachev about the visit, the Soviet leader said that he had spent several weeks traveling the length and breadth of France in a Renault car, rolling up nearly 5,000 km on the odometer. It was certainly an extraordinary journey for a Communist official. But if Gorbachev had conceived any new ideas about the Soviet Union's ideological opponents, he kept them to himself.

Life in a backwater of southern Russia must have begun to grow weary for the Moscow-educated couple. Gorbachev continued his correspondence courses at the Stavropol Agricultural Institute, insisting that he take his exams just as any other student would, despite his position as the city's top official. He received his diploma as an agronomist-economist in 1967. Raisa was awarded her degree of candidate of philosophical sciences from the Moscow State Pedagogical Institute the same year. She continued her academic career in Stavropol, teaching at the city's Pedagogical Institute, which is housed in an old theological seminary a few blocks from Lenin Square. But the Gorbachevs were already reaching the boundaries of what life in Stavropol could offer them. It must certainly have crossed Mikhail's mind that while he was administering a provincial capital that ranked 110th among Soviet towns and cities in population, his old law school friend Zdeněk Mlynář had already been promoted to the Central Committee of the Czechoslovak Communist Party.

Mlynář came to visit Gorbachev in 1967, arriving by airplane in Kamenny Vody, a resort town in Stavropol Krai. Gorbachev, wearing a Panama hat, was there to meet him with a car. The two embraced and set off on a tour of the region. They talked and had a few drinks through the afternoon and late into the evening. Gorbachev expressed his support for deposed Premier Khrushchev's destalinization campaign but questioned his erratic lurches in agricultural policy. Brezhnev, Gorbachev told his Czech friend, was better than Khrushchev in this respect, but the Stavropol party leader still had complaints about excessive interference from Moscow in provincial affairs.

Gorbachev seemed almost wistful when Mlynář explained how the Czechoslovaks were going about their own destalinization program, cleaning house at the very top of the Communist Party in a reform movement that would come to be known as the Prague Spring. "Perhaps there are possibilities in Czechoslovakia because conditions are different," Gorbachev said. When the two men finally arrived back at the Gorbachev apartment late at night, much the worse for wear, Raisa was furious. It was the last time Gorbachev and Mlynář would meet. The Prague Spring came to an abrupt end with the Warsaw Pact invasion of August 1968. When Gorbachev visited Czechoslovakia as part of an official Soviet delegation in 1969, Mlynář was in political disgrace, and thus the two were unable to see each other.

The Stavropol city party boss had told the Czech Communist that he viewed Brezhnev as only a transitional political figure. He was proved wrong. After the hectic days of Khrushchev, Brezhnev brought stability and order to the Soviet bureaucracy. But there would be no more daring innovations to threaten the job security of party apparatchiki. What reform measures were introduced to prod an increasingly sluggish centralized economy proved piecemeal and largely ineffective. The Brezhnev era would later come to be labeled the "time of stagnation," but it was marked by steady advances in Gorbachev's political career. In 1968 he leapfrogged the post of third secretary to become second secretary of the Stavropol Krai party committee, a position that included the region's agricultural portfolio. A year later, he was elected for the first time as a Deputy to the Supreme Soviet, the Soviet Union's parliament, and assigned to the parliamentary commission for the protection of the environment. That was an important subject for the Stavropol region, where drought and soil erosion had long been a major problem.

The next giant stride in Gorbachev's progress to Moscow came in April 1970, when he was appointed first secretary of the Stavropol Kraikom, the territorial party committee. Gorbachev had in effect become governor of the Stavropol territory, though he wielded considerably more power than the Governor of an American state. Despite the extreme centralization of political and economic decisionmaking in Moscow, regional party bosses form a key power bloc at mid-level in the Soviet hierarchy and have the clout to advance or brake policy decisions made in the Kremlin. Since the local party structure exactly mirrors the way power is divided in Moscow, territorial party First Secretary Gorbachev presided over a local politburo, a party secretariat and a regional central committee—just as if he were a minor-league Brezhnev.

The Stavropol territory presented problems for local party officials that were unique among provincial regions in the Soviet Union. The vagaries of geography and the ethnic diversity there left their distinctive stamp on those who have governed the region. Indeed, Stavropolitans contend that once a leader has been steeled by the special conditions of life in Stavropol, he is Moscow material. As a local political expert put it, "It is almost like a process of natural selection. The weak do not survive. Only an active, thinking leader who is more daring in decisions can succeed here." Gorbachev too had to graduate from the Stavropol academy of hard knocks.

Covering a land area that is roughly the size of Belgium, Switzerland and three Luxembourgs put together, the territory contains an example of almost every type of landscape and climatic zone to be found in the Soviet Union, from alpine meadows and permafrost belts to deserts and sun-parched steppes. Stavropol does lack one feature: although located on a corridor stretching between the Black and Caspian seas, it is landlocked and dry. As an old joke has it, there are many rivers in the Stavropol region but no water. Excluding, of course, the famous mineral springs at health spa resorts like Mineralnye Vody (Mineral Waters) and Kislovodsk, where Kremlin leaders have frequently taken the waters—and the measure of the local party leaders who come to meet them at the airport or train station and ensure that their stay is a pleasant one.

The task of ensuring that the nuts and bolts of the territorial bureaucracy were oiled and functioning smoothly would have been the domain of the local government committee. But as *kraikom* boss, Gorbachev had the responsibilities of both chief executive officer and ideological chaplain for the territory. This entailed delivering hundreds of speeches to party groups on the latest policy directives from Moscow and oral reports on what had transpired at Russian Republic and central Communist Party gatherings. Unlike other party functionaries, Gorbachev conducted these instructional sessions with animation and humor. He spoke, in the words of one Stavropol political journalist, "as if he were a living, breathing person." Gorbachev also traveled the length and breadth of Stavropol to visit collective farms and inspect crop damage, pushed forward the construction of an irrigation canal to cope with the region's chronic water shortages and encouraged the introduction of new production techniques into factories, reforms that already foreshadowed some of the experiments in economic self-management that would emerge a decade later with *perestroika*.

Gorbachev may appear to have burst full-grown onto the world scene from out of nowhere, but there were glimpses of a new type of political leader in the making during his Stavropol years. Long before *glasnost* became a household word, the Stavropol party chief was already displaying a keen interest in the press and apparently devoting part of his morning just to scanning the local newspapers. At least, that was the time when he always made his telephone calls to the editorial offices of *Molodoi Leninets*, the local youth newspaper, with comments on the day's issue and suggestions for future topics. Alexander Mayatsky, a former managing editor of *Stavropolskaya Pravda*, remembers how Gorbachev would sometimes come up to him on the street, grab him by the lapel and launch into a discussion of his latest column, encouraging him to tackle topics like milk production that were often outside the journalist's field. Says Mayatsky: "If Gorbachev found something interesting, you had the impression that it would occupy him day and night, waking and sleeping."

Gorbachev saw to it that complete documents from regional party gatherings were made available to the press, and he set up regular monthly press briefings for Stavropol-region newspaper editors. At these gatherings, he or other ranking party officials would explain new programs and field questions on a broad range of topics. It was standard operating procedure elsewhere for editors to coordinate their newspaper's coverage and editorials with local party officials, but Gorbachev discouraged the *Stavropolskaya Pravda* staff from always running over to party headquarters before making decisions. In meetings with newspaper editors, not unlike those he has held with Moscow journalists, Gorbachev used to hammer home the point that it was not simply enough to write ideologically correct articles. They also had to be interesting. Is anyone reading what you write? he would ask, wondering aloud if there was any point in printing stories that no one wanted to read.

The Kremlin's future Great Communicator was very much the populist even in his Stavropol days. During a "walkabout" through one village in the Izolbilnynsky district, the regional party boss asked the assembled villagers how many children they had. Since it was a time when the government was actively campaigning to raise the birthrate, Gorbachev was delighted to find one woman with six sons, and he asked her how she managed so large a family. The peasant woman told Gorbachev that it was not an easy life and that even finding cheap but sturdy material to make clothes was a chore. She recounted how one director of a store had rudely brushed her off when she had asked if she could buy 20 meters of cloth, telling her that since he had not forced her to have six children, she should find a way to clothe and feed them herself. The conversation so upset Gorbachev that he spoke about nothing else in his meeting later with district officials, reprimanding them for their callousness. The store manager was fired. During another meet-the-people tour, Gorbachev was invited home by the family of a local worker who had been decorated as a Hero of Socialist Labor. Gorbachev immediately canceled a more formal dinner with party functionaries to share a modest meal with his constituents.

While Gorbachev was territorial party leader, he usually set out for work on foot each morning from his modest, one-story, 19th century residence on Dzerzhinsky Street. It did not take Stavropolitans long to catch on to the fact that they could avoid making an official appointment at Gorbachev's Lenin Square office simply by discussing their business with him during the brief walk toward Stavropol Krai party headquarters. The Gorbachevs rarely entertained at home, nor were they known to frequent gatherings of prominent Stavropolitans. But the party leader and his wife had the reputation of being avid theater buffs who seldom missed a premiere at the pink-stone-columned Lermontov Dramatic Theater, located just across the park from Stavropol Krai party headquarters on Lenin Square. Gorbachev also came out to root for the local soccer team at the Stavropol sports stadium. According to Maximov, whether it was patriotic plays or military parades, Gorbachev was "always in the front row," even going back to his Komsomol days.

Gorbachev began to gain notice in Moscow and was promoted to full membership on the Communist Party Central Committee in 1971. He was re-elected to the Supreme Soviet in 1974 and appointed chairman of the commission on youth affairs, a tribute to his work in the Komsomol. As Gorbachev rose in the party hierarchy, he was provided with more opportunities for travel outside the Soviet Union. In October 1972 he traveled to Brussels with a delegation of Soviet officials who had been invited by the Belgian Communist Party. In May 1975 he made a visit to West Germany to attend a rally marking the 30th anniversary of the end of World War II. In November 1976 Gorbachev returned to Paris again as a member of a delegation of Communist Party regional and city secretaries, with the French Communist Party as host.

While Gorbachev was developing a new style of leadership in the Stavropol Krai, another up-and-coming regional politician was pursuing a parallel path on the southern side of the Caucasus Mountains in the Georgian Republic. Eduard Shevardnadze also began his career in the Communist youth league organization and held the position of first secretary of the Georgian Komsomol at the same time that Gorbachev held the analogous post in neighboring Stavropol Krai. Thus Gorbachev probably first encountered the man whom he would later pick to be his Foreign Minister at regional Komsomol conferences. As party boss in the south Russian breadbasket, Gorbachev followed with keen interest the Hungarian-style experiments in organizing farm workers into contract teams, a system that Shevardnadze introduced in the Abasha district of Georgia in 1973, when he was first secretary of the Georgian Communist Party. The success of such efforts to encourage more individual initiative among Georgian farmers clearly impressed the Stavropol Krai first secretary. After Gorbachev made his move to the Central Committee Secretariat in Moscow, he repeatedly made fact-finding tours to Shevardnadze's home republic. He also praised the Georgian party organization in a 1984 speech for "persistently [conducting] an interesting search for the best form of managing agricultural production."

Shevardnadze's reputation as a tough opponent of official corruption and his willingness to use such unorthodox methods as public opinion surveys and television programming to root out and expose violators of "socialist legality" must also have earned him the respect of the Stavropol Krai leader. But Shevardnadze and Gorbachev were exceptions to the prevailing norms of political behavior in the stagnant Brezhnev years.

If Brezhnev surveyed the south Russian horizon for rising

political stars, he was more likely to have noticed Sergei Medunov, party boss in the neighboring region of Krasnodar, who ran his *krai* like a private fiefdom. Medunov and his cronies kept firm and lucrative control over building and property permits in this fast-growing resort region on the Black Sea coast. If bribes for services in other areas of the country were counted out in ten-ruble notes, they ran into the hundreds of rubles in Krasnodar, where palms had to be lavishly greased to obtain anything from a hotel room to a job promotion. Letters and complaints to the central authorities were of no avail. When inspectors did come to the region they were sumptuously welcomed and often offered "hospitality services" at a discreet brothel for official VIPs.

Medunov could clearly count on high-level patronage and protection in Moscow. When the 25th Party Congress convened in Moscow in February 1976, Medunov was among the invited speakers. Gorbachev was not. "A regional party first secretary who was intelligent and congenial would have been considered untypical," explains Historian Medvedev. "If Gorbachev had yelled, sworn, been a heavy drinker or a high liver with a rest house outside of town where officials could be entertained by pretty waitresses, that would have been considered normal behavior for a regional party boss of that time. As strange as it might seem, Gorbachev would not so much have inspired fear and respect in party workers as a certain contempt. He was too intelligent."

Gorbachev was not without influential backers of his own within the party's ruling élite. While Brezhnev and his old political comrades in the "Dnepropetrovsk mafia" enjoyed Medunov's hospitality on the shores of the Black Sea, Gorbachev received other Politburo prominents at the famed Stavropol spas, notably Mineralnye Vody and Kislovodsk. Premier Kosygin and Ideologist Suslov would come, separately, for treatment of their heart conditions. KGB Chairman Yuri Andropov, victim of a chronic kidney ailment, would also stay for several weeks to be refreshed in the warm climate away from the turmoil of Moscow. Indeed, Christian Schmidt-Häuer, a West German journalist and biographer, observes that if Gorbachev had been party chief in, say, Murmansk, in the far north, he would never have become General Secretary. But in Stavropol Krai he was on hand to welcome all visiting dignitaries.

Arkady Shevchenko, the Soviet diplomat and former United Nations under secretary who defected to the U.S. in 1978, made a Kislovodsk visit in 1977. According to Shevchenko, Gorbachev's reputation for honesty and energy was impeccable. These qualities undoubtedly brought Gorbachev to the attention of such spa regulars as the dour and ascetic Suslov and the no less austere Andropov. Observes Law Faculty Friend Mlynář: "I believe one of the keys to Gorbachev's success was that he lived simply and that Andropov was impressed with him." According to Shevchenko, Premier Kosygin also took a liking to the up-and-coming Stavropol party boss and may have had an even more profound intellectual influence on him than Andropov and Suslov did. Those two tended to keep to themselves in special dachas, but Kosygin insisted on staying in the main building and mingled freely with the guests. "Kosygin met Gorbachev many times," says Shevchenko. "Kosygin was very interested in everything, and Gorbachev was known not to be corrupt."

When Gorbachev was questioned in 1985 by Indian journalists about who his political patrons had been, he became noticeably defensive and went out of his way to dismiss all the foreign speculation about the Stavropol Andropov-Suslov connection. The Soviet leader traced his rise through the ranks of the party to his election to the Central Committee in 1971. "I had contacts with several leaders. Leonid Brezhnev, Mikhail Suslov, Yuri Andropov and others," said Gorbachev. "I don't think the list should be limited to these two people. Certainly, my political experience benefited from it. Each of them had something to share with me. That is normal."

The Stavropol Krai party chief also received a boost from Kulakov, who had been promoted to the Communist Party Politburo in 1971 and held the key Central Committee Secretariat portfolio for agriculture. When Kulakov decided to test an experimental approach to harvesting grain in 1977, he turned to Gorbachev. The idea, which came to be known as the Ipatovsky method, after the district in Stavropol where it was first put into practice, was radical in its simplicity. Teams of three, four and five combines would move from farm to farm bringing in the sheaves. One extra machine was held in reserve in case of breakdowns, and the work teams were accompanied by repairmen, portable kitchens and even "cultural service" groups that would serenade them in the fields. The armada of combines whipped through the fields of the Ipatovsky district in only nine days, considerably faster than normal. Gorbachev was suddenly in the limelight. On July 16, 1977, an interview with the "hero" of the Ipatovsky harvest was published on the front page of *Pravda*.

Gorbachev was still basking in the glow of success seven months later. On March 1, 1978, one day before his 47th birthday, he was awarded the Order of the October Revolution for his achievements in agriculture. The city of Stavropol that year also received an official decoration to commemorate the bicentenary of its founding. No less distinguished a guest than Ideologist Suslov came to the city in May for the presentation ceremony. The two men were seen to greet each other with warmth, and during a tour of the region, Suslov undoubtedly reminisced about his own chapter in the territory's history, when he had been in charge of local resistance fighters during World War II. The power lines from Stavropol to Moscow appeared to be in perfect working order.

As first secretary of a provincial party organization, Gorbachev would not have been called upon so often to practice the corrosive forms of hypocrisy that ruined ambitious and talented men closer to the seat of power. But he proved as adept as any Brezhnev-era functionary in mouthing the fulsome flattery that the vain and aging Soviet leader expected from his subordinates. When a volume of Brezhnev's war memoirs, titled *The Little Land*, was published in 1978, Gorbachev joined the chorus of sycophantic praise for what was a blatant effort at self-glorification. "In terms of the profundity of its ideological content, the breadth of its generalizations and the opinions expressed by the author, *The Little Land* has become a major event in public life," said Gorbachev in a May 1978 address. "Communists and all the workers of Stavropol express limitless gratitude to Leonid Ilyich Brezhnev for this literary work."

It took one of the more bizarre episodes in the annals of Kremlin politics to catapult Gorbachev into the center of power in Moscow. Almost a year to the day after the triumph on the fields of the Ipatovsky district, Kulakov died. According to the official description of the cause of death, Kulakov's heart had "stopped beating," an unusual phrasing that suggested to many seasoned Kremlin watchers that he had not succumbed to natural causes. How Kulakov died remains a mystery, but the widely held assumption is that he committed suicide by slashing his wrists.

It was becoming apparent in Moscow that Kulakov, who bore the nickname the "Peasant from Penza," after the agricultural area he once headed in the southeast of the Russian Republic, was in deep political trouble. Despite his surname—derived from the Russian word for fist—Kulakov had risen in the party more for his modesty than for his toughness. He was a team player, willing to take on difficult jobs, including the thankless agriculture portfolio. Because of those personal qualities and his relative youth—he was 60 when he died—his name had figured prominently among those in line to succeed the ailing Brezhnev. But the agriculture job was notorious for ending careers and, in the case of Kulakov, life itself.

If the agriculture secretary did commit suicide, it was probably because his performance in the job was under attack and he feared that he was about to be removed from the Politburo. Kulakov appears to have been on the losing side of a major Politburo dispute. On the surface, the conflict seemed to center on the poor harvests that had coincided with his tenure in office. Only two weeks before Kulakov died, Brezhnev in a Central Committee speech had stingingly criticized the performance of the country's agricultural sector. But there may have been a more personal element to the dispute than wheat crops and potato rot. Kulakov was accorded a state funeral in keeping with his Politburo rank, but when his ashes were cemented into the Kremlin wall on July 20, Brezhnev was oddly—and perhaps rudely—absent. Also "on vacation" were his chief aide and eventual successor, Konstantin Chernenko, as well as Premier Alexei Kosygin and Party Ideologist Suslov. Gorbachev, however, remained loyal to his patron in death. The young official added a genuine note of emotion amid the pompous funeral orations, when he said adieu to his "friend and comrade." For the first time, the people of the Soviet Union saw and heard the man who would be their future General Secretary on national television.

Kulakov's death suddenly opened a vacancy in the Politburo and in the Central Committee secretariat. It also removed the one Politburo member who, at 60, was young enough to be considered a successor to Brezhnev. No decision was immediately made to fill the openings, perhaps because the Politburo could not agree on who would least disturb the balance of power in the Communist Party's ruling body. Andropov and Suslov may have lobbied on behalf of Gorbachev. He was a certified agriculture expert and his relative inexperience and lack of a power base outside the Stavropol territory guaranteed that he would not be in a position to try grabbing power all that soon from the Politburo's Old Guard. But Brezhnev, apparently, had doubts about elevating someone so young to the crucial agricultural post in the secretariat.

In September 1978, Brezhnev and his ever loyal aide Konstantin Chernenko embarked on a journey by train through the northern Caucasus to Baku, the capital of the Republic of Azerbaijan. The Soviet leader's progress through the Russian breadbasket took him to Rostov and then to the Krasnodar region for meetings with local officials, including Medunov. When Brezhnev passed through the Stavropol region, Gorbachev was waiting to welcome him at the station at Mineralnye Vody, accompanied by KGB Chief Andropov, who was resting at a nearby spa. The meeting that took place at Mineralnye Vody station proved to be a unique moment in Soviet history that none of those present could have foreseen. There on the narrow platform stood four men who would rule the Soviet Union in succession: Brezhnev, Andropov, Chernenko and Gorbachev.

The stopover in Mineralnye Vody must have persuaded Brezhnev that Gorbachev was the right candidate after all for Kulakov's vacant post in the secretariat. At the November plenum of the Central Committee, the political pieces that had been shaken up by Kulakov's untimely death fell back into place in a new arrangement. Brezhnev advanced Chernenko to full membership in the Politburo, leading to speculation that the colorless bureaucrat was the Soviet leader's heir apparent. Another old Brezhnev crony, Nikolai Tikhonov, was elected a candidate member, along with a newcomer to Moscow circles, Georgian Party Boss Eduard Shevardnadze. The very last promotion to be announced in *Pravda* on Nov. 28, 1978, was laconically worded: "The Central Committee plenum elected Comrade M.S. Gorbachev as a Secretary of the CPSU." The onetime combine operator from Stavropol had now been placed in charge of agriculture for the Soviet Union. After a 23-year absence, he would be returning to Moscow.

4

Summons to Moscow

Gorbachev arrived in a directionless Moscow, a strangely moody city with its excess of red-lettered slogans and gigantic portraits of Brezhnev and the other old men of the Kremlin. They appeared only rarely in public, gargoyles in fur hats frozen in midfrown atop the Lenin Mausoleum. They ruled a country that was drifting, unpowered and unruddered. After a vigorous period of economic and political expansion in the 1960s and early 1970s, some of it at the expense of a troubled and preoccupied U.S., the Soviet Union had settled into a period of torpor. Among the workers of the workers' state there ran a cynical slogan: "They pretend to pay us; we pretend to work." The rubles that workers earned were increasing on the average, but there was little to buy with them. Anything of value seemed to be available only under the table or out the back door. Black markets thrived in every commodity from windshield wipers to birth control pills. A pair of Levis fetched $200. Everybody from doorman to government minister was on the take, and even medals for wartime heroism could be had for the right amount of sausage, the correct carburetor part or a good word in a minister's ear.

In Moscow and in other major centers, the streets were jammed with pedestrians wandering from queue to queue during working hours. The women carried the ubiquitous *sumka,* or large shopping bag, and the men hauled a fat *portfel,* a briefcase containing anything but working papers. Many Soviets shunned work on any pretext, spending their time in queues and seeking out deals in ever present black markets. The verb to buy applied only to such staples as bread and cabbage. When one Russian spotted another with a pair of good boots or a bag of lemons, he asked, "Where did you 'acquire' that?" The implication was that the rare goods were not purchased in the usual way, honestly over a store counter, but were obtained through influence, secret deals and black marketeering. Soviet workers typically did their hardest labor *nalevo* (on the side), and service personnel expected to be paid extra for doing normal work. Even doctors and dentists routinely expected, and accepted, a bottle of cognac or an extra few rubles from their patients.

Payment for such services often was made in vodka, the ubiquitous drug of the Russians. Savvy householders, as a rule, never arranged for plumbers or electricians to come after midday because by that time they would already be staggering drunk from the "tips" consumed in the morning. In such conditions it is not surprising that alcoholism had become a national epidemic. Bored and unmotivated workers drank on the job and off, pouring down vodka in courtyards, alleyways and scruffy beer bars. A frequent drinking habit was to down a bottle *na troikh,* or by three. Three men, often strangers meeting outside a vodka shop, would pitch in together for the price of a bottle and drink it joylessly and immediately in the protection of the nearest alley or doorway. Women drank more discreetly, but to such an extent that some Western demographers attributed the Soviet Union's appalling rate of infant mortality—the highest in the industrialized world—to alcoholism among pregnant women. Partly because of the infant mortality rate, partly because of heavy alcoholism, partly because of poor public health, partly because of bad diet—and, perhaps, partly because of a generalized depression over the shabbiness of life—the Soviet Union was the only industrialized country in the world with a life expectancy for men that was actually declining. In the European part of the Soviet Union there were far more abortions than births. On average, women in the European part of the Soviet Union underwent five abortions in their lifetime and gave birth to only one child. One in three marriages ended in divorce. Though officially denied and unmentioned in public, drug use was becoming a problem among Soviet youth along with gang violence and casual teenage sex. The Soviet Union in the Brezhnev era was a nation on the skids.

It remained a superpower, of course, but there were signs of decline in foreign affairs. The Communist world was in disarray. To the east, the Chinese were turning to Japan and the U.S. for economic development and virtually ignoring their fellow Marxists in the U.S.S.R. To the west, Eurocommunism had become the new direction of Marxist thought and strategy, one that relied upon the Soviet Union for neither inspiration nor leadership. The Solidarity movement was about to sweep a restive Poland. Shortly after Gorbachev's arrival in Moscow, the Soviet army found itself drawn into Afghanistan, fighting a confusing war for undefinable objectives and with no end in sight.

In such circumstances little attention was paid, at home or abroad, to Brezhnev's postmortem snub of Kulakov. And even further beyond public notice was the obscure Central Committee member from Stavropol who played an active role as a member of the funeral commission and delivered one of the eulogies, his first Red Square speech. Yet Gorbachev's presence may be seen in retrospect as the most significant aspect of that gloomy funeral, the beginning of a long and cautiously fought struggle between the stagnant conservatism of Brezhnev and the restless ambition of a younger generation of leaders. At the time of Kulakov's funeral, Gorbachev was 47 years old, a typical representative of the postwar generation's party élite: well educated, dissatisfied with economic stagnation, disturbed by the national habit of laziness and corruption and, most important, eager to do something about it.

Gorbachev did not have long to wait. By November, he was sitting in Kulakov's chair at the Central Committee headquarters on Starya Square. That appointment, in itself, said little about where Gorbachev stood among the Kremlin's power factions. It showed, certainly, that the dominant leaders—Brezhnev, Kosygin, Politburo Member Andrei Kirilenko, Suslov and Chernenko—held him in high regard. Or, at least, it showed that they trusted him not to do to them what they, in their time, had done to Khrushchev. But if they did harbor any fears about Gorbachev becoming a middle-age Turk against them, they insured themselves by giving him the dirtiest and politically the most dangerous job in Moscow. If he became a threat they could always do a Kulakov on him.

They were correct in assuming that Gorbachev could do no more than a mediocre job in running the nation's agriculture, which in fact proved to be the case. The combination of climate and collectivism makes Soviet agriculture a difficult enterprise even in good times. With most of the country's farmland at latitudes north of Minnesota, the quirks of weather reduce Soviet agricultural potential to below the level of the U.S. or Western Europe. And if the weather does not make a mess of things, the system will. On the rare occasions when wind and rain conspire to produce bumper crops in the Soviet Union, poor transportation and inadequate storage quickly turn the abundance into mounds of putrefying waste. Nevertheless, no provincial Soviet politician would turn down a chance to go to the center, even to do the thankless agricultural job.

Gorbachev, in any event, was not the usual provincial politician. In those days, regional party first secretaries tended to be nearly as elderly as the gerontocrats in the Kremlin, but Gor achev was barely into middle age. That is not to say that he was the first to bring the vibrancy of youth to the Kremlin. That had been the rule in the past. The first generation of leaders of the Soviet Union were young and vigorous men when they took power. Lenin, who had been referred to as the "old man" by his awed Bolshevik followers before he had even reached 30, was only 47 when he took power in 1917. Stalin, when he vanquished all rivals for the mantle of succession to Lenin in 1927, was only 48. Khrushchev was 58 when Stalin died in 1953. Even Brezhnev, when he and Kosygin took power from Khrushchev in 1964, was only 57; the average age of the Politburo that year was a mere 59. Michael Voslensky, author of a 1984 study of Soviet leadership style titled *Nomenklatura,* recalled Brezhnev in the 1960s as a "lively, agile man in the Kremlin, with alert eyes in a massive face, self-important in the *nomenklatura* style with a typically southern joviality, constantly making faces and gesturing." That is a description not far different from those recently applied to Gorbachev.

But by the fall of 1978, when Gorbachev arrived in Moscow as junior Central Committee secretary, 20th in rank among the leaders of the Soviet Union, Brezhnev was about to turn 72, and the average age of the Politburo had risen to 70. At 47, nearly a quarter-century younger than the mean age of his political peers and in the pink of good health, Gorbachev would have moved ahead on nothing more than stamina. But obviously he had needed more than stamina to move as far as he had up the ladder of the apparat, and to keep moving in the secretive and dangerous corridors of Moscow's Central Committee headquarters. According to those who knew him on the way up, he was intelligent, energetic and persuasive, and possessed the natural garrulity and innate confidence of a born politician. As important as the virtues he possessed were the vices he did not. Gorbachev was conspicuously lacking in two characteristics typically found in senior-level Soviet bureaucrats of the day. He was neither arrogant nor corrupt. In fact, and in contrast with most Soviet politicians, he was invariably polite, a quality that has remained with him and has become one of his major strengths as a world statesman. His personal charm was effective in disarming potential opposition and rivalry within the Soviet Union, and has been shown to be an asset for Soviet diplomacy internationally since Gorbachev became General Secretary.

And so in the autumn of 1978, Mikhail and Raisa Gorbachev packed their belongings and returned to the city where they had first met. After spending more than two decades in the stifling provinciality of Stavropol, the prospect of tasting once more the rich, bustling, culturally stimulating air of Moscow must have been exciting. By one account, upon their arrival the couple moved into a comfortable Central Committee apartment on Alexei Tolstoy Street. A year later they relocated to more august accommodations on Granovsky Street, where several Politburo members reside. That move came in November 1979, when, at the startlingly young age of 48, Gorbachev was made a candidate member of the Soviet Politburo. Less than a year after that, in October 1980, he became a full member. He was still short of his 50th birthday. Not only was he eight years younger than the next youngest Politburo member, Grigori Romanov, he was 21 years younger than the average for that body.

Other honors, meanwhile, were coming the way of this youthful dynamo. In 1980, Gorbachev was a candidate for the Supreme Soviet of the U.S.S.R., the formal legislative body that in theory represents the highest organ of state sovereignty of the Soviet Union. The Soviets follow the British custom whereby top-level politicians choose their constituency regardless of whether they reside in it. But Gorbachev's choice was intriguing. He opted to represent Altai territory, a minority national administrative unit in Siberia. As it happens, Raisa Gorbachev was born in Rubtsovsk, in the same Altai territory.

The seven years Gorbachev spent rising through the ranks after his arrival in Moscow constituted a valuable period of political grooming for him. He was learning about the levers of power of Soviet politics, about the immense problems of the Soviet economy, particularly in agriculture, and he was getting his first experience of international contact at Politburo level. At the same time, he seems to have taken pains to be unusually self-effacing, not really surfacing as a national figure until 1983.

There were sound political reasons for this reticence. It was, politically, a good time to keep out of sight. The 1978-82 period was the twilight of the Brezhnev years, a time when economic stagnation and political torpor seemed to hatch corruption and intrigue in the highest places. The maneuvering to succeed the puffy-faced, mumbling and nearly incapacitated leader went from discreet to unseemly. A Leningrad literary journal published a tribute to Brezhnev's 75th birthday that included a snide caricature and a tongue-in-cheek assessment of the praises heaped upon him: "Most people think of him as if he had long been dead, so great is the veneration of his talent . . . We shall not have long to wait before we hear the praises, which will be showered upon that author upon his death." Brezhnev's daughter, Galina, was perilously close, through her personal contacts, to a diamond-smuggling scandal involving the director of the Moscow Circus and a deputy director of the KGB. The latter official subsequently committed suicide when the scandal blew up. There were dark suspicions that the scandal had been deliberately uncovered by Andropov as a means of undermining the Brezhnev dynasty and paving the way for his succession to the national leadership. As Andropov's

protégé, Gorbachev took care not to involve himself in such
intrigues, but his support for Andropov obviously helped ensure the elder official's succession when Brezhnev died in November 1982.

Once Andropov took over, Gorbachev was relieved of his
onerous responsibilities for agriculture and was given the party position of Politburo member and Central Committee secretary responsible for ideology, a position of considerable power. The post had long been Suslov's and had been taken over
by Andropov when Suslov died in January 1982. It was considered unofficially the No. 2 job in the party and therefore the
country. So when Andropov gave the position to Gorbachev it
was a gesture of considerable confidence in a trusted supporter. That appointment was the key to Gorbachev's subsequent
rise to the top. It gave him a prominence within the Politburo
that could only increase during 1983 as Andropov, after a fast
start at attempting to restore discipline in Soviet society, faded
into his final illness.

It was also an interesting period in Soviet-American relations. For a few heady months in 1983 Andropov came to be
regarded in the U.S. as a closet Americanophile, a drinker of
good Scotch, a reader of Kurt Vonnegut, a listener to Voice of
America. Whether this impression was the result of wishful
American thinking or Soviet KGB disinformation or both, it
was probably false. Andropov seldom ventured abroad, he
never traveled beyond the Soviet bloc and, aside from a third-
hand report from an émigré who was a schoolmate of Andropov's son, there was no evidence that the austere KGB chief
shared any of the tastes ascribed to him. In any event, he was
terminally ill while he supposedly was displaying the characteristics of a Soviet Renaissance man. Yet the episode may
have been enlightening for Gorbachev. He has shown himself
since to be exceptionally adept at manipulating Western and
particularly American public opinion. Certainly it would be
going too far to credit Gorbachev with creating the image of

the Americanophilic Andropov, but he must have learned something from the phenomenon.

Probably the most valuable lessons Gorbachev learned during the Andropov period came in helping administer a country as vast and complex as the Soviet Union. Andropov's illness advanced to such a degree that his last months were spent in a special medical suite at the Kremlin Hospital complex in Kuntsevo, west of Moscow, where he saw only family members and a few key officials who relayed information to him and decisions from him. Chief among those officials was Gorbachev, who was serving an apprenticeship in power seldom achieved by seconds-in-command in the West, especially by American Vice Presidents. As the principal deputy to an incapacitated leader, he was compelled to take over as crisis manager for such events as the shooting down of a Korean Air Lines passenger plane in September 1983. Gorbachev was thought to be the chairman of the subgroup in the Politburo that coped with the disaster, and certainly the handling of it showed some of the characteristics that he was to develop later in dealing with world opinion. Central to the management of the crisis was a decision to tough it out, which was in itself nothing unusual for the Soviet Union. The crisis committee adopted as the basic cover story an assertion that the U.S. was using KAL 007 as a spy plane, and that line remains unchanged to this day. What was unusual in the handling of the problem was an attempt to get that version of the story, believable or not, before the world public on the Kremlin's own terms. Rather than simply making its spy-plane allegation and then lapsing into silence, Gorbachev's group sent Chief of Staff Nikolai Ogarkov out to the wolves of the Western press to make the case with map and pointer on the television sets of the world. In a way, the tactic worked. The willingness of the Soviets even to offer a public explanation, if not apology, was seen in the West as an improvement on past practice. There was no way the Soviets could win in world public opinion, but the exercise demonstrated that Gorbachev was as good as anyone else in the Politburo at making the best of a bad situation.

Meanwhile, the decline of the Soviet gerontocracy continued. Andropov died in February 1984, and Gorbachev was among the candidates mentioned to succeed him. But it was too soon. Gorbachev faced a powerful contender for the post in Grigori Romanov, the longtime Leningrad party leader and party secretary in charge of the defense industries. He was also the man thought to be responsible for the scurrilous attacks on the dying Brezhnev, particularly the desultory reference in the Leningrad literary journal. In addition, there was tension between the Old Guard and the new, the retainers of the dead Brezhnev and the men brought into the Politburo during Andropov's reign.

In Soviet Communist politics, decisions usually are made by a kind of intuitive consensus that expresses itself in unanimity of vote, though not always of thought. In such circumstances actual votes are seldom taken, or are taken only when there is a certainty that the show of hands will be unanimous. By the time a typical issue comes to decision, those involved already know the outcome and offer their acquiescence. In the confused political uncertainty following Andropov's death it was not apparent whether Romanov or Gorbachev had the most votes for General Secretary. So the Politburo and the Central Committee cautiously deferred its decision until the air cleared, and then elected Chernenko. The decision was also a reward to a skilled but aging political careerist who Brezhnev hoped would be his successor but who had been outmaneuvered by Andropov. Finally, and most important, it was a vote for a man who would not remain long in office. Chernenko was being undermined by another and more implacable foe: ill health, specifically emphysema. He was so weak and ill at Andropov's funeral that he could not even lift his hand to hold on to the casket as it was carried into Red

Square. He could barely walk across a room unaided.

Nevertheless, Gorbachev made it a point to exhibit his own strength publicly. At the end of the plenum that elected Chernenko it was Gorbachev—not the new General Secretary, not Romanov, not any other contender for leadership—who delivered the closing speech. And, strikingly, during Andropov's funeral Gorbachev alone of the Politburo went up to console his bereaved widow Tatiana, a woman whose existence to the outside world had been unknown before her husband's funeral. The gesture, which was warmly human, revealed just how close he had been to the deceased Soviet leader.

Gorbachev was also close to the new leader, a relationship that became increasingly public as Chernenko's health deteriorated. In April 1984, Gorbachev delivered the speech before the Supreme Soviet formally proposing Chernenko as Soviet leader. Gorbachev made a powerful plea for combining the roles of head of state—President or, specifically, Chairman of the Supreme Soviet—with general secretaryship of the Communist Party, arguing that the General Secretary's vital institutional role in formulating foreign policy made the consolidation necessary. (Interestingly, Gorbachev made the opposite argument in 1985 when he rejected the post of Supreme Soviet chairman and gave it to Andrei Gromyko, partly as a reward for his support and partly as a way of getting him out of foreign affairs.)

It is possible that the use of Gorbachev to nominate Chernenko might have been intended by the Brezhnevite Old Guard of the Politburo as a way of flaunting their continuing majority within the Politburo, at least as long as Chernenko still lived. But it also was a clear sign that there had been some significant trade-offs. The old man had made himself acceptable to the younger faction by agreeing not to reverse the policies of discipline and limited personnel purge initiated by Andropov during his brief reign. Gorbachev, in any event, was in a position to make sure of it. He functioned as the de facto "second secretary" for Chernenko as he had for Andropov, taking charge during the times when the General Secretary was too sick to appear for political meetings. Gorbachev alternated the chairmanship of Politburo meetings with his presumed rival, Grigori Romanov. But it became clear through later admissions by Soviet officials that in economic policy, foreign policy and sometimes in other matters, Gorbachev was effectively already acting as General Secretary during Chernenko's last months. Above all, Gorbachev had grasped the levers of decision making, sluggish though these have always been, in the Soviet economy. That on-the-job training must have been decisive in ensuring his appointment as General Secretary on March 11, 1985, when Chernenko finally expired.

If there were any doubts about Gorbachev's extraordinary political skills, his ability to remain at the helm of the Soviet economy after the fiasco of Soviet agriculture in the late 1970s should dispel them. For five years Gorbachev *was* Soviet agriculture, the designated Central Committee secretary in charge of agricultural affairs, and he retained this post until 1983, when he moved into the more politically rewarding job of supervising party personnel matters. Yet the fact is, Gorbachev presided over the worst years on the Soviet farm since the mass starvation of the 1930s.

Almost immediately on his arrival in Moscow, things went wrong through no fault of his own. The year 1978 was a good one for Soviet agriculture, resulting in a record 230 million metric tons of grain (a crop which, ironically, was reaching maturity at the very time the hapless Kulakov was being driven to suicide by attacks on his administration of agriculture). But inadequate preparation for the following sowing season, as well as ruinously heavy rain, meant that the 1979 crop was a calamity: 179 million tons, more than 20% less than the previous year. In 1980, the figure crept back up to 189 million, but in 1981 the harvests were so appalling that the official grain figures were classified as secret. The U.S. Department of Agriculture estimated a total of 155 million tons for that disastrous year. Matters were only slightly improved in 1982, when the harvest was back up to 175 million tons by U.S. estimate. (Soviet grain harvests continued to be state secrets until 1987). Gorbachev, of course, could hardly be blamed for the weather or for the accumulated foolishness of Stalinist collectivism in the Soviet countryside. But as the captain of the ship that was foundering, he was the man at whom fingers would eventually point in reproach.

As it happened, Gorbachev was able to take shelter to a considerable degree behind Brezhnev himself. In May 1982, Brezhnev mounted an ambitious "food program" that would, in theory, put an end to the Soviet Union's chronic agricultural shortages and improve the population's nutrition. The program called for an improved rural infrastructure and the development of what became known as the "agroindustrial complex," an arrangement for bringing the administrative, storage, transportation and processing facilities needed for the overall handling of the Soviet harvest closer to the farms themselves. What the food program did not call for was a family farming contract policy that Gorbachev had developed under a pilot program in Stavropol, and that had been tried with some success in other parts of the Soviet Union (notably in Georgia, under Eduard Shevardnadze). The contract system allowed greater independence to farmers, farm families and farming brigades. Under the program, these people for the first time could count on concrete rewards for higher productivity, that is, real monetary incentives rather than endless moral appeals for harder work.

Gorbachev's interest in launching a contract system and bringing the agricultural establishment closer to the farm was evident from the beginning of his Central Committee secretaryship in Moscow. Like Brezhnev, he wanted to transfer control over agriculture to local agroindustry centers that would have far more understanding of immediate local needs and conditions than distant bureaucrats in Moscow. At the same time, he found it necessary to distance himself from his own "Ipatovsky" scheme of concentrating large amounts of mechanized harvesting machinery on small areas. The system had worked well in some places but broke down when imposed throughout the country. It must have been awkward for Gorbachev to pour cold water on a program whose initial success had been the source of his first national prominence in 1977.

Gorbachev's zeal for expanding the contract system met almost immediate opposition, which evidently continued for years. Nevertheless, in March 1983, he announced in a speech that the Politburo had given approval to the "introduction of collective contracts in collective- and state-farm production." The contracts were to be long term and would apply to autonomous work teams. But Politburo resolutions were one thing; implementation by the thousands of collective farms and local party authorities throughout the Soviet Union was something else. By 1988, the enlarged contract system had made slow headway in most of the Soviet Union because of resistance from collective-farm and local party authorities worried about a possible reduction in their own authority.

That Gorbachev's career seemed not to suffer greatly from the agricultural failures that occurred during his tenure may be a reflection of his unique relationship with Andropov, who appeared at times to be grooming Gorbachev for leadership by giving him the freedom to learn through his mistakes rather than suffer for them. In addition, it was clear that Gorbachev's responsibilities were far broader than mere agriculture, and extended across the full economic spectrum. Even when crops were dying in drought or rotting from too much rain, he busied himself with Soviet economic development generally, leaving particulars of agricultural work to the head of the Central Committee department in charge of it. Significantly enough, when he moved on to economic and personnel matters in 1983, no secretary was immediately designated to replace him, a lapse that suggests that the chief supervisory work had been going on at the department level all along.

Gorbachev's loyalty to Andropov evidently arose from a feeling that in the former KGB chief the Soviet Union had, for the first time, a leader who truly grasped the enormity of the economic problems facing the country. Andropov stressed work discipline as a key to improved productivity, clearly an issue close to the heart of his temperate and hard-working protégé. But Gorbachev's ideas did not limit themselves to the human dimension. He tinkered in macroeconomics, looking at the way the system was supposed to work and seeking reasons for its systemic rather than human failures, as he had in agriculture. During the 1982-85 period, coinciding with the Andropov-Chernenko rule, Gorbachev supervised a "five ministries" program of decentralization and technological innovation. It was yet another attempt to break up the stranglehold on initiative and independence, this time in industry, that still characterized the Soviet economy.

More interesting than the public initiatives, however, were Gorbachev's own ways of educating himself about Soviet reality. Soon after becoming Central Committee secretary, according to his top economic adviser Abel Aganbegyan, Gorbachev started organizing seminars at which economists and other experts could informally, and with considerable freedom, discuss the nation's agricultural problems. "Comrade Gorbachev often used to meet with economists and discussed with them the problems of agriculture," Aganbegyan recalls. "In our institute [the economics section of the Academy of Sciences], the person who met with him was Academician [Tatiana] Zaslavskaya. I also used to meet with him to discuss ordinary problems of the economy. He often used to gather economists to discuss problems and systems of management, how to speed up socialism and economic development, problems of distribution. These meetings were very useful. Of course, everybody said what he thought." The meetings would take place in the Central Committee building in Moscow, or occasionally at a dacha outside the city.

For her part, the distinguished Zaslavskaya, a member of the Academy of Sciences who is also president of the Soviet Sociological Association, is considerably more modest about her role in the formation of Gorbachev's economic ideas. Speaking to TIME's Traudl Lessing in Vienna in the 1987, Zaslavskaya said she had never had a tête-à-tête with Gorbachev and had only actually met him five or six times, always in the company of a small group of people. "I have spoken before him at these meetings," she said, "and he listens very attentively—he is a good listener—and I know that our relations are excellent. During some of my meetings," she went on, "I sat next to him. It is incredible what power and drive emanate from Mr. Gorbachev. One feels as if it were a strong field of energy. His vitality is extraordinary and yet, although you feel this tension, he is a good listener and waits for you to finish."

Zaslavskaya, incidentally, is no teenage romantic. She is 60 years old and, at considerable political risk, pioneered sociological research in the Soviet Union two decades ago, when it was not even a recognized field of scientific research in the country. Her view of human nature is strikingly un-Marxian. Throughout the past seven decades of Soviet history, official propaganda and theory has asserted, as did Marx, that there is no such thing as human nature, only class nature. A corollary was that Soviet society, under supposedly nonexploitative economic principles, was in the process of creating the "new Soviet man," a figure of mythical selflessness, courage, diligence and wisdom. Zaslavskaya disagrees: "I believe that, given the nature of man, we will not create a different human being. We must accept man as he is."

That last sentence, on the need to "accept man as he is,"

may not exactly epitomize the Gorbachevian approach to economic problem solving, but it comes close. Gorbachev remains
a committed Marxist. What seems to have happened as he has
come closer to the reality of socialism in his country is that he
seems comfortable discarding the more esoteric and unde-
monstrable aspects of Marxist philosophy. That certainly does
not make him anything like a pragmatist, as that dangerously
imprecise word is often used, much less someone on the way to
reinventing capitalism. What it does is make him a person
comfortable with economic and philosophical paradoxes. He
is thus able to pursue economic results for their own sake,
without losing sleep over formal definitions within the Marxist-Leninist canon. No other Soviet leader since Lenin has
had this quality, which might best be called "dialectical
flexibility."

Gorbachev had only limited experience of foreign affairs
when he became a full Politburo member in October 1980. He
had, of course, traveled somewhat: to France, Italy, Belgium,
West Germany, East Germany and Czechoslovakia. He had
also been close friends with one foreigner, Zdeněk Mlynář, at
an early age, and thus understood the difference between ideology, which he and Mlynář shared in common, and national
origins and sentiments. But he had not negotiated with any
foreign officials in a formal sense, and he had not been exposed to a direct clash of wills and perspectives in interpreting
the world. He was obviously not ignorant of the West: he was
well read in general, and as a Central Committee member he
would have had access to far more candid accounts of what
was happening in the outside world than was available to the
average Soviet citizen.

What is surprising, therefore, is that the first time Gorba-
chev may have actually sat down and talked at length with an
American was not until 1981, in Moscow. The man was John
Chrystal, then 67 years old and a longtime visitor to the Soviet
Union. Chrystal, a farmer as well as a banker (by 1988, he was

Chairman of the Banker's Trust of Des Moines), describes himself as a liberal Democrat. He had met with senior Soviet officials from Nikita Khrushchev on down from the 1950s. Every other year he had visited the Soviet Union for an extended period to look at agricultural performance in two separate parts of the country and to offer his friendly advice on how production might be improved. Since he was apparently quite uninterested in the conventional matters of Kremlinology, and since he was at odds with a hard-line U.S. approach to Moscow, the Soviets were appreciative and welcoming. In 1981, on his regular visit to the Soviet Union, his hosts made a great fuss over the fact that he was going to visit an important and senior Communist Party official at the Central Committee. It turned out to be Gorbachev, a name that at the time meant little to Chrystal.

The meeting took place in what evidently was Gorbachev's corner office and which, in stark contrast with the heavily Victorian fittings of most Soviet official locales, was furnished with light colored, comfortable and modern-looking Scandinavian furniture. There were two other sharp changes from standard Soviet practice in meetings with foreigners. First, apart from the interpreter, no one else was in the room except Chrystal. Second, the table was devoid of the paraphernalia—mineral-water bottles, cigarette packs, assorted glassware and so on—that have traditionally characterized Soviet negotiating style. It struck Chrystal how different Gorbachev was from all the other Soviet officials he had met. "There was a presence about him," Chrystal recalls. "He gave the impression of being a guy who was forming a vision, and had self-confidence and perseverance. He just wouldn't let a subject go until you were done."

The two men talked the entire afternoon, covering the entire gamut of agricultural questions as well as larger issues of economic management. Chrystal, whose basic attitude toward the Soviet Union has always been friendly, was struck by how tough Gorbachev was in his perceptions of the U.S. Gorbachev seemed to Chrystal to believe down to the last word *Pravda* editorials about American society being made up of huge armies of the near starving. Chrystal comments, "He does believe, never having been here, that the U.S. has abject poverty and quite a lot of it. My impression is that he thinks there are whole towns that are just sort of destitute." Chrystal, who admits to no particular interest in ideology, says he was also struck by the firmness of Gorbachev's commitment to the system he served. "He is a committed Marxist," says Chrystal flatly. Then, interpreting *glasnost,* a term that was not in currency during the 1981 meeting with Gorbachev, Chrystal notes, *"Glasnost* is not American *glasnost;* it is a different product."

A Canadian who visited Gorbachev in the fall of the same year had a similar impression of Gorbachev's view of the U.S. Eugene Whelan, then Agriculture Minister in the Liberal government of Prime Minister Pierre Trudeau, spent ten days in Moscow with a Canadian official delegation. The tone of the meeting was pleasant and innocuous until the subject of the U.S. came up. "He was going on," recalled Whelan, "about how the U.S. was the aggressor, how it was making weapons. He said the U.S. was returning to the conditions of the 1950s." When the Canadians remonstrated, Whelan said, that the widespread perception in the U.S. and elsewhere in the West was that the Soviet Union had armaments far beyond those legitimately needed for defense, Gorbachev became irritated. "That is erroneous," the Russian replied, "and recalls the days of [Secretary of Defense James] Forrestal."

Two years later, in the spring of 1983, Gorbachev had his first direct experience of North America. As a member of the Supreme Soviet, an agricultural specialist and a Politburo member, he was invited by Canada's Parliament to take a close look at Canadian farms and food production. He spent ten days in the country and would have stayed longer, but had to return abruptly for unstated political reasons. He visited Ottawa, the federal capital, as well as parts of Ontario and then headed west to Banff and the prairies of Alberta. He pottered around farms, factories, schools, supermarkets and vineyards.

The visit also marked Gorbachev's first encounter with a man who would later become an important part of his management team: Alexander Yakovlev, then the Soviet Ambassador to Canada and, in effect, a political exile. Yakovlev had been a rising star in the Central Committee apparatus in 1971 but fell afoul of Suslov over an obscure ideological dispute involving Russian nationalism. Yakovlev lost his Central Committee job, and, partly on the basis of his studies at Columbia University in New York City during the late 1950s, was sent to Canada to oversee the routine work of U.S. watching, which is the main function of the Ottawa post. For Yakovlev, this was a McLuhanesque experience of monitoring American television, reading American publications and absorbing American culture at its most basic level. From his Canadian listening post he gained an intuitive understanding of how American public opinion is formed and, of course, manipulated. His first important opportunity to make use of that knowledge came during the Gorbachev trip. The two men sat up late at night shortly after Gorbachev's arrival in Canada and hit it off well. Yakovlev, for all his familiarity with sound bites, beer commercials and *Saturday Night Live,* remained as he had been when he worked in the Central Committee in Moscow, an acerbic and bitter critic of the U.S. Gorbachev appreciated the briefings Yakovlev gave him during the Canada visit. When he became General Secretary two years later, the hard-headed Yakovlev returned to the Central Committee building as Gorbachev's chief of propaganda and trusted media adviser. But Gorbachev was not without his own sense of public relations. His Canadian hosts found him affable, able and effective as a Soviet communicator.

Jim Wright, an official of the Canadian Ministry of External Affairs, was with the delegation for much of the Canadian trip and observed Gorbachev closely, as the Russian took in such local color as, for example, a bull semen operation in Calgary or answered abrasive questions from a parliamentary foreign affairs committee in Ottawa. "He stood out like a sore thumb," says Wright of the Soviet leader, who in 1983 already seemed to Canadian official analysts to be the man to watch in the Soviet hierarchy. Wright was struck by how easily Gorbachev seemed to gravitate to women and children, as well as how impressed the visitor was with Canadian farming methods. At one point on a cattle farm he asked to talk to "some of the workers."

"We really don't have any people on the farm," said the nonplussed farmer, who with his family and a handful of day laborers worked a spread of several hundred acres. Gorbachev was astonished. Wright and others who spoke Russian heard him muttering under his breath: "We are not going to see this [in the Soviet Union] for another 50 years."

Gorbachev, though, demonstrated the same brittleness on ideological matters that has recurred throughout his public career. Asked crudely in Ottawa by a Canadian Member of Parliament why there were so many spies in the Soviet embassy in the city, Gorbachev snapped that the man was just repeating "American provocations." Once while his official host, Agriculture Minister Whelan, was showing him what was in the Canadian newspapers during an airplane ride across country, the two came upon full-page supermarket advertisements featuring the best price deals of the day. Whelan waxed about the wonders of free enterprise and competition, but Gorbachev suddenly cut him short. "Gene, you don't try to convert me to capitalism," he said in a firm but friendly manner, "and I won't try to convert you to Communism."

Whalen, though, was struck by a candid comment Gorbachev made when the topic of Afghanistan came up. "That's a posture that we are involved in, and it was a mistake," Gorbachev conceded. In mid-1984, Gorbachev became chairman of the foreign affairs commission of the Supreme Soviet. Though there was no executive power in this position, it was an indication that the Soviet leadership wanted him to gain as much experience of the Soviet foreign policy apparatus as possible.

In June he took his next trip to the West, to Rome, for the funeral of Italian Communist Party Leader Enrico Berlinguer. Antonio Rubbi, a member of the leadership of the Italian Communist Party and head of its foreign affairs section, was struck during the visit by Gorbachev's frankness about the Soviet Union. Rubbi and other senior Italian Communists had an unexpectedly candid talk with Gorbachev over dinner during the brief visit. "You had the impression that he was very critical of the situation in the Soviet Union," Rubbi recalled. "He said there was too much centralization and there should be decentralization. He was also saying that the [15 Soviet] republics should have more power." For Rubbi, a veteran visitor to the Soviet Union who speaks fluent Russian, it was the first time *any* Soviet official had even admitted there was a nationality problem, much less criticized the concentration of power in Moscow. For his part, Gorbachev was struck by the sight of hundreds of thousands of Italians, many of them giving the clenched-fist Communist salute, paying tribute to the dead Italian Communist leader without being organized by the authorities to do so.

By the end of the year, the demise of Chernenko was almost in sight. He had been out of the public eye for days on end, and Gorbachev was essentially running the Soviet Union. In December, in response to British Prime Minister Margaret Thatcher's efforts to improve relations with Moscow, the Soviets decided to accept a long-standing invitation for a senior official to visit Britain. Gorbachev was the man selected, and the tour, from start to finish, had the air of a dress rehearsal for foreign trips by a future state leader. Gorbachev's Canadian visit had received scanty press coverage because nobody knew who he was; by the time of the 1984 trip, however, it was apparent that he was one of only two or three people likely to succeed Chernenko.

The British tabloids had prepared to cover a rather formal visit that might be interrupted by anti-Soviet demonstrations. But when Gorbachev and Raisa descended together from their plane at Heathrow Airport, he in a well cut suit and smiling affably, she relatively glamorous and actually at his side, Fleet Street salivated for the remainder of the visit. Raisa was almost mobbed as she toured Stratford-on-Avon and brought out her American Express Gold Card (no credit limit) for purchases in London's tony Harrod's department store. Raisa had originally been invited on the Canada trip but had been unable to go. The London visit was thus the first occasion in which she could play the role as, in effect, Soviet First Lady (though Gorbachev, of course, had not yet taken over).

Gorbachev dazzled the usually unimpressed British with references to C. Northcote Parkinson, originator of a satirical study of bureaucratic habits ("I've got news for you," he told a British industrialist, "he's in Moscow now"), and an assertion that he had read the late British novelist C.P. Snow's *The Corridors of Power*. He also delighted his hosts with flip comments about usually serious subjects. Taken to the British Museum reading room, where Karl Marx did most of his research for *Das Kapital* and other works, Gorbachev cracked, "If people don't like Marx, they should blame the British Museum." But he displayed a more abrasive side when taken to task by a Conservative Member of Parliament over persecution of religious groups in the Soviet Union. "You govern your society, let us govern ours," he replied brusquely. "I could give you a few facts about human rights in the U.K. For example, you persecute entire communities, entire nationalities." The reference was presumably to the British role in Northern Ireland, and it did not endear him to his audience. Displaying, as ever, his skill at responding to moods and tones, Gorbachev softened the blow by noting, over lunch with the M.P.s afterward, "Truth comes out of heated discussion."

At this point, Gorbachev might have gone over in Britain as just a better dressed and more mercurially charming version of various Soviet heavies who have occasionally been invited to Britain. His reputation, however, was not simply saved but made by Margaret Thatcher. After hours of heated discussion and slashing argument with Gorbachev, she grandly proclaimed, "I like Mr. Gorbachev. We can do business together." Subsequently, when she visited Moscow last summer to reciprocate Gorbachev's visit to Britain, the hours of debate went on longer and at times became very intense, though never, according to one British observer, ill mannered. "Gorbachev seems to regard political debate as perfectly normal," commented a British official familiar with the talks.

Along with other Western officials, however, the British were struck by how simplistic Gorbachev could become when talking about the U.S. He brought up at one point the "military-industrial complex," and plainly seemed to believe that the U.S. President was told what to do by arms manufacturers. One of the stops on the Britain visit was Chequers, the official country residence of British Prime Ministers. Thatcher wanted to have discussions with Gorbachev in a setting less formal than No. 10 Downing Street in London. The two sat down for 3½ hours of discussions while Raisa roamed through the long gallery upstairs, fascinated at the valuable collection of literary first editions and such items as the letters of Napoleon.

Gorbachev had to cut short his British visit because of the death of Defense Minister Dmitri Ustinov. He returned to Moscow having charmed the British no less completely than if a street mugger had joined the Salvation Army. From then until the death of Chernenko the following March, he was preoccupied in running the Soviet economy and attempting to come to terms with the radical changes that would be needed to keep the Soviet Union functioning into the next decade and beyond. Perhaps mindful of the superiority of Western economic management and distribution during the British visit, Gorbachev was particularly somber when he addressed the Central Committee at the end of 1984. He told his audience, "We cannot remain a major power in world affairs unless we put our domestic house in order." Three months later he found himself the man burdened with directing that task.

5

The Reformer

*ll the officials walked bare-
headed after the coffin . . . Not even indulging in the trivial talk
which is usually kept up by persons attending a funeral. At that
moment, all their thoughts were concentrated on themselves:
they were wondering what the new governor-general would be
like, how he would set to work and how he would take them.*
—Nikolai Gogol, *Dead Souls*, 1842

At 1 p.m. on March 13, 1985, the leaders of the Soviet
Union assembled at Moscow's Hall of Columns for yet another Red Square funeral, the fourth in 28 months. Konstantin
Chernenko, in office as head of the Communist Party barely
more than a year, was joining Leonid Brezhnev, Yuri Andropov and Dmitri Ustinov among recent arrivals to the Bolshevik burying ground beside the Kremlin wall. But this time the
stately gloom of official mourning was relieved by an under-
current of suspense, a sense that something new was happen-

ing: leading the procession was the brisk new General Secretary, Mikhail Gorbachev.

Like Gogol's mourners, the other officials in that day's cortege may have been thinking not of the wasted corpse in the coffin. Instead, they probably were wondering what the new General Secretary would be like, how he would set to work, and how he would take them. Had they known the answers, they might have regretted the decision, made only 48 hours earlier, to elevate their youngest Politburo colleague to the leadership of the Soviet Union. Within a dozen months Gorbachev would tear asunder the complacent, bureaucracy-bound world they had built for themselves during the Brezhnev era. Several would be in disgrace, others in forced retirement, and still others barely clinging to diminished perquisites of power. They, and the entire country, would be immersed in a heady and disturbing turmoil of *glasnost* and *perestroika,* words whose meanings on that raw March afternoon were virtually unknown to the outside world, and were obscure even to Soviets.

By most accounts, there were enough misgivings about Gorbachev so that he very nearly failed to gain the general secretaryship. A combination of chance and political opportunism carried the day—or more precisely, the night—at a hurriedly called meeting of the Politburo on March 10 that lasted until the next morning. At least one vital factor in his nomination was the chance absence of three key members. Vladimir Shcherbitsky, the Ukrainian party leader, was in San Francisco; Vitali Vorotnikov, a colorless government administrator, was in Yugoslavia; and Kazakhstan Party Chief Dinmukhamed Kunaev was still en route from his home in the city of Alma-Ata. Two of the three were to suffer under Gorbachev: Kunaev dismissed and disgraced for his long and corrupt reign in Kazakhstan; Shcherbitsky repeatedly criticized and barely holding onto his office through the sufferance of the new party leader. Of the three absentees, only Vorotnikov might have backed Gorbachev in that night's Kremlin showdown.

But there was more to Gorbachev's election than fortuitous absenteeism. The political maneuvering in preparation for Chernenko's death was complex and Machiavellian. Gorbachev had served effectively as Second Secretary during much of Chernenko's illness, and he was visibly primus inter pares on the Politburo in the period of public discussion preceding the Feb. 24, 1985, elections to the Supreme Soviet of the Russian Republic. But that fact did not guarantee his ascendancy. Far from it. Apart from Foreign Minister Andrei Gromyko, Gorbachev had no obvious supporters in the Politburo. Indeed, Chernenko had implicitly indicated in his last public appearances that his own preferred successor was Viktor Grishin, powerful head of the Moscow party organization.

Why Grishin failed to move up is an intriguing question. According to some reports, never confirmed but certainly plausible, the KGB made it clear to the Politburo that it held embarrassing dossiers detailing Grishin's corruption during his years as Moscow party chief. That would have been enough to prevent his election to the leadership. Who made those dossiers available, and why? KGB Chairman Viktor Chebrikov is a prime candidate because of his close association with the late Yuri Andropov. The why is more obvious: a deal between Chebrikov and Gorbachev. Perhaps as evidence of that, Gorbachev as General Secretary retained Chebrikov as head of the KGB and quickly promoted him to full Politburo membership.

It is probable that Grigori Romanov, the longtime Leningrad party boss, nominated Grishin during that nighttime Politburo meeting. He would have voted for anyone rather than Gorbachev, his main rival for power in the last months of Chernenko's life. Certainly it is hard to imagine that anyone would have nominated Romanov, an arrogant and disliked Politburo member whose ruthlessness as Leningrad party leader might have worried the remainder of the Politburo.

Selection as the candidate of the Politburo was only the first stage of the process. On the following day, about two-thirds of the 300-member Central Committee met to confirm the nomination of Gorbachev, by no means a forgone conclusion. The Central Committee was peopled by men and women brought up in the Brezhnev tradition, and their support for the upstart Gorbachev was not certain. That was obvious from the official announcement that the selection took place *edino-dushno* (with one spirit) instead of *edinoglasno* (with one voice, unanimously). In effect, Gorbachev's selection was by consensus, perhaps without any formal vote at all, or if so, with the highly unusual occurrence of votes abstaining or even numbered against Gorbachev. In a vote for the position of General Secretary, it is not normally a case of Comrade X standing against Comrade Y, a competitive procedure that Communist dogma rejects, but of votes for people proposed as a result of broad discussion and, usually, consensus.

But clearly this *edinodushno* consensus was not simply and easily arrived at. What seems to have tipped the scales in Gorbachev's favor was a remarkable speech by Gromyko, the cold and normally dispassionate Foreign Minister. On this occasion, however, he burned hot. Gromyko delivered an extemporaneous oration that became famous for a single, telling description. "Comrades," he said, "this man has a nice smile, but he has teeth of iron." He went on to assure the members that Gorbachev was up to the mark in Gromyko's own vital area of expertise, foreign affairs. "It is rather clearer to me than to other comrades that he can grasp very well and very quickly the essence of those developments that are building up outside our country in the international arena. I myself have often been surprised by his ability to distinguish quickly and exactly the heart of a matter and to draw the right conclusions in the interests of the party." The fact that the Foreign Minister felt it necessary to argue so forcefully is perhaps an indication of the thinness of Gorbachev's support.

Gromyko's remarks have never been published widely in the Soviet Union. Indeed, there has been little public disucussion of how closely fought was the contest that brought Gorbachev to power. But in January 1987, the weekly magazine *Ogonyok* published reflections of Historical Dramatist Mikhail Shatrov on the process of political change in the Soviet Union. Shatrov, a well-connected and politically astute playwright, offered the following cryptic account of the succession:

"March 1985—this was a struggle not for power, but for an idea, for the necessity and possibility for a democratic renewal of the country, a struggle to return to the ideas of October [the Bolshevik Revolution]. Was there an alternative? From the point of view of the basic interests of socialism there was never one. But we must not forget that in real life there was. Slogans like 'Let us turn Moscow into an exemplary Communist city,' often covering up lies, corruption and other consequences of a lack of democracy, might have appeared in the whole country. We must not forget about this threat, which really existed in March and could have led to the return of 'boundless power,' even if not immediately. The problems suffocating the country could be decided either along the paths of democratization or suppressed by a heavy hand. There was no third alternative."

The reference to corruption in the Soviet capital makes it plain that opponents of Gorbachev must have attempted to argue for Grishin. The abrupt "retirement" of Romanov in the months after Gorbachev took power suggests that he was involved in the "draft Grishin" maneuvering. Chebrikov's role is harder to pin down; in March 1985 he was still a nonvoting member of the Politburo.

Whatever the expediencies required, Gorbachev did not look back. Chernenko's corpse was barely cold in the ground when Gorbachev commenced an astonishing foreign policy festival, a hectic series of one-on-one meetings with the dignitaries who came to pay their respects. They came away impressed. Vice President George Bush, the senior U.S. representative at the funeral, said his 85-minute chat with the new Soviet leader left him "high—high on hope, high that we can make progress in Geneva, high for an overall reduction of tensions." French President François Mitterrand found Gorbachev a "calm, relaxed man." Canadian Prime Minister Brian Mulroney judged that he was "clearly in command." West German Chancellor Helmut Kohl observed: "You do not have the impression that you are listening to a Tibetan prayer wheel." Pakistani Ruler General Mohammed Zia ul-Haq might have preferred a prayer wheel to the dressing down that Gorbachev gave him for Pakistan's support of the Afghan rebels. All, regardless, agreed with what Britain's Margaret Thatcher reaffirmed after her Moscow meeting: he was a man with whom they could do business.

The new General Secretary also sought to show his own people that they had a new and vigorous leader before them, one who would be less remote than his predecessors. His image was that of a man of modesty and candor. No giant portraits were allowed to go up in the city either of himself or of the other members of the Politburo. Down came the infamous "murderers row" displays, 30-ft.-high Politburo posters that had dominated main avenues. Within a month of the Chernenko funeral, Gorbachev began appearing at factories, hospitals and schools, trailed by TV cameras and crowds of surprised and admiring citizens.

A test of Gorbachev's touch as a man of the people came when Soviets realized that he intended to place severe limits on the country's most used and abused drug, alcohol. In a sweeping May 16, 1985, decree, he ordered major cuts in the production of vodka, increased fines for public drunkenness, sharply reduced the number of outlets selling liquor and cut their hours, and raised the drinking age from 18 to 21. Overnight, long queues materialized outside bottle shops, and the nation was swept by anti-Gorbachev jokes, mostly benign or even friendly. He was referred to as "mineral water secretary" and, instead of *gen sec* (short for General Secretary), he was called *gen sok* (*sok* means juice).

Other vodka jokes had an edge. In one, an enraged tippler leaves the queue outside a liquor store, declaring, "I'm going to the Kremlin and shoot that s.o.b." An hour later he returns, downcast. "What happened?" the others ask. He replies, "You should see the size of the queue over there."

As always, Soviets found in the vodka shortage a reason to laugh at the system as well as its leader. One story has a tired old man, shabbily dressed, emerging with his bottle after a three-hour wait. His hands are unsteady and he drops the bottle. It shatters. The other drinkers take pity on the old fellow and pass the hat for the price of another bottle. The old man joins the queue, waits another three hours, gets another bottle, but again he drops and breaks it. The others in the queue take pity again, pass the hat, give him the money. "Look, fellows," says one. "If the old guy has to get in the queue again, the store will close before he gets to the counter. Let's put him at the head of the line." The others agree, and the old man is moved to tears by their kindness. "God love Russia," he cries. "In what other country could a thing like this happen?"

If there was widespread bitterness about the booze shortage among many men, the antialcohol campaign was generally welcomed by women fed up with their husbands' drinking habits. Many industrial managers also supported the program, knowing from sad experience the toll that alcoholism takes on productivity. Others viewed the campaign as a long-term issue that would produce results only after a generation or more. "This policy is not something that will be successful this year or next year or even in ten years," said an Islamic diplomat who approves of the campaign. "It will be successful if the next generation does not grow up thinking that every social occasion has to turn into a drinking bout. This is a policy for the future."

Nevertheless, many doctors and sociologists recognized that draconian laws and quasi-prohibition would work only in the short run, and they were right. Within months of Gorbachev's antialcohol restrictions, there were sugar shortages because of widespread moonshining, and every bottle of cheap cologne in the country had been sold. "The alcoholics still get their vodka," a mid-level Soviet official said. "Maybe it costs them more and it is more trouble to find, but they still get it. The rest of us don't want to spend all that time standing in a queue, so we are the ones who suffer." Gorbachev has not wavered in his determination to put an end to the national binge, although he has permitted periodic adjustments in hours of sale to accommodate those who merely wish to buy a bottle of wine for a birthday party.

In the early months of his leadership, Gorbachev was more concerned with survival in a dangerous political arena than with problem drinkers. He launched a party and government housecleaning that soon took on the proportions of a purge, sweeping thousands of superannuated bureaucrats into retirement or, in some cases, into prison for corruption. It was a shocking time for the old Brezhnev-era bosses who had been running their national and regional fiefdoms like princelings of the old empire, seldom troubled by interference from Moscow so long as they paid the proper tribute and kept their people quiet. Their first hint of trouble came in May 1985, when the new General Secretary went to Leningrad on one of his public forays. In a speech to party activists there, he issued a warning: "We must all change our attitudes, from the worker to the minister. Anyone who is not prepared to do so must simply get out of our way." Later, a prominent Moscow editor found an apt analogy for the changes Gorbachev was about to bring to the Soviet Union. "This is an evening of dancing in a society which has never danced," said the editor, Vitali Korotich of *Ogonyok*. "And in a multinational disco like this, a lot of people are going to step on each other's toes."

Gorbachev stepped on toes by the hundreds of thousands. When he took power, the party was beginning its quadrennial public discussion process in preparation for the 27th Party Congress, at the beginning of 1986. Gorbachev used the process as an opportunity to carry out what amounted to a bloodless purge among the party's "cadres," or full-time officials. He also began forced retirements and replacements of scores of senior ministers. Among the first to go was Leningrad's Grigori Romanov, Gorbachev's opponent in the midnight Politburo meeting that followed Chernenko's death. Scandalous rumors concerning Romanov began circulating in the capital, with officials sympathetic to Gorbachev passing them along to foreign diplomats and journalists so that they would spread among the populace via foreign radio stations. The rumors said that Romanov was a boozer and a carouser who abused his authority and bullied his subordinates in Leningrad. According to one story, he had ordered the famed Hermitage Museum in Leningrad to supply a set of priceless Sèvres china for his daughter's wedding banquet. The party turned rowdy, and several pieces of the service were shattered by drunken guests. The story fit neatly with his name: Romanov was the imperial dynasty overthrown by the Bolsheviks in the October Revolution. In midsummer the man people were now calling "the last of the Romanovs" had been overthrown in his turn, retired "for reasons of health." The rumors this time said he was hospitalized for alcoholism.

Romanov was one of the best-known of Gorbachev's political victims, but there were others. By the time the Party Congress began, 60% of government ministers had been replaced. In some republics, such as Kazakhstan, there were new party first secretaries in more than half of the oblasts, regional power centers roughly equivalent to counties. Gorbachev also swept some of the deadwood from the armed forces.

He demonstrated both determination and powers of persuasion by replacing such long-serving officers as Admiral Sergei Gorshkov, 77, builder of the country's modern navy, and General Alexei Yepishev, 79, the head of the military's political administration. The apparent ease with which he retired these old soldiers and sailors showed how right Gromyko had been: this comrade had teeth of iron.

In fact, the coiner of that phrase was one of those who soon felt its bite. Under Gromyko, the Foreign Ministry had long been an unassailably independent power center, largely free of interference from the party bureaucracy. It was also a bastion of nepotistic conservatism, the Soviet equivalent of England's old-boy network. Of all the institutions of Soviet power, none seemed more impervious to serious reform than the Foreign Ministry. Yet at a Supreme Soviet session in July 1985, Gromyko was replaced as Foreign Minister by Eduard Shevardnadze, the amiable, white-haired Politburo member from Georgia who had virtually no diplomatic experience. As the ministry and the world would soon learn, the Georgian's easygoing exterior disguised an able administrator and a tough negotiator who would totally revamp the ministry and, with it, Soviet foreign policy.

Gromyko, the iceman of the Kremlin, was rewarded for getting out of the way by taking the mostly honorific job of chairman of the Presidium of the Supreme Soviet, or President. The Soviet presidency is a ribbon-cutting and medal-pinning post, and it neatly removed Gromyko from the foreign policy process. But it left him with a seat on the Politburo and access to the many perquisites he had become accustomed to during his many years in power. The move also showed potential opponents that Gorbachev could reward as well as punish.

As Gorbachev began to feel politically secure in his new job, his vision appeared to expand beyond the present and into a future that stretched to the end of the century—which, given a normal life-span, would fall within his term of office. Some of his goals were laid out at the end of August 1985 in an extraordinary interview with TIME, his first conversation with a Western news organization. In a two-hour Kremlin session with the magazine's editors and in extensive replies to written questions, Gorbachev displayed an almost messianic sense of urgency about arms control and relations with the U.S. "The situation in the world today is highly complex, very tense," he said. "I would go so far as to say it is explosive." At another point, he used a metaphor that he was to repeat often in the future: "Time is passing, and it might be too late. The train might have already left the station . . . We must muster the political will and the wisdom to stop this process, and begin the process of eliminating weaponry, and the process of improving, invigorating relations between the Soviet Union and the United States."

It was clear that his urgency stemmed largely from concern for the domestic economy. It was a mess. As recently as 1975, Soviet economic output was about 58% as large as that of the U.S. But by 1984 that figure had fallen to 54%, and has probably continued to slide since then. In his TIME interview, Gorbachev outlined plans for using "such tools as profit, pricing, credit and self-sufficiency of enterprises" to revive the economy. He concluded by saying, "Ponder one thing: What are the external conditions that we need to be able to fulfill those domestic plans? I leave the answer to that question with you."

In various other forums during the following months, Gorbachev set forth a 15-year program for change in the Soviet Union and around the world, a program that amounted to a new Communist vision for the 21st century. It was more modest than earlier, grandiose predictions of a Soviet Union richer than America, a promise made most memorably, perhaps, by Nikita Khrushchev, who in 1961 projected confidently that the per capita production of the U.S.S.R. would surpass that of the U.S. by 1970. Gorbachev's program was also less menacing than the Marxist notion of world revolution. His vision was ambitious, but not beyond the dreams of a practical man. It included:

▶ An arms-control agenda that proposed to eliminate nuclear weapons by the end of the century, and in 1987 made possible the first superpower agreement outlawing a class of nuclear armaments.

▶ An across-the-board relaxation on freedom of expression, centered upon his famed *glasnost* policy, and an unprecedented thaw in the arts and journalism.

▶ Civil rights reforms, including the release of large numbers of political prisoners, easing of restrictions on foreign travel, and revision of the Soviet criminal code.

▶ Economic reforms—the *perestroika* program—that place greater emphasis on individual incentives and the marketplace as a means of improving a notoriously stagnant economy.

▶ Gradual movement toward greater "democratization" in Soviet society, including worker election of managers and secret ballots in lower-level Communist Party elections.

▶ A complete reorganization of the Soviet foreign policy and propaganda establishment, resulting in startling improvements in relations with the rest of the world and in the Soviet Union's public image.

Gorbachev pursued these goals largely through his considerable skills as a communicator. He succeeded with surprising ease in winning the attention, if not always the acceptance, of a suspicious world, and especially of an often hostile U.S. Administration. He was adept in choosing the right time and the right place to launch his many arms-control initiatives. For example, he marked the 40th anniversary of the atom-bombing of Hiroshima by declaring a unilateral moratorium on underground testing of nuclear weapons, challenging the U.S. to do the same. The Reagan Administration steadfastly refused to pick up that challenge, but Gorbachev nevertheless extended the moratorium in three- and four-month increments.

Despite the propaganda content of the Gorbachev arms-control agenda, it represented genuine flexibility and was enough to bring about the Geneva summit meeting with President Reagan. That encounter was notable more for its atmosphere than for its accomplishments, but atmosphere may have been the entire point. Geneva was the "fireside summit," an intimate session symbolized by the picture of the world's two most powerful men modestly seated in a modest cottage before a roaring fire, taking the measure of each other. What they found should have surprised neither: strong opinions backed by strong wills. Reagan implacably insisted on the necessity of his Star Wars program. Gorbachev just as steadfastly denounced it. "It is not convincing," he said. "It is emotional. It is a dream. Who can control it? Who can monitor it? It opens up an arms race in space . . . Why can't you believe us when we say we will not use weapons against you?" Reagan's reply: "I cannot say to the American people that I could take you at your word if *you* don't believe *us.*"

No trust, in other words. But the exchange did establish that, to paraphrase Margaret Thatcher, Gorbachev was a man with whom Reagan could do business, Evil Empire or no Evil Empire. From Geneva came Reykjavík and out of Reykjavík came the Washington summit and the INF treaty. Next on the agenda: Moscow and START in 1988.

In the meantime, Gorbachev pressed on with his nearly monthly arms-control initiatives. Some of his ideas were no more than minor shifts in Soviet positions, presented for no other reason than propaganda. But as in the TIME interview, he projected a sense of urgency that, sincere or not, played effectively to public opinion. After each summit, he dispatched his emissaries to pitch the Soviet proposals. The tactic worked. The world was swept with "Gorby fever" to such an extent that opinion polls in Western Europe sometimes showed him to be more popular and more highly regarded than the U.S. President. Gorbachev was even scoring hits in Eastern Europe, where endemic postwar resentment of the Soviets gave way to grudging admiration and sometimes genuine public affection for this new Soviet leader.

It was not always deserved. Many of Gorbachev's accomplishments fell short of his stated goals, sometimes intentionally so. The INF treaty signed in Washington could have been concluded long ago had the Soviets accepted the original U.S. "zero option" in Europe and stringent verification procedures, and if Gorbachev had not wasted more than a year linking and delinking and relinking INF with other aspects of arms control. The credit given him for improvements in human rights is misplaced when one considers that his policies are less than are expected and demanded of Western industrialized countries. The Soviet economy, a vast and ramshackle structure of bureaucratized ministries and hidebound central planning, cannot be reformed by ideas that amount to little more than tinkering. Gorbachev's "democratization" is a pale imitation of the Jeffersonian concept of that word. He is not a man to tolerate opposition, loyal or otherwise, to the "leading role" of the Communist Party. And his foreign policy changes have been mainly in style, not substance: it has yet to be proved that the long-term Soviet goal of a pan-Marxist world has substantially changed.

Yet in the opening years of his leadership, Gorbachev aroused a sense of excitement and optimism about the future of the Soviet Union and the countries under its power. He altered the style of the East-West relationship in making the Soviet Union more credible to a suspicious world, and to itself as well. As *Ogonyok* Editor Korotich remarked, "There will always be somebody in the West who will assert that we would deceive the world. But what is important for us is not to prove that we are not trying to deceive the whole world. What is important is that we live in such a way that we do not deceive ourselves."

That need to end self-deception gave rise to the most obvious, successful and spectacular of Gorbachev's innovations, *glasnost*. As well known as that word has become around the world, there is still no English translation that fully carries its Russian meaning. It is usually translated as "openness," but it is both more than that and less than that. More, in that *glasnost* also means publicity, which is more than merely being open; it implies that facts should also be actively propagated. Less, in that *glasnost* is regarded as a tool of the party, a means by which the party can more effectively govern the country. The concept is no more than a distant cousin of freedom of speech or of the press, as understood in the West. Yet as a policy and as a concept, it has brought profound changes to the Soviet Union's view of the world and of itself.

Gorbachev indicated early in his tenure that he recognized the need for a spiritual revival and a measure of democratization as essential to economic renewal. Indeed, he speaks of *glasnost* as a substitute for multiparty politics. He made that point to a gathering of writers in 1986, a year after coming to power, and refined and repeated it in subsequent speeches. In Vladivostok in July 1986, he said, "We do not have any opposition parties, Comrades. That is why [criticism and self-criticism] are essential for the normal functioning of both the party and society."

That is demonstrably true, but not universally accepted and understood in the Soviet Union, where *glasnost* has come by fits and starts. The policy very nearly failed its very first test. That came on April 26, 1986, when Unit 4 of the Chernobyl nuclear power station, 80 miles from Kiev, went out of control and exploded, spewing a giant plume of radioactive particles into the atmosphere. At the time, Gorbachev and his minions said nothing, gave no warning either to their own citizens downwind of the disaster or to neighboring countries about to taste the fear and uncertainty of the world's worst reactor accident. Even after monitors in Sweden picked up the first shocking hint of a major accident at Chernobyl, and after the world was swept by rumors of mass death and destruction, the Soviets stonewalled behind a bland announcement that an accident had occurred and that it was being brought under control. Gradually and grudgingly, Soviet officials released details that brought the rumors under control. And some sections of the Soviet mass media, armed with their new weapon of *glasnost,* began to delve into the disaster with admirable zeal.

But for Gorbachev himself, it was a signal failure to abide by his principles, to perform according to his style of candor. It was a failure of leadership, unexplained then and now. For 18 days this accomplished communicator was the man who wasn't there. He dropped inexplicably from sight, had nothing to say to the Soviet people or the world about Chernobyl. Not until May 14 did he go on television, somber in a dark suit, with a 25-minute speech that was more defensive than explanatory. He complained bitterly that "we faced a veritable mountain of lies, most dishonest and malicious lies," which he attributed not to the Soviet failure to issue timely reports on the accident but to the desire of "certain Western politicians" to "defame the Soviet Union." It was not his finest half hour.

But it was the only significant lapse since his coming to power, the only time that Gorbachev had failed to do what was necessary to make the best of a bad situation. After the crisis passed, he seemed to recover. As if to make up for the failure of Chernobyl, he turned his attention to a similarly embarrassing subject: the Soviet human rights record. He showed unusual sensitivity to the nearly constant criticism of Soviet repression of dissidents, partly, perhaps, because he agreed with some of it. In his Vladivostok speech he had declared, "Those who attempt to suppress the fresh voice, the just voice, according to old standards and attitudes, need to be put in their place . . . We have a law: those persons who organize persecution for criticism are liable to criminal prosecution, and legal proceedings will be brought."

Evidently with those thoughts in mind, Gorbachev ended the year 1986 with an extraordinary gesture. One evening in December, technicians suddenly showed up to install a telephone in the apartment of Andrei Sakharov, the dissident physicist and Nobel Peace Prize laureate who had been banished to the closed city of Gorky nearly seven years earlier because of his outspoken views. The puzzled physicist soon learned why he was so abruptly receiving a telephone: at 3 p.m. the next day it rang. Gorbachev was on the line. The two men chatted briefly, and Gorbachev told the physicist he was free to return to Moscow to do what he called "your patriotic work." Gorbachev attached no preconditions, and when Sakharov returned in triumph to Moscow a few days later, he did not hesitate to declare that the Soviet Union should withdraw its troops from Afghanistan, the very issue that had caused him to be sent into exile in the first place. This time, however, he was able to make his point without secret police harassment.

Perhaps one good reason for Gorbachev to free Sakharov was that the Nobel prizewinner's ideas on many subjects are precisely the same as Gorbachev's ideas. For example, the Soviet leader obviously was unhappy with the Afghanistan war and probably agreed completely with Sakharov's objections. And, significantly, Sakharov has been critical of the U.S. Strategic Defense Initiative, although for different reasons from those given by Soviet spokesmen. In the end, Sakharov's ideas clearly were not as harmful to Gorbachev as was the public relations stain of the dissident's continued exile. Freeing him was as much the act of a practical politician as of a humanitarian.

Nevertheless, the release of Sakharov was one in a series of similar gestures. Hundreds of people serving terms in prison camps and exile were released during what amounted to a broad amnesty for "political" crimes ranging from alleged anti-Soviet agitation to the teaching of Hebrew. Many of the most prominent political prisoners were also allowed to emigrate, while others have continued to pursue the activities that originally put them in jail. Sergei Grigoryants, for example, went to prison for, among other things, publishing a dissident journal. When he was freed in February, he immediately set about organizing another such journal, aptly titled *Glasnost*. While Grigoryants and his colleagues subsequently suffered police harassment for their efforts, they nevertheless managed to produce several issues of their journal and, at the beginning of 1988, remained free.

One of the most delicate areas that *glasnost* has opened to self-scrutiny is the country's Stalinist past. Within months of Gorbachev's accession to top leadership, Soviet artists and writers began peeling away the layers of silence, deception and euphemism from the nation's post-revolutionary period, filling in what Gorbachev has called the "blank pages of history." Long suppressed manuscripts came out of desk drawers and banned films were rescued from studio shelves to be hungrily devoured by people who had known the truth of their history only through rumor or Western radio stations. Although censorship has not been eliminated under Gorbachev, it has been narrowed to such taboos as military secrets, pornography and direct attacks on the socialist basis of Soviet society.

There remains the powerful effect of self-censorship and post-censorship. It is doubtful that direct criticism of individual Soviet leaders, especially Gorbachev, would see the light of day unless the party cleared it, as in the case of the fierce criticism of fallen Moscow Party Leader Boris Yeltsin or the denunciations of the disgraced former Kazakh leader Kunaev. Some editors have been reprimanded after the fact for political reporting that went further than the top leadership was willing to accept, and such warnings were likely to have a chilling effect on their future work. But a broad range of subjects opened up nevertheless—enough to keep writers, movie-makers and editors busy for years to come. Already, Soviets have been able to see such work as director Tengiz Abuladze's film *Pokayaniye* (Repentance), with its depiction of a ruthless fantasyland dictator who resembles Lavrenti Beria, Stalin's secret police chief, and who behaves like a local Stalin. The film was seen and cleared by Eduard Shevardnadze in 1983 when he was party leader in Georgia, but it was shelved again before it could reach the public. It was only after Gorbachev came to power, and picked Shevardnadze as his Foreign Minister, that *Repentance* made it to the movie houses. Another groundbreaking work was Yuris Podnieks' documentary *Is It Easy to Be Young?*, a harsh indictment of Soviet society's failure to engage its youth. The film's treatment of drugs, alienation, greed, pacifism and the psychological distress of Afghanistan war veterans would have been banned as subversive under Gorbachev's predecessors, and its director would probably have been imprisoned, if he had succeeded in making the movie at all.

The fact that the film was made and, more surprisingly, exhibited on general release throughout the country, demonstrated Gorbachev's recognition that the Communist Party is in danger of losing its younger generation and that it cannot be reclaimed without some doses of painful honesty. "Gorbachev realizes that the party had lost contact with the population, especially with youth," said a Western diplomat specializing in Soviet domestic policies. "He is trying to find the language of youth so contact can be re-established."

The blossoming of the film industry was matched in publishing. New novels on Stalinism, some of them suppressed for more than two decades, finally made their appearance under Gorbachev's *glasnost* policy. Anatoli Rybakov's *Deti Arbata* (Children of the Arbat), which tells the story of the first wave of Stalinist purges from 1934 to 1937, had been announced for publication in 1966 and again in 1977 but was suppressed both times. The book finally appeared last year. Another long- suppressed novel that surfaced under Gorbachev was Vladimir Dudintsev's *Belyee Odezhdy* (White Clothes), an account of the suppression of the science of genetics during the Stalin era. Those books, already written, were pulled from desk drawers. Others were beginning to come out of typewriters, promising a Russian literary renaissance—if, of course, the curtain of censorship is not drawn again.

The daily press and television also underwent a profound and positive change under the policy of *glasnost*. Newspapers, encouraged by Gorbachev and his propaganda aides, began ferreting out inefficiency and corruption at the local level to an extent never imagined in the past. With surprising speed, journalists and editors learned to work with the vigor and crusading dedication of their colleagues in the West. Several newspapers, such as the Moscow regional daily *Sovietskaya Rossiya* and the multilanguage weekly Moscow *News,* achieved reputations as fearless muckrakers. At times, however, it appeared that the editorial zeal was a function of political vendetta. *Sovietskaya Rossiya* conducted an admirable investigation into the scandalous state of Moscow housing construction, gathering evidence of malfeasance that led eventually to the ouster of the Moscow party committee first secretary, Gorbachev's old rival Viktor Grishin. Had Grishin been an ally of Gorbachev's rather than a rival, it is doubtful that *Sovietskaya Rossiya* would have been so bold. Indeed, once Grishin was safely out of the way, *Sovietskaya Rossiya's* editor was rewarded with promotion to a higher post, and the newspaper soon lost its muckraking zeal.

Other journals and journalists, however, have continued to crusade against corruption and to fill in history's blank pages. The weekly *Ogonyok* has plunged into such touchy subjects as the war in Afghanistan, youth gangs and banned poets. Over the course of a year the magazine published an anthology of 20th century poets that included many writers whose work was suppressed for decades or, in some cases, had never been published in the Soviet Union. This trove of buried treasure included poems of Ivan Bunin, banned for many years in his homeland, even though he was the first Russian winner of the Nobel Prize for Literature (1933).

Ironically, the Nobel literature award for 1987 also went to an exiled Russian poet, Joseph Brodsky. But gone were the days when such an event would be deemed an insult to the Soviet Union and virtually a subversive act by the recipient, as had been the case in 1958 when Novelist Boris Pasternak was forced to decline the prize. By contrast, in the Gorbachev era the Soviet reaction was to reclaim Brodsky as one of their own and to schedule publication of his work in the literary journal *Novy Mir*. In such an atmosphere it was also possible to clear the name of Pasternak, whose *Doctor Zhivago* was finally published in *Novy Mir* in 1988. But even under Gorbachev, it has proved impossible for the Soviets to come to terms with Alexander Solzhenitsyn. The author of *The Gulag Archipelago* remains in exile in the U.S. and unpublished in his native land except for his novella *One Day in the Life of Ivan Denisovich*, which appeared during the thaw of the early 1960s.

For all that they have gained, Soviet intellectuals are not willing to give Gorbachev and the party leadership full credit for the changes. *"Glasnost* is not something that comes down from above,"* said Poet Yevgeni Yevtushenko. "It is no gift. We worked very hard for it, and it has been a long battle since Stalin's death. We had some victories and many defeats, and there were times when we had unpublished *glasnost,* voiceless *glasnost."* That was a play on words: *glasnost* comes from the Russian word *golos,* voice. "Many of the people now in the government leadership were young men sitting in the balconies when I was reading poetry in the 1950s," Yevtushenko said. "Gorbachev himself is a man of my generation, and he was a student at Moscow State University in the '50s. He was a man of the balcony too."

Yevtushenko acknowledges that Soviet policy on artistic freedom is still unsettled. A backlash is possible. "It is very uncomfortable now for mediocrities in the bureaucracy to hear all this criticism," he said. "These 'armchairologists' don't like it. The relationship between political power and writers has always been one of competition and tension. They used to say that Russia had two czars, one in the Winter Palace and one in Yasnaya Polyana [Leo Tolstoy's home]." The uncertainty of Soviet policy is one reason Yevtushenko cautiously calls the age of *glasnost* a "pre-renaissance," and not yet a renaissance in the arts and letters. "We are heirs to great art, great music, great literature, and we should be modest in light of that."

Yevtushenko and many other intellectuals firmly believe that stagnation in the Soviet economy is a direct result of Stalinism and the refusal to come to terms with it. Economic renewal, they say, can only come with spiritual renewal. "The relationship between *glasnost* and economic reconstruction is the same relationship between the air and the soil," Yevtushenko said. "The air can be quickly refreshed, but after that it takes a long time for the soil to become refreshed."

Rybakov, author of *Children of the Arbat,* said much the same thing. Stalinism, he asserted, "destroyed initiative, independent thought, and it created a fear of taking chances. It created a huge bureaucratic apparatus accustomed to acting only on orders from above." He said the first step in restoring the economy is to repair the Stalin-damaged psyche of the entire country. "We must have everybody at every step of the social ladder feeling free and brave and competent to make decisions," he said. "Then, and only then, will come important economic reforms." Such acts as the release of Andrei Sakharov from internal exile are vital to restoring the national psychology, Rybakov explained. "The decision on Sakharov was not an act of political opportunism," he said. "It is part of the process of change that must take place. We need people to speak up freely and, more important, to work freely. In these times, it is impossible to banish a person to Gorky for his views." Rybakov himself was exiled for three years in 1933 for "anti-Soviet agitation" and was further denied the right to live in some three dozen major cities, even though he won medals for heroism in World War II. He was allowed to live in Moscow only after he was "rehabilitated" in the late 1950s. His book's publication has brought him vindication.

The air will be further cleared with a series of legal reforms initiated under Gorbachev. Among the changes: repeal of some of the more noxious sections of the criminal code banning "anti-Soviet agitation and propaganda," the clause most often used to send dissidents to the Gulag. Also due for revocation are the use of banishment, or internal exile, as punishment, some restrictions on the practice of religion and some uses of the death penalty, especially in economic crimes. Already, Soviet authorities have made basic changes in rules concerning forced psychiatric treatment, including the key step of putting "special" psychiatric hospitals under the Ministry of Health instead of the Interior Ministry.

Among Gorbachev's least noticed and least heralded reforms has been a small but significant relaxation in the most fundamental human right of all, the right to leave the Soviet Union. A total of 9,000 Soviet Jews were allowed to emigrate during 1987, the highest annual figure since 1979 and an order of magnitude greater than the 943 allowed to leave in 1986. Similarly, total emigration has been climbing as well. The number of citizens—including Jews, Armenians, ethnic Germans and others—allowed to leave the country in 1987 exceeded 20,000, up from 5,000 the year before. On a less publicly noticeable level, thousands of Soviets were permitted to travel abroad for temporary family visits. The consular office at the U.S. embassy has been swamped as never before with visa applicants, and airline representatives report sharp increases in the numbers of Soviet passengers traveling to the West.

Another new and surprising development was a relaxation on restrictions on working abroad by top-level sports and cultural figures, who are now free to arrange foreign performing tours as long as the tours do not interfere with their professional obligations in the Soviet Union and as long as no financial burdens are placed on the Soviet state. That limits such travel to top-name performers who can command substantial fees in the West. But it is at least a change from previous practice, which required a lengthy bureaucratic approval procedure in the Ministry of Culture—a process so tedious, and so often ending in refusal, that few performers tried it. Under the new rules, approval is virtually automatic if the scheduling and financial restrictions are met. Soviet hockey and soccer players have begun picking up contracts with Western professional teams, and it is commonplace for artists and writers to pursue artistic endeavors abroad. The Bolshoi Ballet's prima ballerina, Maya Plisetskaya, for example, signed a contract as artistic director of the Spanish National Ballet in Madrid. In the other direction, former defectors were allowed to return for visits to a homeland that had once denounced them as traitors, Dancer Rudolf Nureyev prominent among them.

The changes were partly the result of regulations that went into effect at the beginning of 1987. Many critics complained that the new rules merely codified past practice and predicted that they would make travel abroad for Soviets more difficult, not less so. The rules specify that Soviets may go abroad to join or visit close family members—spouses, parents or siblings—and require authorities to give answers to visa applications within one month, or three days in cases of emergency. A significant exception applies to those who are alleged to have had access to state secrets, which is a reason given for refusal to grant exit permits to a number of prominent Jewish refuseniks. But as always in the Soviet Union, the letter of the law is less important than the spirit of those who administer it. Under Gorbachev, a tincture of generosity has been added to that spirit. There are still cases of arbitrary action by the authorities, and would-be emigrants are still treated as pariahs by former friends and co-workers—application to emigrate usually leads to dismissal from work. Yet, for the most part, the new rules are being observed. More citizens are able to vote with their feet against, or for, Gorbachev's Soviet Union.

The General Secretary's almost uncanny ability to exploit apparent disasters was demonstrated with the arrest and temporary imprisonment of an American news correspondent, Nicholas Daniloff of the magazine *U.S. News and World Report.* The Daniloff case had the earmarks of a KGB operation gone awry, an absurd frame-up staged to retaliate for an earlier FBI arrest of a Soviet United Nations employee. The problem was that Daniloff's seizure violated an unwritten rule, observed since the time of Stalin, against using journalists as pawns in superpower spy games. The rule grew out of the obvious fact that arresting reporters is a guaranteed method for getting a bad press, and the Soviets got plenty of it. But instead of going to ground, Gorbachev moved quickly to use the incident to haggle with the Reagan Administration. With astonishing ease Gorbachev—and his able Foreign Minister Shevardnadze—managed to parlay Daniloff's freedom into the Reykjavík summit, the neutral-ground meeting that Gorbachev had been seeking for six months and that the White House had steadfastly rejected.

Gorbachev was on a roll. Even the abortive climax of the Reykjavík summit, at which the two leaders came within a "yes" of putting together the arms-control agreement of the century, was turned to advantage. Whether or not he actively planned to tantalize the Americans at the Hofdi House session and then yank away the prize at the last moment, Gorbachev was clearly prepared for the failure of Reykjavík to produce an agreement. He immediately dispatched his diplomats around the world to blame the Americans for failure. Within two hours of the talks' breakdown, the theme of the Soviets' argument was put forth by Gorbachev in a pre-departure press conference. He presented a carefully reasoned explanation that the failure was the fault not of President Reagan but of the "military-industrial complex" that held him in thrall. It was an explanation that revealed both a shrewd understanding of the popularity of the President and Gorbachev's own skewed view of the way America is governed.

As for the governing of his own country, Gorbachev's concept of "democratization" is an example of a political mentality that may be instinctively democratic but has been conditioned by a lifetime of Communist politics designed to enclose every freedom inside a thicket of rules and controls. "A house can be put in order only by a person who feels that he owns the house," he said in a major 1987 speech. "Workers and collective farmers are far from being indifferent about who heads the enterprise, workshop, section and team. Since the well-being of the collective is made dependent on the abilities of the managers, the working people should also have real opportunities to influence the election process and monitor their activities."

But on close examination, his specific proposals are far from democratic. He called for multiple candidates, but only in the nominating process, not in the election itself. And he conceded at the same time that elected governmental bodies have little power. "Their work is often a formality," he said. "Only secondary matters, or even questions that have already been decided in advance, are brought up for discussion."

Of greater importance to the running of the country are Gorbachev's views on choosing party officials by secret ballot. He said that party secretaries at the district, city, regional and republic levels should be elected by party committee members casting secret ballots for more than one candidate. At present, secretaries are usually picked by local party bigwigs and then presented to the committees as a single candidate, to be accepted or rejected by a show of hands. Obviously, few committee members are willing to risk the displeasure of their superiors by raising a hand in opposition. The secret ballot, however, would bring a measure of democracy to the Communist Party only, a ruling élite numbering about 18 million members of a national population in excess of 280 million. Nevertheless, Gorbachev repeatedly declared that democratization is a vital necessity to the Soviet Union's future. "Some comrades apparently find it hard to understand that democracy is not just a slogan," he said. "They must change their views and habits so as not to find themselves outside the mainstream of life. This is our persistent advice to all who are still doubting and slow." For those who may still be doubting, he promised that his reforms would not undermine the system. "The point at issue assuredly is not any breakup of our political system," he said. "Socialist democracy has nothing in common with permissiveness, irresponsibility and anarchy."

When Gorbachev talks of "democratization," of course, he is hardly exhorting citizens to go out and organize their own political parties. "The goal is not to install a Western-style multiparty republican system," writes Historian Moshe Lewin in *The Gorbachev Phenomenon,* a book scheduled for publication in 1988, "but rather to increase citizens' participation in political life, to enhance political and other freedoms and to return the party to a political role, instead of a basically bureaucratic-administrative one." Lewin, a U.S. expert on the Soviet Union, suggests that Gorbachev might also want to return the party to its roots: "The Bolshevik party, which was literally buried by Stalin and Stalinism, was a political party, with lively debates and factions. The party operated democratically, even during the civil war. It took at least eight years of struggle before the Bolshevik party was transformed into some other creature."

In some sense, Gorbachev's goal is to prove what has never been shown in practice, that Lenin and his Bolsheviks were right, that Communism can work. Gorbachev has said the country should become a place where the "workingman would feel that he is the master of his life, where he would enjoy all the benefits of material and spiritual culture, where the future of his children would be secure, where he would have everything necessary for a full and interesting life. And even skeptics would be forced to say, 'Yes, socialism is a system serving man, working for his benefit, in his social and economic interests, for his spiritual elevation.' "

Gorbachev's catchword for creating that kind of socialism is *perestroika*. It is a simple enough word, although it has taken on a heavy load of propaganda freight. To some, it means a return to the basics of socialism. To others, it means free enterprise and the market system. The dictionary definition is simply "restructuring," a word broad enough in its meanings to encompass everything from socialist revival to capitalist flirtation. Perhaps Gorbachev chose the term for that very reason, to include everybody. His ideas, however, are somewhat more precise. He laid them down in his book *Perestroika* and more briefly in a pivotal June 25, 1987, speech at a Central Committee meeting called to endorse his economic plans. He listed five basic principles of *perestroika:*

▶ "A drastic expansion of the margins of independence" of state enterprises by switching them to full cost accounting, including "establishment of a direct dependence of the level of incomes of collectives on the effectiveness of their work."

▶ "Radical transformation of the centralized management of the economy . . . resolutely relieving the center from interference in the day-to-day activity of subordinate economic bodies."

▶ "Cardinal reform of planning, price setting, finance and credit."

▶ "Creating 'new organization structures' to involve science more directly in production and on this basis [achieve] a breakthrough to the world standard of quality."

▶ "Transition from the excessively centralized command system of management to a democratic one; development of self-management; creation of a mechanism of invigorating the individual's potential; precise delimitation of functions, fundamental change in the style and methods of activity of party, government and economic bodies."

Stripped of the verbiage, much of Gorbachev's "new thinking" on economic change is little more than a demand for harder work and more sensible behavior. He criticizes the central-planning bureaucracy without mercy, but he has not dismantled it. His most ambitious *perestroika* project was the abolition of five agricultural ministries two years ago and their replacement with a superministry called Agroprom that was supposed to eliminate bureaucratic bickering between farmers, agricultural machinery producers and fertilizer producers. But after two years, the Soviet press has begun to criticize Agroprom for being even more bureaucracy-bound and unwieldy than the patchwork of ministries it replaced.

Nevertheless, other large-scale reforms are going forward. The newest is *khozraschet,* which translates as self-financing, a principle that became effective Jan. 1, 1988, in 60% of Soviet industrial and agricultural production. What it means, in theory, is that Soviet enterprises must now conduct business and balance their books in such a way that they produce goods and services of a value higher than the resources and labor that goes into them. In the capitalist world, that may seem like a simple enough concept. But for enterprise executives who have never known anything other than state plans and fixed prices, the notion is alien and sometimes frightening. An executive of a factory that produces measuring equipment told *Izvestia* that unreliability in raw-material supplies—a chronic problem in Soviet production—would now mean real hardship for his enterprise and its workers. He said he was facing a shortage of 400 tons of sheet metal at his plant. "It is extremely alarming," he added. "What are we going to do? I don't rule out that in February one of our factories will have to stop work."

There was the nub of the problem. In a workers' state, can factories be allowed to shut down? Can workers be laid off? Unemployment was abolished in the Soviet Union in 1930, and officials often counter foreign complaints about human rights in their country by pointing out that every Soviet citizen has the "right to work," a guarantee that few capitalist countries can match. There was always some structural unemployment in the U.S.S.R.—it takes time for people to change jobs—and considerable overstaffing. Yet under Gorbachev, the principle of full employment may be crumbling. The General Secretary has already decreed that the Moscow-based ministries must shed 60,000 bureaucrats by 1990. The Soviet press in 1987 reported the complaints of 680 workers who had been displaced by the consolidation of two engineering ministries. Most of the victims felt that they had been dismissed unfairly. Because full employment is guaranteed, there are no unemployment benefits as such, though workers who lose their jobs through consolidation can usually continue collecting their salaries for a few months.

Prime Minister Nikolai Ryzhkov told the Supreme Soviet in 1987 that 13% of state enterprises might have to close. Vladimir Kostakov, a Soviet economist, suggested in 1986 that the industrial work force might have to be reduced by as much as 19% by the end of the century in order to meet the kind of productivity targets that Gorbachev is talking about. The General Secretary's closest economic adviser, Abel Aganbegyan, also comes close to endorsing shutdowns and layoffs on a large scale. "Personally, I think it would be wise to close down several thousand enterprises," he said last year. "Not one, not two, not one hundred. I can name several mining enterprises where conditions of work are unbearable, which suffer terrible losses. Why do they exist? It would be easier to erase them by bulldozer and build new ones instead of keeping them running. An enterprise that suffers losses is a burden on the society. It should be closed." But did he believe that such shut-downs really would take place? "If so," he shrugged, "they would be symbolic in nature, if only for the others to under-stand that the possibility exists."

So far there have been a few such symbolic shutdowns, but not on the scale envisioned by Aganbegyan and perhaps favored by Gorbachev himself. The self-financing system may help identify the economic losers and embolden Soviet leaders to close factories and dislocate workers, if not put them out of work. That will be the test of Gorbachev's intentions.

More visible than *khozraschet* in industry are the small-scale reforms in private and cooperative enterprises. Under rules that took effect in 1987, individuals may carry out 29 dif-ferent kinds of small-scale spare-time work such as bootmak-ing, interior decorating, plumbing and using private cars as taxis. This was work that was done in the past, but it was tech-nically illegal. The new rules make it legal and, of course, tax-able. Statistics on compliance have been spotty, but the the So-viet news agency TASS reported that 137,000 Muscovites obtained permits for individual labor within the first three months of its enactment. The rules have made such labor more visible, but it is not clear that they have made more ser-vices available. According to official estimates in 1987, be-tween 30% and 80% of small-scale repairs of such goods as shoes, cars and household appliances were done privately in a black market that had an annual turnover estimated at 16 bil-lion rubles ($24 billion) annually. While private taxis and street vendors are likely to register to do their more open pri-vate enterprise, experts expect that most of the old black mar-ket will remain black.

More open, and more successful in some areas, has been the cooperative movement. Cooperatives operate under differ-ent rules than individual enterprises do, paying higher taxes and coming under closer regulation. Nevertheless, cooperative enterprises, which may range from a small family-operated restaurant to a relatively large television-repair shop, have shown considerable early success. The prototype for such enterprises was the Kropotkinskaya café, Moscow's first cooperative restaurant and an instant hit when it opened last March. It drew thousands of customers with its simple but carefully prepared dishes, its courteous service and plush, prerevolutionary ambience. It thrived perhaps too well. Ill-wishers complained that the eight-member cooperative was getting rich, and *Pravda* criticized the café for returning only 3% of its earnings in taxes in the first six months. The owners responded that they were still paying off state loans, and would eventually be subject to taxes in the 40% to 50% bracket. What the episode showed more than anything was that, after 70 years of Communism, Soviet citizens are deeply suspicious of profit and absolutely scandalized by wealth.

Gorbachev insists repeatedly that his reforms are socialist reforms and that the "socialist basis of society will not be undermined." In a meeting with media officials early in 1988, he criticized both "ultra-*perestroika*" advocates—by which he apparently meant such men as Moscow Party Boss Boris Yeltsin, who had been calling the pace of reform too slow—and criticism coming from the "right." "Voices from that side claim that the 'foundations of socialism' are being undermined," he said. "A legitimate question arises. What is undermining them? People's movement, activity aimed at handling more confidently the affairs of the country where they are the masters? On the contrary, socialism is not weakening. It is gaining strength and, through the people's political and social activity, it is more fully realizing its potential."

Such sermonizing for socialism is one of the things about Gorbachev that observers sometimes find remarkable. Phrases like that one, so leaden on paper, ring with conviction when he puts his expressive eyes and busy hands into their delivery. He makes it sound as if he means it, and he probably does. "I think he sees himself as the Martin Luther of Russian socialism," said an admiring American diplomat after witnessing one of Gorbachev's speeches. "He believes he is taking the Soviet Union back to its Leninist roots."

Much of Gorbachev's agenda for domestic revival was set forth in a 1987 Central Committee speech. He denounced the habits of the past in terms that were intended to shock a torpid society out of its two-decade Brezhnevian slumber. Never before had Soviets heard such language as this from one of their leaders: "The growth of alcohol and drug abuse and a rise in crime became indicators of the decline of social morality. Disregard for the law, report padding, bribe taking, sycophancy and encouragement of toadyism had a deleterious effect on the moral atmosphere of the society."

Although he did not mention him by name, Gorbachev clearly was referring to the leadership of the late Leonid Brezhnev when he recalled the "mass distribution of awards, titles and prizes" and said that "red tape and formalism flourished, extreme intolerance of criticism emerged." He added, "In those years, there were no firm obstacles placed in the path of dishonest, pushy, greedy people intent on personal gain from their party membership."

Gorbachev had criticized the Brezhnev era before, most notably in his keynote speech to the 27th Party Congress the previous February. But never had he pilloried it so scathingly or comprehensively. The speech was especially remarkable because his audience comprised mostly Central Committee members who had been elected during the Brezhnev era; there was only a 42% turnover at the previous party congress, leaving potential opponents of many of Gorbachev's ideas in the majority. When he spoke of "permissiveness, slack discipline, drunkenness, departmentalism, parochialism and manifestations of nationalism," he was talking about many of those sitting before him in the Kremlin hall. The speech was regarded as a challenge to the vaguely defined "opposition" that he complained of almost from the beginning of his tenure in power and that continued to dog his leadership. "Not everyone is marching in step with the demands of life," he said on that occasion. "There are quite a few people who are slow in throwing off the burden of the past, who are adopting a wait-and-see attitude and openly putting a spoke in the wheel."

At times, Gorbachev has sounded like a man who was not winning his battle with the bureaucracy. He spoke almost despairingly of an opposition that is often attacked but seldom specified. "Between the people who want these changes, who dream about these changes, and the leadership, there is an administrative layer—the ministerial and party apparatus—that does not want these changes, does not want to be deprived of certain rights and privileges," he said in a meeting with a group of writers. He raged at one of the biggest of the bureaucratic institutions, the State Planning Committee: "For our Gosplan there are no authorities, no general secretaries, no central committees. They do what they want. And the sort of situation they like best is when everybody has to come to them and ask for a million rubles, or 20 tractors, or 40,000 tractors— when everybody has to beg."

However much he may rail at the opposition, Gorbachev has been compelled to moderate some of his plans to accommodate it. The extent to which he must guard his political flanks was demonstrated in the case of his friend and political ally, Moscow Party Leader Yeltsin. An impulsive and short-tempered politician, Yeltsin sealed his fate in October 1987, when he delivered an unscheduled speech before the Central Committee in which he complained about some members of the leadership. The speech was never published, but insider reports made it clear that his main dispute was with the conservative party ideologist Yegor Ligachev. Whatever Yeltsin said was too much. Two weeks later he was compelled to undergo a "self-criticism" session so severe that he was hospitalized for heart trouble shortly afterward.

Whether for political reasons or because of genuine anger

with Yeltsin, Gorbachev himself led the attack and thus deeply shocked many Muscovites, who had seen Yeltsin as a tough opponent of corruption and privilege. But Gorbachev appeared in the end to have survived the episode intact, and perhaps even strengthened politically. Despite his popularity, the abrasive Yeltsin had alienated hundreds of influential politicians who can make their displeasure felt in Moscow, just as members of Congress can make theirs felt in Washington. "Just think of Yeltsin as the James Watt of Soviet politics," said a Western diplomat in Moscow, referring to the lively but controversial U.S. Secretary of the Interior who was ultimately forced to resign from the Reagan Cabinet.

Despite the unsavory taste left by the Yeltsin affair, Gorbachev has steadily built a majority and even a consensus on the Politburo, the important 13-member voting body that sets party policy. He has assembled a strong core of supporters both in the Politburo and in the Secretariat, the twelve-member group that runs the party on a day-to-day basis. They include his handpicked propaganda chief, Alexander Yakovlev; his foreign policy guide, Anatoli Dobrynin; Viktor Nikonov, who holds Gorbachev's old job as agriculture secretary; and Lev Zaikov, a Leningrader who backed him against Romanov and was rewarded by being brought to Moscow as Yeltsin's replacement. Most of the Brezhnev-era holdovers have gone, including Geidar Aliev, who left because of heart trouble, and Sergei Sokolov, the Defense Minister. Sokolov was forced into summary retirement after a young West German named Mathias Rust flew his single-engine plane unimpeded through hundreds of miles of Soviet airspace, landing near Red Square. The Rust adventure, which was an embarrassment to the much vaunted Soviet air-defense system, enabled Gorbachev to finish what he had set out to do more than a year earlier: bring new blood and new attitudes into the leadership of the armed forces. Thanks to Rust, Gorbachev has his own man, General Dmitri Yazov, in charge of the Ministry of Defense.

A man who is able to build that kind of consensus is not a radical. In a Nov. 2 speech commemorating 70 years of Communist power, Gorbachev demonstrated that fact by refusing to deal with the more unsavory portions of Soviet history. Many had hoped for a *glasnost* updating of Khrushchev's secret speech to the 20th Party Congress, especially because of Gorbachev's repeated insistence that the "blank pages" of Soviet history must be filled in. Such high hopes were not met. Of forced collectivization, Gorbachev used a phrase that might have seemed comic had the subject not included terrible crimes and widespread suffering. Looking at a mass of stone-silent faces, many of them elderly, in the Kremlin's Palace of Congress, he said, "It must be said frankly: at the new stage there was a deficit of the Leninist considerate attitude to the interests of the working peasantry." That was an odd way to describe what was a savage exercise in expropriation, arrest, murder and starvation. Gorbachev treated with similar verbal squeamishness the blood purges of the 1930s in which millions of people, including much of the leadership of the party itself, were wiped out in an orgy of arrests, denunciations, star chamber trials and executions: "Quite obviously it was the absence of a proper level of democratization in Soviet society that made possible the personality cult, the violations of legality, the wanton repressive measures of the '30s. I am putting things bluntly—those were real crimes stemming from an abuse of power. Many thousands of people inside and outside the party were subjected to wholesale repressive measures. Such, comrades, is the bitter truth."

Actually, the truth was that millions, not thousands, were shot, worked and starved to death, not merely "repressed," by Stalin's NKVD. That the Soviet leadership is not ready for a truly candid account of the party's history was confirmed by Alexander Yakovlev, a Politburo member and Gorbachev's chief adviser on public opinion and propaganda. The man who some call "Mr. Glasnost," when questioned about Gorbachev's candor, shot back, "Why do you think that, if he had said millions, he would have been speaking more truthfully than if he had said thousands? I know the rumors that persist in the West . . . but I think many rumors lie on the consciences of certain people."

Both Yakovlev and Gorbachev may have reason to feel uncomfortable with too much candor on the subject of Stalin, who was a man they were taught to love and admire during their formative years. "I can say that I did not take part in the 1920s and 1930s because of my age," said Yakovlev, who is eight years older than Gorbachev. "But I did take part in the war, and I am not ashamed to say that I had faith and believed in the fact that Stalin's leadership was correct."

Still, in its cautious way, the Gorbachev speech opened a narrow window in a notoriously impenetrable wall of history. He mentioned some names that had not been on the lips of a senior Soviet official at any time since they were made "unpersons" in the 1920s and '30s. Of some, he spoke positively. He credited Nikolai Bukharin, who was tried and shot in 1938, with having defended Leninist ideals and for admitting his political errors. The General Secretary could not do the same for Leon Trotsky, who, he said, "displayed excessive pretensions to top leadership in the party, thus fully confirming Lenin's opinion of him as an excessively self-assured politician who always vacillated and cheated." Nevertheless, it was the first time in modern history that any Soviet leader had even mentioned Trotsky's name, and that fact has meaning for Soviet historians, writers and artists. By speaking publicly, if euphemistically, of the Stalin-era crimes and of some towering figures of Soviet history, Gorbachev in effect gave his blessing to others who may wish to treat such subjects far more freely.

Also of some significance was his announcement that a special commission will be established to study and rewrite the party's history, if only because it will provide an opportunity and a forum for Soviet intellectuals to debate what had been a closed and close-minded subject. "This is something we have to do," he said, "the more so because even now there are still attempts to turn away from painful matters in our history, to hush them up, to make believe that nothing special happened." He did not specify who will be on the commission or when it will make its revised history public. But he indicated that the panel will have access to some of the closed archives that contain the evidence of Stalin's crimes. "It is sometimes said that Stalin did not know of many instances of lawlessness," he said. "Documents at our disposal show that this is not so. The guilt of Stalin and his immediate entourage before the party and the people for the wholesale repressive measures and acts of lawlessness is enormous and unforgivable. This is a lesson for all generations." And it is a lesson especially for his own generation, the "children of the 20th Congress."

As Gorbachev settled into his role as world leader, there was a question on virtually everybody's mind, in the Soviet Union and abroad: Can he last? Or more precisely, will hardline Communists and innate conservatism turn *glasnost* into another short-lived thaw? Will *perestroika* peter out into the timid half-measures that characterized the much heralded *perestroika* of the early Brezhnev years?

By nature as well as by habit, the Soviet system has always run on fear and force. Gorbachev is now telling both the rulers and the ruled that it runs badly. But to make the system run well, is Gorbachev willing to lead his comrades toward a future in which command and intimidation are replaced by consent and competition? If he tries, will they follow? And if they do, will the resulting society still be the Soviet Union? Marxists have long relished pointing out the "contradictions" in other political systems. Now Gorbachev is forcing them to face up to some excruciating contradictions in their own. Whether—and how—he can resolve them is one of the most important questions of the decade, perhaps even of the era.

6

One Day in the Life of Mikhail Sergeyevich

In Moscow in early winter, the sun does not rise until 9 a.m. Muscovites, however, are not easily deterred by darkness, much less by cold. After the dreary, drizzly days of autumn, they almost look forward to the onset of winter. The hours of daylight may be short, but each new snowfall leaves the usually gray and grimy capital covered with a fresh coat of clean, cottony soundproofing. Despite the cold, the streets are filled with people, and outdoor ice-cream vendors remain at their posts. Darkness, which comes as early as 4 p.m., does not slow the pace. Summer, when the sun never seems to set, merely stretches out the bustle. During July, average temperatures in Moscow are about the same as in Paris, the ice-cream vendors do an even brisker business than in winter, the parks are a little more crowded, the activities more varied. But whatever the season, Moscow's streets are busy.

Mikhail Gorbachev is very much a Muscovite, having lived in the capital continuously since 1978 and having spent five years there as a student. Thus, on a typical morning, summer or winter, the lights are on early at the Gorbachev house. The First Family has an apartment two blocks west of the Kremlin, but it is not the same one that the Brezhnevs, Andropovs or Chernenkos lived in (there is no official General Secretary's residence equivalent to the American White House).

More often, however, the Gorbachevs stay at their dacha along Rublyovskoye Shosse, on the western outskirts of the city, where the lights are also burning early. The term dacha can mean many things in the Soviet Union, from a worker's one-room shack in a development of similarly modest vacation and weekend homes, to a high party official's prerevolutionary palace in some verdant precinct of the greenbelt around Moscow. Some of these residences are owned by their occupants, though most of the grander ones are properties of the state. Tenants remain there by virtue of their job and face the prospect of eviction if they lose that post.

Since Stalin's day, Soviet leaders have had the use of one of or more of the state's better dachas. Leonid Brezhnev, for instance, occupied one just outside Moscow at Usovo that had been used by Stalin and Khrushchev, as well as a hunting lodge at Zavidovo, 70 miles northwest of Moscow. In his 1976 book *The Russians,* Journalist Hedrick Smith retells the story of how Brezhnev, shortly after becoming General Secretary, had his aged mother flown to Moscow from her home in Dneprodzerzhinsk so he could show her his new domain. After taking her around the grounds at Usovo, he whisked her in his private helicopter to Zavidovo. There, in the banquet room with its huge fireplace, he finally asked her, "Tell me, Mama, what do you think?" She looked around at the baronial splendor and replied, "Well, it's good, Leonid. But what if the Reds come back?"

Gorbachev's dacha remains something of a mystery. It is in an area marked by an international no-entry sign, a red circle with a yellow bar across it, an emblem known in Russian as a *kirpich* (brick). The neighborhood is patrolled by security vehicles. The entire area to the north of Rublyovskoye Shosse is closed to foreigners, presumably because of the district's complex of residences used by high officials. Some foreign visitors have been invited to Gorbachev's dacha as guests, notably Indian Prime Minister Rajiv Gandhi and his Italian-born wife Sonia. Indeed, the Gandhis seem to be genuine personal as well as official friends of the Gorbachevs. Raisa and Sonia appeared to hit it off well during the Gandhis' 1985 visit to Moscow. During a return visit in 1987, the Gandhis were invited to an intimate family dinner at the Gorbachevs' home. Given Raisa's reported aversion to entertaining, not many outsiders have seen the interior of either of the Gorbachev's Moscow-area residences, and no details about their size or furnishings have been made public.

In 1978, when Gorbachev was summoned to Moscow to become party secretary in charge of agriculture, he and Raisa were admitted to a lavish, highly stratified network of privileges and perquisites, of which the official dacha is only one element. In addition, members of the Moscow élite (and their counterparts in smaller cities, though on a more modest scale) enjoy special apartments, medical care and other advantages not available to the average Soviet citizen. This system of official privilege began under Stalin, flourished under Brezhnev and is only starting to be curbed by the current General Secretary. One of Gorbachev's more interesting reforms has been to abolish the special stores open only to bureaucrats. The theory behind the move is that the people who control the Soviet economy should know what it is like to stand in line waiting to be sold inferior goods by surly shop clerks.

The Gorbachevs have probably not had to suffer such indignities since they returned to Moscow. Like other senior Kremlin families, they most likely have their groceries delivered—a practice common enough in Western cities but almost unknown in the Soviet Union. Writes Smith: "The Soviet system of privileges has its protocol: perquisites are parceled out according to rank. At the top, the supreme leaders of the Communist Party Politburo, members of the powerful party Central Committee, government ministers and the small executive group that runs the Supreme Soviet, or parliament, get the *Kremlovsky payok,* the Kremlin ration—enough food to feed their families luxuriously every month—free . . . The value and quality of the rations are arranged in descending order, according to the rank of those receiving them." Gorbachev has required that those who receive the *Kremlovsky payok* pay full price for the ration, which can run considerably more than the 100 to 120 rubles a month that an average family of four spends on food. But ration recipients still enjoy food of a quality unavailable to ordinary citizens at any price.

To be fair, salaries of the leaders who run this nation of more than 280 million are exceedingly modest by Western standards. Gorbachev's pay is undisclosed, but it is probably not much more than the 900 rubles a month ($1,400) reportedly earned by Brezhnev. By contrast, the U.S. President receives $200,000 a year, plus $50,000 for expenses, $100,000 for travel, $20,000 for entertainment, and other perquisites that can rival those of his Soviet counterpart.

Just as the President is outearned by tens of thousands of American business, professional, sports and entertainment figures, so is the General Secretary of the Soviet Communist Party far from the best-paid worker in the worker's state. Soviet authors and entertainers can earn royalties in the tens of thousands of rubles a year. The top statutory salaries are pulled down not by party officials but by skilled workers in dangerous or remote locations, like the Siberian gold miners who get 700 rubles to 1,200 rubles a month. Yet they have little to spend it on besides elaborate vacations inside the country or black-market electronics equipment. Because of the general lack of consumer items and quality food and clothing, people who earn more than about 700 rubles a month have more money than they know what to do with. Perquisites, not cash, are essential for a comfortable existence.

One major emblem of status in the Soviet Union is the chauffeur-driven car. At the top of the pyramid is the ZIL, a hand-assembled, $100,000-plus luxury behemoth that vaguely resembles a Lincoln Continental. Roughly the top two dozen Soviet officials are thought to merit ZILs. Next comes the Chaika, a spacious limousine with the bulging contours of an early 1970s American sedan. Cabinet ministers, top military leaders and visiting foreign dignitaries usually rate these autos, which can be bought by foreigners for $85,000 each. The sight of a Chaika barging down a main Moscow street in the center lane reserved for official cars is so common that it is referred to as the "Chaika lane." At the third stratum of the automotive élite is the Volga, a four-door sedan that resembles American midsize cars of a decade ago. They are nearly always black in Moscow, although many provincial officials prefer them in white.

With the coming of *glasnost,* even the official car has been spoofed in a new film, *Forgotten Melody for the Flute,* Director Eldar Ryazanov's comedy about the mid-life crisis of a *perestroika*-era bureaucrat. Soviet moviegoers hoot at the opening scene, when columns of official cars carrying self-important apparatchiks to their ministries come to a screeching halt so that a policeman with a white baton can wave a single speeding limousine into the center lane.

Stalin was known to travel in a five-car parade, and sometimes rode in an American-made Packard. Khrushchev cut the motorcade to four vehicles. Brezhnev maintained that number. If he had thoughts of reducing it further, they probably vanished when a disgruntled lieutenant took a shot at the Soviet leader's motorcade at a Kremlin gate one day in January 1969.

When Gorbachev started his general secretaryship, Muscovites admiringly described him as *skromny* (modest) because he used only one ZIL to move around the city, plus a modest Volga sedan with security agents aboard. He also traveled generally within the 80 kilometers-per-hour (50 m.p.h.) speed limit, in contrast to Brezhnev, whose fleet roared down the center lane at speeds in excess of 80 m.p.h. Over time, however, Gorbachev's motorcade grew, apparently to enhance his personal safety. There have been rumors, never confirmed, of attempts on his life. In any case, security precautions appeared to increase in early 1986. A burly, powerful-looking man with thinning hair combed straight back—his personal-security chief—began to appear at his side in most photographs.

By 1988 the General Secretary was moving in a phalanx of four ZILs: one in front with flashing lights and security men staring out the side windows, then the car Gorbachev occupies, then an outriding limousine also filled with security men, and finally a curtained ZIL bristling with antennas. This final car is clearly heavier than the others, as evidenced by the deeper roar from its tires and engine and the floating motion of its suspension. It is probably a communications car containing the equipment necessary for ordering military alerts and, ultimately, the launch of nuclear weapons. Moscow authorities in 1988 limited the use of sirens and flashing lights by a large number of official cars, though the General Secretary's motorcade still uses a siren that sounds a discreet European *wee-waw* to move other cars out of the "Chaika lane."

Like people everywhere, Soviets are fond of automobiles. Brezhnev, for instance, owned and drove a number of expensive foreign autos—including a Rolls-Royce—most of them gifts of foreign governments. Gorbachev is not known particularly to share this fascination. The General Secretary has probably never owned a car. He does, however, know how to drive, having operated a combine in his youth. He also no doubt chauffeured himself around Stavropol Krai in a state-owned vehicle when he was a young Komsomol official, though he commuted on foot to his office. Even after his return to Moscow in 1978—from the first day, he rated an official car—he was never seen sitting in the front seat with his driver, a frequent affectation of high Soviet officials who wish to show their enduring solidarity with the working class.

As his Moscow motorcade has grown, so has the entourage that Gorbachev takes with him on foreign trips. He flies out of Vnukovo II, a special airport on the outskirts of Moscow reserved for high-level travelers. His plane is an Ilyushin 62, the mainstay of civil aviation in the Soviet Union and Eastern Europe. The plane is based on a 1960s-era British airliner, the VC-10, which is no longer in civilian service, and also resembles the Boeing 707 that President Reagan uses.

When Gorbachev arrived in Paris in October 1985, three ZILs were flown in for him: the one in which he rode, the communications vehicle and a third car for the local Soviet Ambassador and other top officials. One of the ZILs broke down in Paris, forcing the occupants of the third car to take French Citroëns. As a result of that experience, when it came time for the Geneva meeting with Ronald Reagan, four ZILs were flown in; the fourth one was presumably a spare. The Reykjavík meeting, more a working session than a full-blown summit, required only three ZILs. For the Washington summit in December 1987, however, the Soviets did not spare the hardware: Gorbachev's motorcade contained as many as eight ZILs. Among them was the communications vehicle, traveling, as always, about 50 yards behind the rest of the pack.

The Gorbachev retinue on these foreign trips is small by U.S. standards. In Geneva, it numbered roughly 140 people, including a press corps of about 30, and two dozen experts— scientists, arms-control scholars and similar specialists— whose principal job appeared to be meeting with local journalists to pitch the Soviet line. By comparison, Reagan brought more than 500 Americans to Geneva with him, not counting the several thousand U.S. and other foreign journalists who

chev presides over the highly secretive Defense Committee, which includes four or five other top leaders.

He is said to be especially effective in a conference room, where he can display his phenomenal memory for detail as well as his personal warmth. He makes those present feel that he knows precisely who they are, that he is knowledgeable about their work and that he cares about it. Says one aide: "He can spout off a page of information at a time."

Gorbachev also displays those qualities in sessions with foreign visitors. During his 1985 Kremlin interview with the editors of TIME, for instance, he kept a stack of photocopied papers—evidently briefing material or news summaries—on the table in front of him. They were neatly underlined in red, green and blue; the visitors were unable to figure out his color coding. At one point, he picked up one of the sheets from the pile and quoted from a translation of a syndicated column written by American Journalist Mary McGrory. He also expressed an interest in the various magazines published by Time Inc., and was appreciative when Henry Grunwald, then its editor-in-chief and later U.S. Ambassador to Austria, promised to send him copies. Since then, Gorbachev has received a weekly packet of magazines from Time Inc. It is not known whether the General Secretary, whose foreign-language skills are rudimentary at best, ever sees them. Raisa, however, told TIME Correspondent Nancy Traver during the Washington summit that she reads the magazine regularly.

The General Secretary keeps in close touch with his top half-dozen aides, conversing with them daily in person and on the telephone. It is not unusual for one of these men to receive several calls a day from the General Secretary asking for information on one subject or another. On foreign-policy matters, Gorbachev relies for advice almost totally on Anatoli Dobrynin, his top international-affairs adviser, and Foreign Minister Shevardnadze. Gorbachev most often calls on Politburo Members Alexander Yakovlev and Yegor Ligachev to discuss domestic policy. Premier Nikolai Ryzhkov is a specialist on economic issues, and Viktor Nikonov is the Secretariat's agriculture expert.

The Soviet leader rarely sees middle-level officials—say, anyone below the rank of Dobrynin. Lesser Kremlin aides are sometimes allowed to attend meetings with Politburo members but seldom alone with the General Secretary. Said one middle-rank official who has attended such meetings with Gorbachev: "He's not someone you call 'Misha,' but on the other hand you can talk to him easily. As we say, he doesn't stand on Chinese ceremony. There's not a lot of bowing."

He exercises firm control over his appointments calendar, unlike Brezhnev, who in his later years was led from ceremony to ceremony by his aides and sometimes had only a vague idea of whom he was meeting or why. "Gorbachev decides whom he will see and whom he will not see, and he does not like to have meetings just for the sake of ceremony," says a senior Foreign Ministry official. "He likes something a little different. For example, when he heard that there was a group of American teachers of Russian visiting Moscow, he immediately invited them to a meeting, and he enjoyed that very much. He likes for his meetings to produce a real conversation, a real exchange of information. He is bored by formal meetings where everybody just sits there."

Gorbachev calls regular meetings of senior officials in various professions or industries. He holds a session with agricultural, industrial or defense officials about once a month. He has had at least two meetings with top Soviet editors. The sessions frequently go on for five or six hours at a time, with Gorbachev asking those present to air their opinions freely. Sometimes his remarks are pointed. At a meeting with social science teachers described by U.S. Historian Moshe Lewin, Gorbachev complained that instruction in many socioideological disciplines had become "something boring, formal, bureaucratic." From now on, he said, the order of the day was *kazennoe,* which means roughly the "breaking of former stereotypes."

One of the most dramatic elements of Gorbachev's managerial style is that, more than any of his predecessors, he gets out of the office and meets average citizens. He makes these forays into the provinces on a systematic basis, about one trip every two months or so. On these occasions, he typically presides over one or two meetings of local political, civic and industrial leaders. The gatherings are usually televised, and they probably convey a flavor of how he runs his closed meetings in the Kremlin: he talks about various local or national problems, often interrupting to ask, "Isn't that so?" or "Do you agree with that?" in such a way that the audience usually responds with a murmur of assent.

In August 1987, for instance, he visited the Ramensky agro-industrial complex near Moscow. Zealous local officials at the Zavorovo state farm had built a special staircase to spare their distinguished guest the indignity of climbing down an eroded hill into the potato fields below the main road. They need not have bothered. When the Kremlin delegation pulled up in black ZIL limousines, Gorbachev stepped out, took one look at the brand-new wooden construction, gave a dismissive wave of his hand and scrambled down the steep incline in his neatly pressed gray suit, leaving his surprised entourage to run after him. That playful moment was witnessed not only by the five-man potato-growing team, patiently waiting to meet the Soviet leader at the edge of a furrowed field, but by millions of other Soviets who happened to watch *Vremya* (Time), the nightly news broadcast.

The conversation that followed, recorded by a television camera peering over the shoulders of the farmers like an unseen spectator in a crowd, was typical of the Gorbachev style. Slipping into the melodious Russian spoken in his home region of Stavropol, where a hard, guttural *g* becomes a soft, aspirated *h,* the onetime combine operator tried to put the diffi-

On a chow line in Alberta during his ten-day tour of Canada, 1983.
Courtesy Hon. Eugene F. Whelan, P.C.

Sampling whiskey at a Canadian distillery, 1983. *Courtesy Hon. Eugene F. Whelan, P.C.*

In Ottawa, his first encounter with lobster, 1983. *Courtesy Hon. Eugene F. Whelan, P.C.*

With granddaughter in
Moscow, 1985.
V. Kuzin—TASS

Daughter Irina and her husband Anatoli in Red Square, 1987.
Boris Yurchenko—Associated Press

Folk dancing with Rumanian allies in Bucharest's Square of Victory, 1987.   *Y. Lizunov/A. Chumichev—TASS*

Saluting the crew of a nuclear submarine during tour of a naval base in Severomorsk, north of Leningrad, 1987.   *V. Kuzin/N. Malyshev/A. Chumichev—TASS*

The onetime combine driver checks the crop at the "Borets" collective farm outside Moscow, 1987.   *A. Chumichev/Y. Lizunov—TASS*

With the gusto of a Western politician, Gorbachev works the crowd in Bucharest, 1987.   *A. Chumichev/Y. Lizunov—TASS*

Pressing the flesh during an impromptu stop on a Washington streetcorner, 1987.   *Y. Lizunov—TASS*

A grim-faced President Reagan bids farewell after talks break down in Reykjavík, Iceland, 1986.   *David Hume Kennerly—TIME*

The summiteers smile for photographers during their successful meeting in Washington, 1987.   *Diana Walker—TIME*

Raisa makes friends in Iceland during the Reykjavík summit,
1986.   *Rudi Frey—TIME*

dent potato growers at ease with a bit of small talk. He asked about the general mood at Zavorovo.

"Good. Businesslike," replied the men, standing in dirt-smudged caps and khaki work clothes beside a row of well-tended agricultural equipment, like soldiers at a military review.

They could not have provided Gorbachev with a better opening. It was a predictable response that he has heard innumerable times. As ever, the Soviet leader was ready with a comeback that has become a major leitmotif of his on-the-street discourses. "You know, I always hear the same answer," said Gorbachev, grinning: Good. Normal. Excellent." Then the twinkle in his brown eyes disappeared as he broached the topic of *perestroika,* his program to restructure the Soviet economy: "There are always problems. And right now we have a lot of them. If we didn't, we wouldn't have undertaken such major tasks with you."

The Kremlin visitor clearly had a few things on his mind that he wanted to share with these rural Russians. "Except for vodka, do you have everything here?" he asked, alluding to his antialcoholism campaign. When the farmers dutifully mumbled that everybody appeared to be satisfied, Gorbachev cut through the usual formalities to touch a sore spot that he knew was bothering both his audience in the field and in front of TV sets across the country. No, said Gorbachev, there was really no reason to be satisfied. The Central Committee had been receiving letters complaining about shortages, and in particular, about the lack of sugar. One farmer summoned up the courage to declare that it was the season for making jams and jellies, and sugar was in great demand. But by then Gorbachev had launched into a televised lecture on the dangers of alcoholism.

"I have something I want to say to you, and the correspondents should communicate it to the whole country," Gorbachev went on, lowering his voice so that his tone did not sound overly strident. Turning to look at one of his aides as if in confirmation, the Soviet leader said he had come prepared with a few facts and figures, and rattled off from memory statistics on sugar use in the U.S. and Western Europe to illustrate his point that Soviet annual per capita consumption had jumped ten kilograms (22 lbs.) above medically established norms. The reason? Moonshine. Gorbachev said that amateur distillers had been buying up sugar in large quantities to make home brew and get around his stringent regulations on the sale of alcohol. "Let's talk straight with one another," Gorbachev said. "Isn't it time to bring the making of moonshine to an end? . . . Those sorts of people belong back in the times when the dinosaurs lived." The line left the potato farmers laughing.

This careful melding of audience, setting, message and medium during that Zavorovo farm visit was a good illustration of Gorbachev's communications skills. Former KGB Chief Yuri Andropov was the first to realize that, after the isolation of Brezhnev's declining years, it was time for the ruling circle to venture out from behind the Kremlin's crenelated walls and be seen mixing with the *narod* (people). Andropov died before he had much opportunity to put that principle into practice. He did, however, make one visit to Moscow's Sergo Ordzhonikidze machine tool factory for a stilted talk with workers that was dutifully recorded in *Pravda*.

Gorbachev wasted no time before continuing the practice. In April 1985, a month after he became General Secretary, he traveled to the industrialized Proletarsky district of Moscow to visit supermarkets, chat with workers at the Likhachev truck factory, discuss computer training with teachers at school No. 514, and talk of the need for pay hikes with the staff of city hospital No. 53. He even found time to sip a cup of tea with a young Muscovite couple after showing up at the door of their apartment.

Only still photographs of that early walkabout in the Proletarsky district were shown on the evening news. On subsequent trips from Kiev to Khabarovsk and from the Siberian oil fields of Tyumen to the wheat fields of Kazakhstan, TV cameras were on hand as Gorbachev polished his skills in impromptu encounters with citizens who proved to be either diffident and tongue-tied or brutally frank. The Soviet leader may often have delivered brief homilies that sounded like animated *Pravda* editorials, but he displayed a natural talent for finding humor in any situation.

When he was hemmed in by jostling Leningraders, and a woman in the crowd yelled out to him, "Just get close to the people," Gorbachev laughingly exclaimed, "How can I get any closer?" He proved fast on the draw when farmers in the Tselinograd region of Kazakhstan started to blame lower crop yields on the fickle weather. "Comrades," said Gorbachev, "the weather is here to stay in our country for the next 100 years. Rain or no rain, we still need the harvest." After angry consumers in the Far East city of Komsomolsk peppered him with complaints about everything from the lack of furniture and children's clothes to shortages of fruits and vegetables, Gorbachev told them, "We have many problems—a pile of them in fact. What we need here is a big bulldozer!" By the time Gorbachev arrived in Czechoslovakia in April 1987, he was jubilantly pressing the flesh with the self-assurance of a seasoned Western politico and was winning shouts of *"Druzhba! Druzhba!"* the Russian word for friendship, from the normally Russophobic residents of Prague.

No matter how his drive to modernize the Soviet economy may fare, Gorbachev has clearly wrought a dramatic turnabout in the Kremlin's approach to public relations. Lenin was prescient enough to recognize the tremendous power of the young film industry as a propaganda tool, but he was first and foremost a fiery orator in the 19th century mold. Stalin, short of stature and with a thick Georgian accent, fostered his cult of personality by appearing at the center of carefully staged political tableaus like a silent, monumental piece of statuary.

Nikita Khrushchev fascinated the West—and embarrassed a few of his more sophisticated countrymen—with his pungent peasant proverbs, finger-wagging lectures and shoe-banging pranks, but they were the overblown theatrics of a ham actor from the provinces. What difference did it make if the ebullient Soviet leader did not somehow fit the contours of a television screen as well as his summit partner John F. Kennedy? At the time, only 22 of every 1,000 Soviet households had TV sets. In the next two decades, the number of televisions per 1,000 people in the Soviet Union increased more than tenfold, to 249, but the aging leadership in the Kremlin was slow to tap the full potential of the communications revolution. Brezhnev, Andropov and Chernenko had good reason to avoid the close scrutiny of the TV camera. All too often it captured the cortisone-bloated faces, shuffling footsteps and wheezing breath of sick men.

Not so with Gorbachev. Knowing that when he talks with oil-field workers in Tyumen or wheat farmers in Kazakhstan, he is sending a message that can be seen and heard from Karelia to Kamchatka, he has enthusiastically appropriated the electronic press as a pulpit for *perestroika*. He is comfortable before the camera and has learned the simple truth that the best way to play to the lens is by appearing to ignore it.

There is something reassuringly ordinary about Gorbachev's round face with his slight double chin and bald pate topped with a few unruly wisps of graying hair. With the exception of the port-wine-colored birthmark on his forehead, there are no distinctive characteristics like bushy eyebrows or warts and a bulbous nose to inspire the cartoonist. It is the eyes that energize these placid features and give spark to a beaming smile that can just as suddenly turn into a pursed-lip glare. He knows the use of eyes. In chats with the crowds, Gorbachev occasionally says he can tell who is sincere by looking into his eyes. Those who meet him are always struck by the eyes. When he reaches out with a firm handshake, he fixes each well-wisher in his line of vision for a fleeting moment, an eye-lock that no one forgets. The eyes, he told onlookers in Prague, never lie.

Russian is a language that must be spoken with the hands, arched eyebrows, an occasional shake of the head from side to side or a shrug of the shoulders. Gorbachev is a master of linguistic gestures. He slashes the air in a modified karate chop or spins his hands one over the other like a pinwheel. Sometimes he extends them, palms up, in a gesture of vulnera-bility, only to fiercely clench them in fists a moment later. When he entered the hall of the Starnikovsky farm to talk with livestock breeders during a tour of rural Moscow in the summer of 1987, he deliberately veered away from the row of seats on the tribunal, perching on the edge of the table so he would be free to respond to the audience. It was a small but telling gesture. His ailing predecessors needed a solid lectern where they could anchor their arms for support.

Gorbachev's prepared speeches may seem long, dogmat-ic and dull to Westerners accustomed to political addresses full of carefully crafted aphorisms and tailored for prime-time television. But even if there are few rhetorical raisins among the bland Marxist-Leninist platitudes, Gorbachev is an out-standing orator in comparison with his predecessors. Soviets turned off their televisions whenever Brezhnev or Chernenko stepped to the podium. But they listen to Gorbachev, and what they hear is often startlingly blunt. In an address in the city of Murmansk in November 1987, for example, Gorbachev talked about ending subsidized food prices, pointing out that baked goods were so cheap, "you can see children using a loaf of bread as a football."

He is not one to wallow in vague generalities. In a June 1987 speech to the Central Committee, Gorbachev singled out several high ministers and party leaders for criticism, includ-ing the head of the powerful State Planning Committee, and he praised individual potato growers and livestock farmers by name for their contributions to *perestroika*. Sometimes his ideas have a Lincolnesque ring to them. In his address on the 70th anniversary of the Bolshevik Revolution, Gorbachev spoke of the need to develop a sense of self-government in the Soviet Union, "a government of the people, exercised by the people themselves and in the interests of the people."

His oratorical training at the law school of Moscow State University probably shows to best advantage when Gorbachev speaks without a prepared text. At the end of his farm tour through the Ramensky region, Gorbachev made an impromptu pitch for his *perestroika* policies to local party activists: "We are talking together, looking each other in the eyes, and I want to say one more time—there must be no wavering. We need to decisively restructure. All of us need to restructure ourselves."

Gorbachev is, of course, no Marxist Peter the Great, determined to force the party faithful to perform the modern-day equivalent of shaving off their beards and donning Western garb. But he does occasionally display an almost impish impatience with hollow ceremonies and pompous speechmaking. He has a penchant for doing and saying the unexpected, leaving functionaries confused and disoriented.

During a visit to Leningrad's Baltic shipworks in November 1987, he emerged from a brief welcoming meeting with the plant manager to chat with a small group of party activists and workers gathered outside. "I've already found time to criticize your director," he cheerily announced, while the target of his joke stood grinning uncomfortably beside him. Later, when Gorbachev toured the shop floor and a spokesman for the assembled workers began a droning, predictable welcoming speech in which he expressed the wish that *perestroika* might develop even faster, the Soviet leader interrupted him with a playful *"Davai! Davai!"* ("Let's get on with it!") The crowd erupted with laughter and the surprised spokesman never fully recovered his composure to finish his memorized lines.

Among the many imponderables of the Gorbachev era is the question of whether the Soviet leader can resist the temptation to use his popularity to promote a cult of personality. During the 27th Party Congress in 1986, Gorbachev grew impatient when a prominent Soviet film director repeatedly mentioned him by name. When the man turned to express his thanks once more to "Mikhail Sergeyevich, for your brilliant lesson," Gorbachev finally interrupted with a brisk one-line reference to a grade-school grammar exercise: "Let's stop declining Mikhail Sergeyevich!" The auditorium broke into applause and laughter. According to a widely told anecdote, the new General Secretary made a call to *Pravda* Editor-in-Chief Viktor Afanasyev to ask him if he had the works of Lenin handy. When the newspaper editor said he did, Gorbachev reportedly told him to "be good enough to quote him in the future—and not me."

Since then, however, Kremlin biographers have been adding a few predictable hagiographic touches to the official biography. A portrait of the Soviet leader in a compendium of his speeches, published in the U.S. under the title *Gorbachev: Mandate for Peace,* (Paperjacks Ltd.; New York; 1987), glowingly observes that "Mikhail Gorbachev's natural gifts, inquiring mind, his self-discipline and energy, and his love of the land stood out even in childhood." As a Communist Youth League worker, the biography asserts, he was "able to captivate people with his brilliance . . . His originality of thought and his charm attracted people to him." Perhaps future editions might want to include Gorbachev's own thoughts about those who are solely concerned about image. As the Soviet leader told villagers at the main settlement of the Borets (fighter) Collective Farm outside Moscow: "It's bad when you see that someone doesn't really work that hard and has special pretensions of being chic and glamorous. That raises the question of what you do with such a person. It's always more visible to the people when someone starts to lose touch with the collective and with society."

Gorbachev himself could hardly be accused of being chic and glamorous. He dresses carefully, conservatively and perhaps expensively. He has had several of his well-fitting suits made abroad, in Italy and Britain. A tailor who once worked at the prestigious British firm of Gieves and Hawkes on London's Saville Row told an acquaintance that he had taken Gorbachev's measurements for two custom-made suits during the Russian's 1984 visit to Britain. The finished products were delivered to Moscow shortly afterward. Starting prices for suits at Gieves and Hawkes run in the $600 to $700 range, the equivalent of several months' wages for many Soviet workers.

Despite the low foreign reputation of Soviet clothing, Gorbachev probably need not send abroad for his suits. Part of the network of special privileges for high Moscow officials is a small number of special hand-tailoring establishments that cater to the élite. If Gorbachev's suits seem to look better than, say, Brezhnev's or Chernenko's, it is likely that he pays more attention to the tailoring. Until recent years, Soviet men have not been especially clothes conscious, and any inclination in that direction has long been considered frivolous and unmanly. One of the hallmarks of the Gorbachev era is the sudden appearance around the world of Soviet officials who are younger and better educated than their predecessors—and whose suits fit.

The General Secretary keeps a $1,000 gold-and-stainless-steel Rolex watch on his left wrist. During his 1985 Paris visit, he was seen wearing shoes so new that they bore no scuff marks on the soles, a possible indication that he had bought them on the trip. Gorbachev probably sends his shirts and underwear to a special laundry near Moscow's Ukraine Hotel that caters to senior officials. He favors white shirts, heavy on the starch. They are thought to be of Soviet manufacture, though he could have picked up a few imported shirts on his travels. One item of the general-secretarial apparel is unmistakably Russian: his dull, vaguely metallic neckties. Soviet men are known for those distinctive cravats.

On a typical day in the life of the General Secretary, he leaves the office and heads for home around 6 p.m. Occasionally, the Thursday Politburo meeting will run late, and his motorcade is not seen heading westward along Kutuzovsky Prospect toward the dacha until 9 p.m. or even later. Even on days when he leaves at the normal hour, he brings work home with him. He takes a long summer vacation—about five weeks in 1987—some of it probably spent in his home district, which is, after all, well supplied with resorts. When he is on holiday, aides regularly forward papers to him, and he sends work back. In the period before the Washington summit, nearly everyone in the Politburo worked seven days a week. In normal times, Gorbachev puts in a six-day week, taking only Sunday off.

Not much is known about his leisure pursuits, aside from his theater attendance with Raisa. The General Secretary did, however, attempt to discuss the subject with an interviewer for Italy's *L'Unita* in 1987. "As to free time," he said, "I do not have any now, and not only I but all the members of the Soviet leadership. This is not normal but is dictated by the times, by a situation resembling revolutionary periods when one must give oneself entirely, regardless of anything." Perhaps realizing that he had gone on too long—and not answered the question—he concluded by saying, "As you can see, we didn't get anywhere in our talk about relaxation and free time."

The Gorbachevs have a daughter, Irina, born in 1959, who is a physician and is married to another doctor, and two known grandchildren. The extent to which the Gorbachevs guard their family privacy can be measured by some of the things that are not known for sure: Irina's married name (only the first name of her husband, Anatoli, has been disclosed); the granddaughter's name (it has been reported variously as

Oksana and Xenia, though Western intelligence officials believe the latter is correct); her age (she was probably born in 1980); and the sex and name of a second grandchild (Gorbachev proudly told former U.S. President Jimmy Carter, who visited Moscow in the summer of 1987, that one had just been born, but would disclose no more than that).

Indeed, for a man who leads one of the world's two major superpowers—and who has introduced a new measure of openness in official Soviet disclosure of all sorts—relatively little has been made known about his personal habits or how he spends his days. But then, the Soviet Union is not the West, where private lives of public figures—whether politicians or popular entertainers—are considered fair game for the press. Many Soviet citizens are not especially curious about such matters when it comes to Gorbachev, and some people would even consider such curiosity to be unseemly.

But Muscovites can be excused if, watching that distinctive four-ZIL motorcade roar westward along Kutuzovsky Prospect toward dacha land in the evening dusk, some wonder what kind of day their leader has had at the office. Did he make progress in his plans to restructure the Soviet economy, bring more openness to government, improve the quality of life for the average worker? Perhaps his fellow residents of the capital also wonder what sort of existence Gorbachev is heading for at the end of his ride home—and whether, someday, some of the comforts, privileges and perquisites their leader enjoys might be theirs too.

7

Raisa

Mikhail and Raisa Gorbachev were dining with Margaret and Denis Thatcher toward the end of the 1984 visit to Great Britain that first brought the Soviet leader-to-be to the attention of the West. After days of public relations triumphs, Gorbachev was feeling pardonably expansive. The talk got around to the subject of the working class, and he proclaimed that in the Soviet Union "we are all working class."

"No, we are not," his wife interrupted. "You are a lawyer."

Gorbachev hastily retreated. "Perhaps you are right," he conceded. "Perhaps it is just a sociological term."

Of all the visit's memorable events, that exchange was perhaps the most striking. For the wife of a member of the Soviet Politburo to contradict her husband in public was stunning enough. For her to do it in front of a foreign leader was unheard of. And for her to get away with it—indeed, to win

191

Gorbachev's indulgent acquiescence—well, it was a signal that a world accustomed to ignoring the wives of Soviet leaders would have to start paying attention to Raisa Maximovna Gorbachev, a woman with a mind of her own and no intention of hiding in her husband's shadow. Since the Thatcher dinner, Raisa has gone on to fill—or more precisely, create—a role familiar enough in the West but entirely new to the U.S.S.R.: First Lady. Working the crowds with her husband in joint appearances from Murmansk to Bucharest, presiding over midsummit teas with Nancy Reagan, cutting the ribbon to open an exhibition of American paintings in Moscow, chatting knowledgeably about art and literature with foreign dignitaries and helping to establish a fund that encourages the development of young people in the arts, she has become perhaps the most visible Soviet female since the women who helped shape the Revolution.

The most controversial as well. Moscow buzzes with stories about Raisa's fondness for furs, jewelry and stylish gowns, as well as dark speculation about the political power she supposedly exercises by whispering in Gorbachev's ear. A legend has grown up about a viciously anti-Raisa videotape supposedly making the rounds in Moscow. Allegedly put together by critics, it is said to show her shopping in fashionable London stores during the 1984 visit and charging purchases on an American Express card. The shopping trip and the credit card were real—the latter belonged to Raisa herself—but foreign correspondents in Moscow have been unable to find anyone who claims actually to have seen the tape. Nonetheless, the persistence of the rumors about the tape gives a clue to the public suspicion that has led some of Raisa's Moscow critics to refer to her as the "czarina."

Just what it is about the General Secretary's wife that might upset some of her fellow citizens may be difficult for some Westerners to understand. Many of the whispered accusations seem prompted by little more than male chauvinism—

a vague feeling that it is improper, even somewhat scandalous, for a woman to be so prominently visible. Thus the complaint of a Foreign Ministry official when Raisa accompanied her husband to the 1986 summit meeting with Ronald Reagan in Reykjavík (Nancy stayed home on that occasion): "Why does she want to push herself to the front rank? Who chose her to represent the Soviet Union?" The answer to that question is rather obvious: her husband, the General Secretary.

Other criticisms reflect plain jealousy. Raisa may not quite be the "Bo Derek of the Steppes," as a hyperventilating British newspaper christened her on the 1984 London visit, but she is a slender, pretty, auburn-haired woman who dresses with a stylishness beyond the means and dreams of most Soviet women. At times, her fashion sense has seemed inappropriate to some fellow citizens. The note of disapproval is obvious in the voice of a young Moscow professional woman, who complained that on a recent Gorbachev visit to the port city of Murmansk, Raisa was seen in two different outfits the same day: "That may be O.K. for Paris but not for Murmansk, where people get meat and butter only once a month."

To be fair, Raisa is for many Soviet women a source of fascination and even inspiration. "Our other First Ladies were nice, but they looked like grandmothers," said Irina Salgus, 59, a teacher in Moscow. "Raisa is the first to look like a modern woman. We're all interested in how she's dressed. When she makes a trip, we sit in front of the TV to see what she has on. That's how we find out what's modern. We want to copy her." Salgus acknowledged, however, that the General Secretary's wife was not universally admired. "Some conservatives think it's not good for her to appear everywhere with her husband," she said. "You might hear that from a cab driver. But the new generation thinks it's O.K. Oh, some think that she shouldn't act like the General Secretary, that a woman should know her place, but I like her."

In the opinion of some foreigners who have met her,

Raisa is more attractive than she appears in photographs, with her warm smile and an almost porcelain complexion. She is clearly less comfortable than her husband at working the crowds. As she accompanied Mikhail past ranks of farmers on a state farm near Bratislava, she kept repeating a single remark, delivered in her thin, high-pitched voice: "Thank you so much for coming. Thank you so much for coming." Raisa generally keeps in the background during her husband's walking tours, but she will occasionally prompt him. When the two were preparing to return to their car after mingling with a small knot of bystanders that had gathered outside a Prague war cemetery, Raisa happened to notice a mother pushing her young son in their direction. The General Secretary's head was turned away. Addressing him as she always does in public, she said "Mikhail Sergeyevich" and motioned for him to look around. Mikhail Sergeyevich obeyed and, of course, the motorcade was delayed for several minutes while he took the boy in his arms and invited him to come to Moscow.

Soviet editors and television producers, aware that Raisa is a controversial figure, treat her with caution. She is frequently pictured in the press at her husband's side during public appearances, but the captions either fail to identify her or refer vaguely to "M.S. Gorbachev and spouse." Soviet TV evidently considered Gorbachev's views on his political discussions with Raisa too hot to handle. In an interview in late 1987, Tom Brokaw of the American network NBC asked the General Secretary, "Do you go home in the evenings and discuss with her national politics, political difficulties and so on in this country?" Gorbachev replied, "We discuss everything." Brokaw persisted: "Including Soviet affairs at the highest level?" Gorbachev repeated, "We discuss everything." In the version of the interview shown in the U.S.S.R., however, the first question was edited to have Brokaw ask merely whether Gorbachev discussed with Raisa "questions of public life," and the second question was dropped entirely. Presumably, Soviet viewers would have been shocked by the thought that Gorbachev solicited his wife's opinions on "Soviet affairs at the highest level."

That such affairs should be considered none of a wife's—even a Soviet First Lady's—business is a fascinating commentary on gender relations in the U.S.S.R. Women were granted complete legal and political equality with men at the time of the Bolshevik Revolution, and that concept has been enshrined in the Soviet constitution. But in fact the Soviet Union is a male-dominated society in which women are expected to defer to their husbands even more than in most capitalist countries. It is true that Soviet women work outside the home to an extent unknown in the West. The trend began during the labor shortages caused by the country's forced-draft industrialization in the 1930s and the slaughter of World War II, when most working-age men were conscripted and millions died at the front. The condition has persisted. Some surveys indicate that as many as 85% of all females ages 20 to 35 hold full-time jobs. Though more than half are in white-collar positions, with an especially heavy concentration in the trade and service sectors, women fill many heavy, menial jobs as well. In Soviet food markets it is women, not men, who haul sides of beef and bushels of potatoes; in garbage-collection areas of apartment complexes, it is women who shovel refuse to be hauled away into trucks. A sight that never fails to impress first-time visitors to the Soviet Union is the brigades of older women, heavily muffled against the cold, clearing ice off city sidewalks with hand-held scrapers. Soviet law supposedly bars women from some particularly heavy or dangerous industrial jobs, but the law does not always seem to be observed; in 1985, female workers in a metallurgical factory sent a letter to *Rabotnitsa* (Workingwoman) magazine complaining that they had to move 254 tons of metal per shift. At the same time, equality in the numbers of women at work has not brought them anything like equality in status. As in most parts of the West, men are still the main breadwinners; studies show that women's pay averages 70% or less of men's wages, about the same ratio as in the U.S. More than 70% of Soviet doctors and teachers are women, but those professions pay poorly, and senior physicians, hospital administrators, school principals and the like are still nearly all men.

As in other societies, Soviet women carry the main burden of shopping, homemaking and child rearing. Custom demands that men give their mothers, wives and daughters flowers or small presents on International Women's Day (March 8, a popular Soviet holiday) but emphatically not that the men lend a hand with the housework. Few men do. Holding down a full-time job and shouldering almost the entire burden of running a household make the lot of the Soviet female dreary indeed. As British Journalist Martin Walker puts it in *The Waking Giant,* a 1985 book about the U.S.S.R., "The average Soviet woman spends her life rushing. She gets up early to prepare breakfast, takes her child to the day-care center, goes to work, shops in her lunch hour and even in work hours, travels back to pick up the child, to prepare an evening meal, to clean the flat."

Shopping is a constant headache. Few Soviet families own cars, and even in those that do, the women hardly ever drive. Soviet women travel to the stores by crowded bus and subway lines, which means hours of lugging heavy parcels around. Stores are often jammed with pushing and shoving crowds, and the peculiar Soviet shopping system forces women to stand on line three times to make a single purchase: there is one line to select merchandise, another line to pay for it and obtain a receipt, a third line to pick up the item bought. Stores do not supply shopping bags. A Soviet woman carries her own net bag called an *avoska,* a word derived from *avos* (meaning maybe).

Their harried lives give Soviet women little time to participate in public affairs. Only about a quarter of the members of the Soviet Communist Party are women, and membership in the party is a prerequisite for exercising any influence in public affairs. On the other hand, women are well represented in local government; they make up slightly more than half of the 2.3 million deputies to local soviets (councils) across the country. But females become increasingly rare at the higher levels of the Soviet bureaucracy. Only about 5% of senior party positions like regional first secretary are held by women. Alexandra Biryukova in 1986 became the first woman in 25 years to serve among the eleven secretaries of the Party Central Committee secretariat (she is in charge of consumer goods and light industry). There has not been a woman member of the ruling Politburo since Ekatarina Furtseva in the early 1960s, and there are no female government ministers. Presumably because of women's lack of political clout, the Soviet system pays little attention to the particular needs of women. Tampons, for example, are not made in the Soviet Union, and even externally worn sanitary pads are uncomfortably thick. Women use ordinary cotton batting, and there are occasional shortages of it, and of so many other items in Soviet life.

As with women in general, so with Soviet leaders' wives. The generation that made the Bolshevik Revolution included some prominent women leaders, notably Alexandra Kollontai, an outspoken advocate of women's rights and the world's first female ambassador (to Norway in the 1920s). Nadezhda Krupskaya, Lenin's wife, was a writer, social worker and formidable public figure in her own right. But Joseph Stalin's two wives were hardly ever seen in public, and with rare exceptions Kremlin wives have remained resolutely in the background ever since. The image of the Soviet leader's spouse created by Nina Khrushchev, Viktoria Brezhnev and Anna Chernenko, to the extent that there was any public image, was of a square-figured, kind-faced but dowdily dressed *babushka* notably ill at ease on the infrequent occasions when she was glimpsed. An unkind joke making the rounds in Britain in

1987: Raisa Gorbachev is the first Soviet leader's wife to weigh less than her husband. Perhaps the nadir of invisibility was reached by Tatiana Andropov. Until the day her husband Yuri died in 1984, Western observers were unsure whether he had ever been married or, if he had been, whether his wife was still alive. Tatiana settled that point by showing up weeping at the General Secretary's funeral; it was evidently the only public appearance of her life.

Raisa Gorbachev, however, is representative of a new type of Soviet woman, the well-educated professional. She is, for instance, every bit as accomplished an intellectual as her husband, and has even been heard to boast, with unassailable justification, that her academic credentials are superior to his. Yet much about Raisa's origins and early life remain obscure. The Soviet government did not get around to issuing an official biography of the leader's wife until her husband met Ronald Reagan for the third time, at the Washington summit late in 1987. And then the publication was so sketchy, exactly five sentences, as to make her husband's uninformative official biography seem positively chatty by comparison.

It is now known that she was born Raisa Maximovna Titorenko in Siberia. There was speculation recently that her ancestry might be non-Russian, always a serious matter in the ethnic-conscious Soviet Union. At the time, mid-1987, the subject was especially touchy. Crimean Tatars, who had been forcibly moved to Siberia in the 1940s by Stalin because of doubts about their wartime loyalty, were demonstrating in Moscow for a return to their homeland. Some of Gorbachev's critics were insinuating that he had allowed the demonstrations to take place because his wife, with her slightly Tatar facial features, was a Crimean Tatar. As if to dispel any doubts about her ethnic background, Raisa insisted in reply to shouted questions at the Revolution Day celebrations in Red Square in November 1987 that she is "absolutely Russian."

People who knew her as a student at Moscow State University in the 1950s had the impression that she came from a privileged background; one former student asserts that her father was a professor. There has even been some talk that he might have been the Maxim Titorenko who was a Soviet economist in the 1920s and had been exiled to Siberia by Stalin. There is no evidence to support that theory. Raisa's official biography states that she was born in the Siberian town of Rubtsovsk in Altai Krai and that her father was a railway engineer.

The Kremlin biography does not give Raisa's date of birth, which has been reported as being as late as 1934. Diplomats who processed her visa papers before Gorbachev became General Secretary report that Raisa was born Jan. 5, 1932. As is the case with her husband, the biography is silent about whether Raisa has any siblings. Zhores Medvedev, the Soviet biologist who now lives in exile in Britain (and stays in close touch with Soviet affairs through his brother Roy), asserts that Raisa has a sister who married a man named Shipakhin, who thus became Gorbachev's brother-in-law. In his 1986 book, *Gorbachev*, Medvedev reports that Shipakhin was a decorated World War II veteran and in 1965 was appointed party secretary of Zheleznovodsk, a spa town in Stavropol Krai, where Gorbachev was then a rising party official. According to Medvedev, however, Shipakhin "became a liability to Gorbachev, since he was partially implicated in a local corruption case in 1977. He was dismissed and demoted to a minor post in the local consumer system." Medvedev does not disclose his sources for the report, and apparently nothing else has appeared in print in the Soviet Union or elsewhere about Raisa's family.

By the early 1950s, Raisa was a philosophy student at Moscow State University. Her good looks, sophistication and sense of style attracted a number of male admirers, among them an earnest young provincial named Mikhail Gorbachev who was studying law and lived on the same floor of the shabby Stromynka Student Hostel. She, in turn, was attracted by his candor, his wide interests and the political skill he was displaying even then as an organizer for the Komsomol. As noted earlier, Mikhail had a good bit of competition for the bright, popular Raisa's attention, but they eventually saw each other steadily and were married early in 1954. The following year they graduated and moved to Mikhail's home region of Stavropol in southern Russia, where they lived for the next 23 years while he rose through the Communist Party apparat.

Even in this backwater, Raisa maintained her intellectual interests and followed her own career. She got a job teaching at a local school, and continued to teach throughout their years in Stavropol. She also became something of a pioneer in Soviet sociological research. In 1967 she won the degree of candidate in the philosophical sciences, the equivalent of a Ph.D., from the Moscow State Pedagogical Institute by submitting a dissertation with the forbidding title "Emergence of New Characteristics in the Daily Lives of the Collective Farm Peasantry (Based on Sociological Investigations in the Stavropol Region)."

Zhores Medvedev explains the procedure Raisa had to go through to obtain her degree: "The examination of a dissertation is formidable in the Soviet Union. The dissertation must be defended at an open meeting. A successful defense requires agreement by a secret ballot of the members of the academic council (consisting of 12-15 members). The council nominates two 'official opponents' who add their critical comments to the public report by the candidate. The research work is presented as a typewritten manuscript and 200 copies of a detailed synopsis of the work have to be printed and distributed to related institutes and departments for comment at least one month before the presentation." And even after a successful defense, the "dissertation has to be submitted for official confirmation by the All-Union Qualification Commission, which holds an independent review and approves the work at a closed session of one of its specialized councils." Only then is a diploma issued by the Ministry of Higher Education.

Visitors to the Lenin Library in Moscow can still find on file a synopsis of the thesis on collective farming by "R.M. Gorbacheva" (the Russian style of her name; married women take the husband's family name, modified with a feminine ending). People who have read the work find it remarkable for a number of reasons. To begin with, Raisa used methods that were then highly unusual in the U.S.S.R. She sent out questionnaires that drew 3,000 replies, and conducted follow-up interviews during visits to five collective farms. She also cited other theses, an uncommon practice in the U.S.S.R. Says Christian Schmidt-Häuer, the West German journalist and Gorbachev biographer: "Few doctoral researchers and social scientists work at such depth" in the Soviet Union even today.

Raisa was candid about the bleak living conditions on the farms. She found that nearly all housing lacked such amenities as central heating, sewerage or a water supply, even though half the farmers she studied had moved into new or renovated houses between the mid-'50s and 1965. She also discovered that wage differentials on the collective farms were much greater than they were supposed to be under official state doctrine. In Schmidt-Häuer's view, that conclusion "drew attention to a state of affairs not accepted by Soviet sociological literature until very much later—that in terms of wages and education 'class differences' within one and the same class can be greater than those between industrial workers and collective farmers."

Other conclusions were more in line with what later observers found to be Raisa's dogmatic Marxism and her alleged haughtiness. An American who has read the thesis reports that Raisa was annoyed to discover that in half of the villages she visited, peasants continued to celebrate the religious festivals of Christmas, Easter and the Day of the Trinity. They also enjoyed the game of dominoes, and for some reason that too irritated Raisa. She recommended "enlightened ceremonies" and visits to the theater and to good movies to take the peasants' minds off religion and dominoes. The American reader's overall impression of her dissertation: "Highly dogmatic and didactic."

The thesis undoubtedly helped Raisa push her academic career toward a pinnacle when the Gorbachevs returned to Moscow in 1978. She won a coveted appointment as a *dotsent* (lecturer) in Marxist-Leninist philosophy at the couple's alma mater, Moscow State University. Having a husband who had been promoted out of provincial obscurity to be a member of the national hierarchy—as boss of all Soviet farming and, within two years of their arrival, as a member of the ruling Politburo—could not have hurt either. In any case, she continued to teach at Moscow State University until Mikhail was named General Secretary of the Communist Party in 1985. Only then did she give up her academic career for the new unofficial post of full-time First Lady.

While not much is known specifically about Raisa's teaching, it is possible to draw a picture of the milieu in which she worked. Moscow State University is the showpiece of the Soviet educational system, drawing the brightest students from the most influential families. The 24,000-member student body includes some talented youngsters from obscure provincial backgrounds, like Mikhail Gorbachev and Raisa Titorenko in the 1950s. But a large proportion of its students are sons and daughters of the country's party and intellectual élite, with a heavy representation from the Moscow area, since the U.S.S.R. is a heavily centralized country. An occasional slow student gets in as a result of having influential parents who pull strings. But the majority of undergraduates are bright and hardworking. They know well that their performance in the university, and the recommendations they receive from their professors, will go far toward determining their status for the rest of their lives.

Marxist-Leninist philosophy is a required course. Every

student at every institution of higher learning in the Soviet Union must take it. No one can receive a degree unless he or she passes the final exam in Marxism-Leninism, regardless of marks in other subjects. At Moscow State University, the highest exam mark is 5. Students whose grades drop below 4 at any time during their academic careers lose the state stipends that cover their living expenses while they are attending classes. Those who score below 4 on the final exam may still, however, receive their degrees (passing mark is 3).

Marxist-Leninist philosophy courses bear little resemblance to the study of philosophy as that subject is known in the West. They are instead a relentless drilling in the tenets of "scientific socialism" divided into yearlong courses on historical materialism, dialectical materialism, political economy (half on socialist economy, half on capitalist economy) and a course on "History of the Communist Party of the Soviet Union." At Moscow university, professors lecture for two hours at a time in large halls to classes of about 150 students each. Attendance is always taken, and Marxist-Leninist philosophy is one class it is most inadvisable to cut. The lectures are supplemented by weekly two-hour seminars involving 30 to 35 students. The professor calls on them individually to comment on the material covered in the mass lectures, thereby testing their comprehension.

Students, as might be expected, often regard Marxist-Leninist philosophy as something to be endured stoically. One commented to an American reporter that the subject is "more boring than you can even conceive, yet it is such an integral part of education in the Soviet Union that every student spends almost a third of his time on it." The professors, however, tend to be true believers, their convictions deepened by the same endless repetition that drives their students to distraction. No wonder then that foreigners who have talked to the Gorbachevs often describe ex-professor Raisa as a more doctrinaire Marxist than her husband. Even Mikhail has commented that "she is the atheist" of the two.

Raisa was in a very different role, however, when she stepped onto the world stage in 1984. The setting was London, where she accompanied Mikhail, by then a member of the Politburo and already widely expected to be on the verge of attaining supreme power, on a six-day visit. That he brought her along was surprising enough, given the previous invisibility of Kremlin wives. When she turned out to be a woman of sophisticated taste in fashion and considerable intellectual polish, the British went wild over her. Traveling in a Rolls-Royce flying Soviet flags on the fenders, she stepped out in ensembles that included a splashy white satin outfit with gold lamé sandals. She passed up a pilgrimage to Karl Marx's grave in favor of a trip to the Tower of London to see the British crown jewels, and later dropped into Cartier's to buy a $1,780 pair of diamond earrings. She discussed British literature knowledgeably with a Foreign Ministry official and then one-upped him deftly by asking his views of modern Soviet writers (he had not read any). She reportedly called out a cheery "see you later, alligator" in English to one British host. Though Raisa usually speaks in Russian and uses an interpreter, she has learned some English and French, which she says is self-taught; she speaks them with a heavy accent.

Gorbachev is reported by the British press to have joked "that woman not only costs me a lot of money but also a lot of worry." Nonetheless, he took an obvious delight in showing her off, realizing that she was a major public relations asset. At Marks & Spencer, the popular British department store, Raisa posed so engagingly for photographers that they chipped in to buy her a farewell bouquet of flowers. Her sharp reminder to her husband at dinner with the Thatchers that they are not working class went unreported at the time; not surprisingly, it has never been published in the Soviet Union.

Since then, Raisa's appearances overseas have for the most part built on her London triumph, with only a few jarring notes. Some snapshots:

Paris, 1985. Accompanying Gorbachev on his first trip to the West as Soviet leader, Raisa charms Danielle Mitterrand, the First Lady of France, by laughingly pleading as she inspects Mitterrand's newly decorated office: "Give me some advice. I'm a beginner at this job." Inspecting Impressionist paintings at the Jeu de Paume museum, she shows a discriminating appreciation of art (a constant interest; she would later impress U.S. officials with her knowledgeable comments about the 19th and 20th century paintings in a display of American art that opened in Moscow in November 1987). She banters easily with Pierre Cardin at a showing in his salon, pronouncing his creations "not commercial" and adding, "I respect them as works of art." After a tour of the sights of the city, including the bookstalls along the Seine, in the company of Danielle Mitterrand, she coos, "I'm in love with Paris." The punctilious Paris fashion press takes her to task for wearing a dark wool suit twice, and at the Cardin salon she interrupts a procession of models to ask that lights be turned out because they are shining in her eyes. Laurence Masurel, a reporter for *Paris Match,* comments, "She must not be that easy to get along with every day; she knows what she wants." Nonetheless, Masurel's magazine gushes, "The image of the Soviet Union has changed by virtue of a woman's face."

Geneva, 1985. At the first Reagan-Gorbachev summit meeting, Raisa puts on an effective sideshow. Visiting a clock-and-watch museum, she displays a jeweled antique timepiece to U.S. television crews and warbles, in English, "It's bea-u-tee-ful." Shown a display of restored watches and clocks, she gets in a plug for disarmament: "This is what we should be doing, restoring things instead of destroying things." At the University of Geneva, she engages a startled rector in a conversation about the relationship between philosophy and physics, and declares herself an appreciative reader of Swiss Writer Friedrich Dürenmatt. On various occasions around town she strides with undisturbed aplomb past her first hecklers, one shouting in Russian, "KGB are killers!" The highlights of her performance are two teas with Nancy Reagan at which they alternate as hostesses and make First Lady chitchat. Nancy's aides report, not for the last time, that she finds Raisa a bit pedantic and inflexible. But they hold hands briefly while facing photographers, and afterward Nancy asserts for the record, "I think she was a very nice lady."

Reykjavík, 1986. Raisa decides at the last minute to attend what is billed as a "working" summit, reportedly after first sending word that she would not go. Some Americans are miffed at what they interpret as an upstaging of Nancy Reagan, who stays home, and some officials on Raisa's side are less than enthralled by her presence. This being one summit devoted to serious, though largely fruitless, negotiation rather than to ceremony, her activities are thoroughly overshadowed. On the scene, however, she performs creditably enough. She visits a class of schoolchildren and, at her request, a farm chapel. Standing in front of a simple altar with two candles burning on either side of a crucifix, she asserts, "I am an atheist, but I know the church, and I respect all faiths. It is, after all, a personal matter . . . I believe in the natural goodness of people, and I firmly believe that no one wants war, especially nuclear war."

Washington, 1987. At the third summit, Raisa, vivacious and voluble, dazzles the U.S. capital with her strobe-light smile. At the National Gallery, when employees gather to applaud her, she stops to chat, noting that she is "glad to see so many of the staff are women." On a White House tour, she launches into a sermonette on modern life: "In our age, all of us have to work. We have professional duties. We have family duties as well as social duties. A person in the 20th century is at a loss to distribute his or her time." At a tea for prominent women, Raisa declares herself a "great admirer" of the work of Joyce Carol Oates, and specifically mentions reading two of

Oates' novels, *A Garden of Earthly Delights* and *Angel of Light*. Oates, writing in the New York *Times* Magazine, later recalls, "Mrs. Gorbachev, petite, stylish, a beautiful woman only slightly past the bloom of her beauty, held my hand in both of hers and told me that my books are 'much read' and 'much admired' in her homeland. 'You are the one who writes of women well? And of politics?' " After the tea, another guest, Maryland Senator Barbara Mikulski, marvels, "This is the first person I've ever met who talks more than I do."

To some who met her at the Washington summit, however, Raisa appeared well informed but nervous—"like a student who had studied hard for an exam and wanted to show off everything she knew," as one diplomat put it. At one State Department luncheon, Raisa endeared herself to the guests but infuriated the hosts by trying to hold a personal conversation with all 180 people in the receiving line. The line moved so slowly that the lunch did not conclude until 4 p.m., barely leaving time to prepare for a dinner that began two hours later.

The most serious strain came between Raisa and Nancy Reagan. Even before the summit, White House aides sniped that Raisa took two weeks to respond to Nancy's invitation for an afternoon tea. Other American sources, however, say it was Mrs. Reagan who stalled in issuing an invitation that Mrs. Gorbachev had requested for a tour of the White House. In any event, when the First Ladies finally did get together, "their face-off in front of the fireplace [in the White House Red Room] was extraordinary," says one diplomatic observer. Raisa began by asserting, "We missed you in Reykjavík." Nancy, clearly taken aback, replied, "I was told women weren't invited." Mrs. Reagan, one observer points out, was recuperating from cancer surgery and mourning the death of her mother: "She was clearly not feeling very well. And Raisa didn't seem to have a psychological feel for what she was doing. She's very well informed and very curious, but she tends to talk more than she listens."

At one point, Raisa observed for the third time that 20 million people had been killed in the Soviet Union during World War II. "Yes, you mentioned that," Nancy replied dryly. When Raisa remarked that the U.S. had not had a war fought on its own territory, Nancy mentioned the Civil War, and "then Raisa began lecturing her about that," says one diplomatic source. Things went no better when Mrs. Reagan finally did take Mrs. Gorbachev on a tour of the White House. Raisa peppered Nancy with questions: Was that a 19th-century chandelier? Did Jefferson live here? And, by the way, when was the White House built? Nancy, confessing "I'm not much help," had to turn to an assistant curator to supply the answer: between 1792 and 1800. Asked if she would like to live there, Raisa annoyed some Americans by replying, "This is an official residence. I would say, humanly speaking, that a human being would like to live in a regular house." By summit's end, the White House felt obliged to put out patch-up stories. In one version, Raisa asks Nancy in puzzlement, "What is this about our not liking each other?" and Nancy gamely replies, "Such stories are so trivial and silly."

Largely as a result of the summits, Raisa is probably better known overseas than at home. She has received saturation coverage in the Western press, down to her measurements (36-24-36, according to Paris dressmakers who were supplied the figures, in centimeters, by Moscow), where she has her hair hennaed (the salon of the International Hotel in Moscow, say some reports) and how she selects her clothes. The source for the latter is Raisa herself, who was quizzed on the subject in (where else?) Paris. Asked if she deals with Slava Zaitsev, a well-known Soviet designer, she replied, "No, I don't go to Slava, though many of my friends do and tell me I should too." Then does she design her own clothes? "No, no. I am shown models, and I choose according to my tastes, which are very classical." Favorite color? "I like them all, and I wear them all." One Moscow designer Raisa is known to patronize is Tamara Mokeyeva, 58, who fretted a good deal about dressing her properly for the Paris trip.

Back home, Raisa has been somewhat less visible. Her evident reluctance to do much high-level entertaining is a source of some contention in official Moscow, though she does occasionally shepherd around visiting dignitaries' wives; for example, she took Sonia Gandhi, wife of the Indian Prime Minister, on a tour of Moscow art galleries in 1985. She accompanies her husband to many cultural events. While living in Stavropol, they attended not only virtually every play that opened but also many dress rehearsals. In Moscow last fall they found time while preparing for the Washington summit to take in the opening night of *The Peace of Brest,* a historical drama about Lenin's early years in power. Raisa has joined Gorbachev on some of his celebrated walkabouts to hobnob with the citizens, though she has not done much except stand around and look friendly. She has given only one interview to the Soviet press, a round-table discussion with representatives of textile mills, fashion designers and editors of the magazine *Rabotnitsa.* She said nothing particularly provocative. Sample comment: "On the whole, Soviet people are not poorly dressed now. Of course, there are still many problems in this area . . . and if we speak of consumer goods, we are all acquainted with the difficult questions concerning variety, quality, competitiveness, questions which need to be resolved more quickly."

Recently, however, Raisa has become more prominent at home too. She has begun making a few appearances on her own. In November, for example, she showed up on Soviet television to cut the ribbon opening the Moscow display of American art organized by Armand Hammer, the veteran businessman and trader with the Soviets. Mikhail was nowhere to be seen. She was instrumental in creating the Soviet Cultural Fund, an organization dedicated to encouraging the development of young people in the arts. The fund is independent of the widely criticized Ministry of Culture.

By Western standards, all that might seem minimal activity for a First Lady. But in the U.S.S.R., it has been enough to set off a whispering campaign accusing Raisa of conduct unbecoming a Soviet wife. Gregory Freidin, a Soviet expert writing in the American magazine *New Republic,* believes the criticism reflects something more than straightforward male chauvinism and simple envy, though these qualities certainly are involved. An unconscious tradition has grown up in the Soviet Union, he believes, that leaders are in effect married to the state, which receives, or ought to receive, their total attention and devotion. Thus a human wife who is notably prominent appears almost as the "other woman," stealing attention owed to the state.

What Gorbachev thinks of such speculation, if he is even aware of it, is unknown. The two are tight-lipped about their private lives. But they give every indication of being close. In Paris in 1985, the French press was struck by Gorbachev's actions as he strode into the French National Assembly to give a speech. His gaze roved restlessly over the audience until he spotted Raisa in the front row; then he gave her a tender gaze and smiled as if her presence reassured him. Raisa, for her part, told a dinner host the next day, "I'm very lucky with Mikhail. We are really friends, or if you prefer, we have great complicity."

In any case, Gorbachev has made clear that he resents foreign—and, by implication, Soviet—criticism of his wife. The criticism broke into the open after the November sacking of Boris Yeltsin, the Moscow Communist Party boss who had been an enthusiastic supporter of Gorbachev's reforms but complained that they were proceeding too slowly. Rumors circulated in Moscow, and eventually appeared in the British press, that Yeltsin had hastened his downfall by attacking Raisa. Supposedly he accused her of taking a large salary for her work with the Cultural Fund. Foreign Ministry officials indignantly denied that Yeltsin had said anything of the sort and noted that Raisa serves on the fund without pay. They went so far as to upbraid the British reporter who had printed the rumors. Soviet officials later made clear that they were speaking for Gorbachev, who was angered by the reports. A top Soviet official went so far as to suggest that Gorbachev's occasional testiness with reporters during the Washington summit could be traced to his continuing outrage over the foreign press reports about Raisa's link with the Cultural Fund.

If Raisa has any effect on policy, it has been so subtle as to be a matter of conjecture. She is said to be responsible for one of the minor triumphs of *glasnost:* the republication of the work of Nikolai Gumilyov, a poet who was executed as a counterrevolutionary in 1921. There is much speculation too that she has been educating her husband about women's issues. If so, the job is incomplete: Gorbachev has talked in ambiguous terms about the subject. In his book *Perestroika,* the Soviet leader spoke of a "weakening of family ties and slack attitude to family responsibilities" as a "paradoxical result of our sincere and politically justified desire to make women equal with men in everything." He raised the "question of what we should do to make it possible for women to return to their purely womanly mission." To NBC Interviewer Brokaw, that sounded as if Gorbachev thought "women should be spending more time at home." The leader quickly replied, "No, I think that a woman should take part in all spheres in life, in all of the processes taking place in society." But in language that would hardly win feminist approval, he continued to speak of women's "predestination, that is, as keeper of the home fires."

Several commentators, however, have discerned Raisa's influence behind a passage in Gorbachev's speech to the 27th Communist Party Congress in 1986 pledging or instituting a number of reforms of particular interest to women. Among them: extension of paid leaves for new mothers and of days off to allow them to tend to sick children; a promise within five years to create a place in a preschool nursery or kindergarten for every Soviet child; and a plan "to extend the practice of letting women work a shorter day or week, or to work at home." There is some talk too that Raisa may have encouraged her husband to start and stick to his antialcohol campaign. Gorbachev, to be sure, had plenty of other reasons. Alcoholism had reached crisis levels that were seriously damaging the economy and the nation's health. It is certainly conceivable, though, that Raisa pointed out to him an obvious consideration: the crusade against vodka, while bitterly unpopular among Soviet men, would win silent approval from many women tired of nursing the hangovers—and dodging the blows—of hard-drinking husbands.

Raisa, however, need not exercise any power-behind-the-throne eminence to be a notable figure in Soviet history. Simply by being herself—an attractive, vivacious, stylish, sometimes bossy and pedantic but always intelligent woman—she has already earned herself at least a footnote in histories of the Gorbachev era, and perhaps much more. Even in the White House, there is no agreed-upon job description for First Lady: the opportunities, duties and responsibilities are pretty much what each occupant chooses to make them. But the wives of American Presidents and other Western leaders at least have some precedents to guide them. Raisa Gorbachev has nothing but a tradition of invisibility that is no longer of any use in the modern world. First Lady of the Kremlin is a position that did not exist before she arrived. What it becomes, and whether it continues to exist, will depend on the content she gives it.

8

Mr. Gorbachev Goes to Washington

Ronald Reagan had dreamed up a real Hollywood scenario for Gorbachev's first visit to the United States. He wanted to take the General Secretary on a whirlwind tour of the country, show him cornucopian supermarkets, glittering backyard swimming pools, prosperous suburbs, skyscraper-studded cities. If the Soviet leader could only see these wonders firsthand, Reagan reasoned, perhaps he would realize that the fruits of liberty, democracy and capitalism were undeniably superior to anything Communism could produce.

Gorbachev had another script in mind. His advancemen made it clear from the outset that he wanted a short, "businesslike" Washington summit. In addition to the signing of the recently concluded intermediate-range nuclear forces (INF) treaty, the official agenda would be limited to talks on strategic-arms reductions, regional issues and human rights. Beyond that, Gorbachev had a personal agenda: selling his policies to the American people through a public relations blitz of orchestrated meetings, television appearances and even a few impromptu handshakes that at times would make him seem more like a U.S. presidential candidate than the leader of a Communist superpower.

In a sense, Gorbachev was a candidate, but not for anything resembling a democratic election. His real constituency was back in the U.S.S.R., where Gorbachev's countrymen were greeting his economic reforms with a mixture of hope, skepticism and outright resistance. The ouster from the Politburo late in 1987 of his erstwhile ally, the reform-minded Boris Yeltsin, had underlined the frictions that persisted within the Kremlin leadership. In factories and on farms across the country, citizens who were being asked to work harder were waiting, with mounting impatience, for concrete results.

Against that backdrop, Gorbachev knew he had to come back from Washington with some clear gains: a reduction of superpower tensions and progress toward further arms-control agreements—both of which were needed to divert resources from the military to the civilian economy. Reagan, for his part, hoped to win Senate ratification for the INF treaty and reach a strategic-arms deal in order to salvage his role in history during the troubled twilight of his presidency. The stage was thus set for the summit of '87, a meeting of high hopes and expectations in which both leaders seemed to have more at stake than in either of their two previous meetings. In addition, this would be the first visit to Washington by a Soviet leader since General Secretary Leonid Brezhnev's in 1973. Perhaps most interesting, it would be the first close look Americans would have at the man who was causing such a commotion in the Soviet Union.

As his blue-and-white Ilyushin-62 descended toward Andrews Air Force Base on the afternoon of Dec. 7, Gorbachev knew that tens of millions of his fellow citizens were waiting to see how their leader would perform in the American spotlight. "The visit has begun," he told U.S. Secretary of State George Shultz, who greeted him at the airport, "so let us hope. May God help us." That invocation of the deity—actually a common Russian phrase—had little to do with religion. But it said a lot about the importance Gorbachev attached to this historic moment. The day earlier, he had scored a clear diplomatic success during a two-hour stopover in Britain, where he met with Prime Minister Margaret Thatcher at the Brize Norton air base near Oxford. After their talks, Thatcher virtually gushed with enthusiasm for Gorbachev and his reforms, telling a Soviet television interviewer that "the whole of Britain was thrilled, thrilled that he came, thrilled at the warmth of the relationship."

Less thrilled were the two or three dozen Jewish protesters who gathered in Moscow's Smolensk Square on the eve of the summit to demonstrate in favor of the right to emigrate. Several hundred burly Soviet plainclothesmen, ironically disguised as peace demonstrators, pushed into the crowd, sliced television cables and ripped cameras from the hands of foreign journalists seeking to cover the event. One U.S. correspondent, Peter Arnett of Cable News Network, was thrown into a police bus and detained for four hours. The scene was an ugly reminder that the strong-arm methods of the past had not totally disappeared and that there were still definite limits on *glasnost*.

That incident seemed far away as the General Secretary's 14-car motorcade sped him and his entourage toward downtown Washington. As he gazed through the tinted windows of his black ZIL 114 limousine, he glimpsed a few sparse groups of bystanders and an incongruous roadside billboard proclaiming REMEMBER PEARL HARBOR/ WELCOME GORBACHEV. (That was a reference to the date of his arrival, the 46th anniversary of the bombing of Pearl Harbor, and it was probably meant to express disapproval of the visit.) Once inside the capital, amid the white marble totems of American democracy, Gorbachev saw a far more dramatic sign of his mission's historic significance: the Red flag, with its gold hammer and sickle, was flying next to the Stars and Stripes on Pennsylvania Avenue and even along the White House drive. Had he come a day earlier, he also would have seen some 200,000 demonstrators on the Mall protesting his government's treatment of Soviet Jewry. During Gorbachev's visit, however, the motley groups of protesters—ranging from Buddhist monks to supporters of the Afghan resistance—were kept well away from the Soviet embassy at 1125 16th Street, four blocks north of the White House, where he and Raisa resided during their four-day stay.

No summit events were scheduled that first evening, presumably to allow the Soviet leader and his wife to catch up on the jet lag that plagued them—but hardly slowed their frenetic pace—throughout the visit. The Gorbachevs dined privately at the embassy with a group of Soviet officials. Before retiring, they reportedly watched a video movie of *Top Gun,* starring Tom Cruise as a daredevil U.S. Navy pilot. At the request of Soviet officials, Jack Valenti, president of the Motion Picture Association of America, had sent the film over to the embassy along with copies of *Platoon,* a hard-hitting Viet Nam saga, and *Cry Freedom,* a film about Stephen Biko, the martyred South African black activist.

Gorbachev was formally greeted on the South Lawn of the White House Tuesday morning. Though technically not a head of state (As President, Andrei Gromyko holds that title), the General Secretary was accorded full state honors, complete with heraldic trumpets, a 21-gun salute and a dazzling array of full-dress military honor guards in both colonial and modern uniforms. After the U.S. Army band finished the Soviet national anthem, last played at the White House during Brezhnev's visit, President Reagan stepped up to a clutch of microphones on the red-carpeted dais and welcomed his visitor. "I have often felt that our people should have been better friends long ago," he said, setting the tone of amity and good feeling that was to dominate the summit. "But let us have the courage to recognize that there are weighty differences between our governments and systems—differences that will not go away by wishful thinking or expressions of goodwill, no matter how sincerely delivered. This uncomfortable reality need not be reason for pessimism, however. It should provide us with a challenge, an opportunity to move from confrontation toward cooperation." As he listened to the Russian translation of Reagan's remarks, Gorbachev nodded in approval, a gesture he frequently repeated over the next few days.

The Soviet leader responded in kind, proclaiming the Soviet people's "vital stake in preserving and strengthening peace everywhere on earth" and echoing Reagan's hope that the two nations could advance toward the goal of reducing their strategic nuclear arsenals by 50%. Unlike Reagan, however, Gorbachev added the phrase, "in the context of a firm guarantee of strategic stability." In the jargon of arms control, that clearly referred to what was the major stumbling block in U.S.-Soviet negotiations: the 1972 Antiballistic Missile Treaty and its implications for Reagan's cherished Strategic Defense Initiative. The Soviets had long claimed that the ABM treaty precluded all but the most basic Star Wars research; the Reagan Administration, under its much disputed "broad" interpretation of that treaty, insisted that more advanced research and certain tests in space were permitted. Confronting, and ultimately finessing, that basic disagreement would prove to be the central task of the summit.

Reagan declined to answer reporters' questions during the brief Oval Office photo session that preceded the first round of talks, but his guest seemed eager to court the American press. Asked if he had brought a surprise arms-control offer, Gorbachev, fashionably dressed in a gray pinstripe suit, replied through his interpreter: "I don't think that policies are made with surprises. Responsible policies, particularly by such countries as the Soviet Union and the United States, have to be well thought over and, on the basis of that, responsible decisions have to be taken." After fielding several other questions—and saying little of substance—he told the departing reporters, "I think you have gotten quite a lot from me."

Reagan got considerably less from the General Secretary, however, during the 30-minute, one-on-one session that followed. The President began, as always, with the prickly subject of human rights. Unless the General Secretary understood how deeply the American people felt about this issue, said Reagan, there was no way of improving relations between the two countries. "How do you think the United States, a nation of immigrants, feels about the fact that you won't allow your people to emigrate freely?" asked the President, pointing to the previous weekend's 200,000-strong Washington demonstration as an indication of popular sentiment. Gorbachev responded angrily. "I am not on trial here," he snapped, "and you are not a prosecutor." The General Secretary charged that the U.S. was organizing a brain drain to encourage some of the Soviet Union's best trained and most talented citizens to leave. He questioned the human rights record of a country that had homeless people lying around the streets of its capital. He asserted that the U.S. had guns trained on the Mexican border to prevent citizens of that country from entering the U.S., while the Soviet Union allowed immigrants in without restriction (a rather weak argument in view of the short waiting line to get into the U.S.S.R.). Replied Reagan: "There's a big difference between wanting out and wanting in."

Although there was little movement on the human rights front, U.S. officials insisted that there was progress in the mere fact that the Soviets were now ready to discuss the issue. "The content of our talks is entirely different from what it used to be," Shultz later explained to reporters. "With Gromyko, we couldn't discuss the issue at all."

Following that initial tête-à-tête, the talks were expanded to include senior U.S. and Soviet officials. Both sides agreed to set up two working groups: 1) an arms-control team with Presidential Adviser Paul Nitze and Marshal Sergei Akhromeyev, the Soviet armed forces Chief of Staff, as co-chairmen, and 2) a sort of grab-bag group, dealing with all the other issues, headed by Assistant Secretary of State Rozanne Ridgway and Soviet Deputy Foreign Minister Alexander Bessmertnykh. Before the two leaders went off to their separate lunches, Reagan gave his visitor a pair of solid gold cuff links identical to the ones the President was wearing. They depicted the prophet Isaiah breaking swords into plowshares—the sentiment of which, though not the precise words of the Biblical source, was a frequent theme in Gorbachev's own speeches.

The two leaders reappeared in the East Room of the White House at 1:45 p.m. for what was the ceremonial high point of the summit: the official signing of the INF treaty eliminating an entire class of nuclear weapons from Europe and the rest of the world. The product of six years of negotiation, the pact called for the destruction of 1,752 Soviet and 859 American missiles and established rigorous on-site verification procedures that, it was hoped, would pave the way for more ambitious agreements on longer-range weapons in the Strategic Arms Reduction Talks (START). Despite their sharp private exchange over human rights that morning, both men radiated warmth and good humor at the signing ceremony, occasionally swapping one-liners like a well-rehearsed vaudeville team. At one point Reagan cited the Russian phrase *doveryai no proveryai* (trust but verify), only to be interrupted by Gorbachev's good-natured observation, "You repeat that at every meeting." When the laughter of the 250 guests died down, Reagan flashed his off-center grin, gave Gorbachev a little bow and replied, "I like it." The audience exploded with laughter again.

"We can only hope," said Reagan, "that this history-making agreement will not be an end in itself but the beginning of a working relationship that will enable us to tackle the other issues, urgent issues, before us." Gorbachev expressed hopes that the date of the treaty signing would "mark the watershed separating the era of a mounting risk of nuclear war from the era of a demilitarization of human life." Mindful of the tough negotiating road that still lay ahead, however, the General Secretary added that "it is probably still too early to bestow laurels upon each other."

The two leaders then sat at a table that was once used by Abraham Lincoln's Cabinet and signed their names eight times on two bulky sets of treaty documents. The U.S. copies were bound in slate-blue leather; the Soviet ones in burgundy red. When they had finished writing, the two men exchanged pens, rose to their feet and shook hands as the audience treated them to an enthusiastic ovation. Seated in the front row, Nancy Reagan turned to Raisa Gorbachev and said, "I think we should shake hands too." Raisa obliged her with a smile and a handshake. Some U.S. officials, moved by both the symbolism and substance of the signing, were seen wiping tears from their eyes.

Reagan and Gorbachev then walked briskly down the central hallway to the State Dining Room, where they each delivered televised addresses to the U.S. and Soviet people under the haunting gaze of Lincoln's portrait. Reagan sounded familiar themes, plugging for "human rights," "faith and family," and "a common dream of peace." Gorbachev similarly spoke of the "sacred human right to live" but also included remarks aimed at his own constituency. He cited Lenin as the originator of current Soviet peace and disarmament policies, for example, and stressed the urgency of making *perestroika* succeed at home. He also referred to the possibility of "substantial cuts in conventional forces and arms in Europe, whose buildup and upgrading caused justified concern." The last point was addressed to those critics in the U.S. and Europe who feared that the elimination of Euromissiles would leave NATO vulnerable to the Warsaw Pact's conventional superiority. Gorbachev was seeking, in particular, to soften INF opposition in the U.S. Senate, which had yet to ratify the historic document that had just been signed with such fanfare.

Each leather-bound volume included the 41-page treaty, two protocols and an appendix. Together, they spelled out detailed procedures for burning, exploding, crushing or harmlessly launching all short-range and intermediate-range missiles within three years—all under close inspection by the other side. The Reagan Administration immediately made three of those documents public. But the fourth, pinpointing the locations of U.S. and Soviet missile sites, remained classified. Administration officials explained that the information was being kept secret to avoid encouraging possible terrorist strikes against U.S. and allied missile installations. The Soviets, however, immediately seized upon the issue to score public relations points by appearing, for once, to be more open than the Americans. "Our impression during the [INF] talks was that the U.S. side was in favor of publication," said Soviet Arms Negotiator Alexei Obukhov, adding that the material would soon be published in the Soviet Union. "This is amazing," commented a Moscow newspaper columnist. "The Americans don't want to publish some parts of the treaty because they are afraid the information will be useful to terrorists. But we are publishing all sorts of things that used to be secret." A few days later the White House reversed its decision and published the full appendix.

Despite the widespread public jubilation that accompanied the treaty signing, Gorbachev's visit was not universally applauded in Washington. In Lafayette Park, across from the White House, motley bands of demonstrators held forth throughout the summit. Berobed members of the International Society for Krishna Consciousness chanted and beat drums for peace. Ukrainian émigrés brandished black balloons as a sign of mourning for their lost homeland. Christian evangelists called on the leaders to abandon their negotiations and leave the future to Christ. Some women's groups demonstrated in favor of SDI; others railed against it. Supporters of the Afghan resistance chanted "Death to Gorbachev!" For five hours on Tuesday, several hundred supporters of Latvian, Lithuanian and Estonian independence held a candlelight vigil.

Several U.S. conservative groups denounced the summit as a Munich-like appeasement. Bill Jones, 40, a follower of right-wing Political Extremist Lyndon Larouche, strutted around in black morning coat and bowler hat doing imitations of 1930s British Prime Minister Neville Chamberlain ("peace in our time") in a dubious English accent. Less flamboyant but similarly scathing were Conservative Activists Richard Viguerie and Howard Phillips, who held a press conference to dismiss their former hero Ronald Reagan as "nothing more than a useful idiot for Soviet propaganda." The New Hampshire Conservative Union rolled a 10-ft.-high Trojan horse into town.

The protesters were only a small sideshow in the giddy, almost circus-like atmosphere that seemed to pervade Washington during the summit. On the whole, the mood was upbeat. Some commentators branded the phenomenon "Gorby Fever,"—although it hardly matched the frenzy of a 1960s Beatles concert or a Super Bowl game. Souvenir vendors hawked I LOVE GORBIE buttons and GORBACHEV TOUR '87 T shirts. Local Top 40 radio stations dedicated songs to the Soviet leader (example: Michael Jackson's *The Way You Make Me Feel*). The Marriott Hotel, site of the main press center for 7,000 accredited journalists, renamed its coffeehouse the Glasnost Café. In addition to covering the main events, the daily press abounded in summit-related color, anecdotes and trivia—including the length (248 in.), width (81.5 in.) and weight (6,800 lbs.) of Gorbachev's 1985 ZIL 114 limousine.

Not the least of the circus acts was the Soviet delegation. Along with 40 or so government officials, the group from Moscow included some 50 journalists, 50 academic experts and about 100 security agents from the KGB. While the Gorbachevs stayed at the embassy, the other visitors bedded down at the Madison and Vista International hotels, both of which were ringed with heavy U.S. and Soviet security contingents. Most of the delegates ate prepaid meals at a special hotel buffet or in their $165-a-day rooms. (One unidentified Soviet, probably Foreign Minister Shevardnadze, luxuriated in the Madison's $1,900-a-day presidential suite.) Alcohol was not supposed to be part of the fare, in deference to Gorbachev's antidrinking campaign. But many of the Soviet visitors quickly discovered, and emptied, the individual minibars in their rooms. Although most of the Soviets were rationed to $20 a day in U.S. currency, scores of them flocked to local shops and discount stores in search of American cassettes and records, blue jeans and assorted electronic gadgets. The hectic pace of summit events—and probably the vigilance of the KGB—kept the delegates from late-night carousing or extensive sightseeing. One of their favorite tourist spots, however, was Lafayette Park, where the Soviets ignored the protesters and snapped pictures of one another against the backdrop of the White House.

Reagan's aides had previously concluded that the press would focus its attention on the General Secretary and his wife, so the President was advised not to make any "grab for the spotlight." While Reagan kept a relatively low profile, Gorbachev launched a full court public relations blitz designed to take his case directly to the American people. Central to this campaign was a series of face-to-face meetings with groups of influential U.S. citizens, handpicked by Soviet officials, with whom Gorbachev wanted to discuss his "new thinking" and what they should be doing to encourage it. The first of these sessions took place on Tuesday afternoon at the Soviet embassy, an ornate beaux arts–style mansion that staff members had been frantically repainting and refurbishing for weeks before the summit. Through its heavy black wrought-iron gates passed a rather mismatched assortment of U.S. intellectuals and artists, including former Secretaries of State Henry Kissinger and Cyrus Vance, Economist John Kenneth Galbraith, Writers Normal Mailer and Joyce Carol Oates, Actors Paul Newman and Robert De Niro, Evangelist Billy Graham, Astronomer Carl Sagan, Singer John Denver and the undefinable Yoko Ono.

The Gorbachevs personally greeted each visitor arriving at the reception with a well-prepared anecdote or a flattering comment on their work. The Soviet leader exuded charm and charisma. Joyce Carol Oates later wrote in the New York *Times* Magazine, "To shake hands with Gorbachev—that is, to have one's hand shaken vigorously by Gorbachev—is to feel the grand conviction, no less powerful because it is absurd, that the man has hurried to you for this purpose alone; that, for a blurred moment, *you* are the center of *his* universe." There was little doubt who was the center of Gorbachev's universe, however, once he began his 40-minute monologue in the embassy's gilded ballroom. Seated at circular tables adorned with white tulips and bottles of mineral water, the guests listened to the General Secretary outline his hopes for domestic reform and world peace. Borrowing a folksy touch from Ronald Reagan, he read part of a letter from an American teenager calling for "one human family." Speaking with disarming candor about his own country's problems, and occasionally addressing remarks to individuals in the audience, he appealed to his listeners to "light a fire" under U.S. and Soviet leaders to keep both governments in step with the "profound sentiments of the people" for improved relations. Billy Graham, who knows good preaching when he hears it, called Gorbachev's talk a "beautiful picture of the world in which we are all brothers."

The discussion period that followed degenerated, according to some accounts, into a sort of free-floating rap session. Alongside proposals for joint U.S.-Soviet space ventures and

AIDS research programs came bizarre suggestions that the two countries should sponsor multilingual Shakespeare plays and that U.S. arms manufacturers start producing computers and consumer goods for donation to the U.S.S.R. On more than one occasion, as a speaker rose to make his proposal or comment, Henry Kissinger was heard asking his neighbors, "Who the hell is *that*?"

The session ended promptly at 6 p.m., leaving the Gorbachevs only one hour to prepare for that evening's state dinner at the White House. Still tired from jet lag and the exhausting rush of summit events, Moscow's First Couple had asked the White House ahead of time to curtail the event so they could get to bed early. Accordingly, the pre-dinner cocktail period was canceled and coffee was served along with dessert rather than afterward. At the Soviet request, there was another departure from tradition: Gorbachev and the other male members of the Soviet delegation would wear dark business suits instead of the black tie that is standard at state dinners.

Nonetheless, it was one of the most glittering White House events of Reagan's presidency. In addition to senior U.S. and Soviet officials, the 126 invited guests included Business Leaders David Rockefeller and Armand Hammer; Musicians Dave Brubeck, Mstislav Rostropovitch and Zubin Mehta; Entertainers Pearl Bailey and Claudette Colbert; Athletes Chris Evert-Lloyd, Mary Lou Retton and Joe DiMaggio (who had brought a baseball for the two leaders to autograph, but unfortunately left it in his overcoat pocket). "I knew this was a special moment," Nancy Reagan recalled thinking as she entered the State Dining Room with her husband and the Gorbachevs. As she said later, "The people were uplifted."

The menu, prepared by White House Chef Jon Hill, was anything but proletarian: Columbia River salmon, lobster medallions, loin of veal with wild mushrooms and champagne sauce, brie with walnuts, tea sorbet in honey ice cream, all washed down with an assortment of vintage American wines.

Apart from the salad, which for some reason he did not touch, Gorbachev downed his meal with gusto. Yet neither he nor the other guests had really come for the food. They were there to take part in a ritual act of concord and conviviality that seemed to symbolize the hopes of peace shared by both sides. "I was stunned by how much that evening moved me," said former Democratic Party Chairman Robert Strauss, who sat at Gorbachev's table. "I've only felt it once before, at the dinner for Sadat and Begin."

In his toast—again sounding like the Great Communicator himself—Gorbachev recalled the story of Lynne Cox, the U.S. swimmer who last August crossed the Bering Strait separating Alaska from Siberia in just over two hours. "On television," said Gorbachev, "we saw how sincere and cordial the meeting was between the people—between our people and the Americans—when she stepped onto the Soviet shore. By her courage she showed how close to each other our two peoples live.

"Without minimizing the great political and ideological distances between us," the Soviet leader continued, "we want to seek and find avenues of rapprochement in areas where this is of vital importance for our two countries and for all humankind." Such expressions of mutual good feeling did not prevent Gorbachev from engaging in an animated dinner table debate with Richard Perle, the former Pentagon official whose hardline defense policies had earned him the nickname "Prince of Darkness." "I don't think either of us persuaded the other," Perle remarked after some spirited but courteous jousting over economic and defense issues, "but he's an intelligent man . . . very engaging, forceful, intelligent."

Van Cliburn, who as a young pianist from Texas won the 1958 Tchaikovsky prize in Moscow, provided the after-dinner entertainment with a recital in the East Room. Gorbachev embraced Cliburn in an affectionate bear hug both before and after his program, and gave the audience an unexpected thrill when he and Raisa joined the pianist in singing the Russian lyrics to *Moscow Nights*. As other members of the Soviet delegation began to add their voices to Gorbachev's pleasing baritone, Conservative Columnist George Will leaned over to Admiral William Crowe, Chairman of the Joint Chiefs of Staff, and whispered, "That song just cost you 200 ships." After Gorbachev's mellow sing-along, Pearl Bailey quipped, "This child may never go home. He was having a ball." But 45 minutes past their scheduled 10 p.m. departure, the Gorbachevs finally made their exit.

The two leaders did well to get their sleep that night, for Wednesday turned out to be what White House Spokesman Marlin Fitzwater called a day of "heavy lifting." Gorbachev's workout began with a crucial bit of salesmanship: a morning meeting with nine congressional leaders, including four of the Senators who would ultimately decide the fate of the INF treaty. The General Secretary began the session, held at the Soviet embassy, with some ad-libbed remarks in which he called disarmament the "most crucial issue in the world today." He warned against "congressional ultimatums" that might compromise the INF agreement and suggested, none too convincingly, that he might have his own problems getting the document ratified by the Supreme Soviet. "We have our conservatives too," he declared. "They are different from your conservatives. Our conservatives are accustomed to a certain way of life, a certain order of things. They need to change their attitude towards life. They won't get the upper hand. The [reform] process is irreversible, although we will not be able to change everything at once."

Most of the legislators were impressed by Gorbachev's intelligence, candor and energy. Said Republican Senator Alan Simpson of Wyoming: "He comes at you with six headlights like a Mack truck." But many of them also let the General Secretary know that some concrete Soviet actions were necessary to improve relations. Senate Majority Leader Robert Byrd suggested that Gorbachev could greatly boost support for the treaty by announcing a timetable for Soviet withdrawal from Afghanistan. Gorbachev replied that Moscow had "no intention of staying in Afghanistan" but wanted assurances that that country would remain "unaligned" after a Soviet pullout. Senate Democratic Whip Alan Cranston of California, a strong INF supporter, asked the General Secretary what could be done to speed the START talks along. "You know what needs doing," replied Gorbachev. He pointed out that the Soviet Union was now sending out "good vibes" and added, "We need good vibes from you." Senate Republican Leader Robert Dole, at that time a pivotal fence-sitter on the INF issue, told Gorbachev that "some Republicans may want to take longer" to study the treaty before deciding whether or not to support it. Mindful of Dole's key role in the upcoming Senate debate, and of the possibility that Dole might succeed Reagan in the White House, Gorbachev pulled the Kansas Republican aside for a private ten-minute chat after the meeting ended. As the Senator left, Gorbachev smiled and wished him good luck in the presidential race. "Thank you," Dole replied. "I'm winning." Dole must have been reassured by Gorbachev's words, as well as by the final INF treaty text; the following week he appeared alongside Reagan in the White House press room and announced his formal backing for the accord. A major obstacle was thus cleared from the road to ratification.

When Gorbachev arrived at the White House at 10:30 a.m., the President invited him into his private study for an informal chat accompanied only by interpreters. Once the men were seated, Reagan pulled out the baseball that Joe DiMaggio had wanted the two leaders to autograph at the state dinner the night before. The President's intention was not merely to fulfill the Yankee Clipper's request. He wanted to use the baseball as a metaphor. What he was asking Gorbachev, in effect, was this: "Are we going to play ball or not? Can we get down to serious business, not only in the next two days but in the months ahead?" The President said he wanted to get going on START as soon as possible. Gorbachev heartily agreed. The two men then signed the baseball and returned to the adjoining Oval Office to begin an hour-long session with their aides.

Reagan delivered a 15-minute speech on nuclear weapons and, for the first time during the summit, brought up the prickly subject of Star Wars. "We are going forward with the research and development necessary to see if this is a workable concept," he said, "and if it is, we are going to deploy it." He reviewed the progress of the discussions to date, observing that if the two nations did come to an agreement on a 50% reduction in strategic warheads, as expected, SDI would become an even more important part of his concept of a transition from nuclear offense to nuclear defense. Yet he was well aware that the Soviets still hoped to hamstring his program and made it clear that he would have none of it.

Gorbachev listened intently and looked Reagan hard in the eyes as he spoke. When the President finished, the Soviet leader replied, "Mr. President, do what you think you have to do. And if in the end you think you have a system you want to deploy, go ahead and deploy. Who am I to tell you what to do? I think you're wasting your money. I don't think it will work. But if that's what you want to do, go ahead." He added ominouslyetā"We are moving in another direction, and we preserve our option to do what we think is necessary and in our own national interest at that time. And we think we can do it less expensively and with greater effectiveness."

U.S. experts were unsure what he meant, but offered several possible explanations: that the Soviets were working on their own defensive system (a fact that Gorbachev seemed to concede in an interview with NBC's Tom Brokaw a week earlier); that they might consider breaking the moratorium on antisatellite systems, which could cripple space-based SDI components; or that they might resort to abrogating existing treaties and rebuilding their nuclear arsenals. What Gorbachev really seemed to be saying was this: the Star Wars question need not be settled at this point in the START process; but if it remains unresolved and the U.S. does deploy, all bets are off and Moscow reserves the right to take any countermeasures it sees fit. He did not mean, as Reagan was later to claim, that he had lifted all objections to SDI. Yet he clearly indicated that he would not make Star Wars a summit breaker in Washington as he had done in Reykjavík. Thus it was up to the arms-control working group to shape the language of the joint communiqué in a way that would accommodate both the Soviet and U.S. points of view and, as Soviet Spokesman Gennadi Gerasimov put it, "postpone our quarrels." That task kept the Nitze-Akhromeyev team busy well into the night.

The Wednesday morning talks then moved from arms control to regional issues. For more than a week before the summit, Soviet aides had hinted that Gorbachev would unveil a schedule for withdrawing his 115,000 troops from Afghanistan within twelve months. He did not. Instead, he told the President he first wanted assurances that a neutral coalition government would replace the Soviet-backed regime in Kabul, and that the U.S. would immediately stop aiding the Afghan rebels. Reagan refused to budge. "What's keeping that plan from moving is your refusal to set a date for withdrawal," he said bluntly. "I am not going to help you with that problem by renouncing aid to the freedom fighters." Although Gorbachev would begin taking steps toward unilateral withdrawal shortly after the summit ended, there was no sign of any imminent movement during the Washington meetings. Nor was any substantive progress made on Central America, the Persian Gulf or other regional issues. On these questions, as on human rights, the summit produced little more than a "frank exchange" of views.

After a lunch at the State Department—with an all-American menu that featured Alaskan king crab, Louisiana shrimp, Maryland crab, Maine lobster and, of course, apple pie—Gorbachev returned to the Soviet embassy to play host to another of his seminar-like discussion sessions. This time, his guests were leading American media executives. Among them: CBS President Lawrence Tisch, Cable News Network President Ted Turner, *Foreign Affairs* Editor William Hyland, Washington Post Chairman Katharine Graham and Time Inc. Editor-in-Chief Jason McManus. Gorbachev began with his by-now standard opening remarks on his reform efforts and the need to improve relations between the two countries. As in earlier sessions, he was strikingly candid about his country's economic problems. At one point, he referred to the Soviet Union as the "world's second ranking power." The remark, which surprised many Westerners in the audience, was consistent with the message he has been stressing at home: that the Soviet Union must squarely face up to the problems in its economic system. Soviet Spokesman Gerasimov later told TIME that it was the first time Gorbachev had put his country's runner-up status so bluntly. Joked Gerasimov: "He conceded—to Japan."

But the General Secretary also betrayed a testiness that, until then, had not been publicly revealed during this summit. What set him off was a question on human rights from Robert Bernstein, chairman of Random House, the publishing firm. "What right does the U.S. have to preach to us, to the rest of human society?" he demanded, repeating the arguments he had earlier made to Reagan about U.S. machine guns on the Mexican border. He then launched into a tirade against the press for its fascination with rumor and scandal. "What a business!" he said. "How irresponsible and how dubious. It doesn't have a very good smell to it." Dismissing press reports of rifts within the Kremlin, he brought his hand down on the table like a knife blade and insisted, "There is no split in the Politburo. There is no split in the Central Committee, and I can assure you there will be none." Perhaps sensing that he risked alienating the very media group that he had so arduously

courted throughout his visit, he added, somewhat apologeti-
cally, "Maybe I was a little emotional, but I was sincere."

Gorbachev's outburst left many listeners uneasy. "Some
of the scales fell away," said one editor. "The inhibitions were
down, and then you began to see the guy who worked his way
up to the top of the Soviet hierarchy. He was potentially much
tougher, much meaner." The session lent some credence to the
claims by White House aides that the sweetness and light of
Gorbachev's public statements did not match the harder line
he took in his private talks with the President.

The final push on arms control began early Thursday
morning, when George Shultz and Paul Nitze arrived at the
Soviet embassy. There they met with Shevardnadze and Akhromeyev to review the progress of the talks and the results of
the working group's late night labors. The two sides then went
off to brief their respective leaders. It was clear that more
work—and time—were needed. Consequently, the scheduled
10:30 a.m. meeting between Reagan and Gorbachev was canceled to allow the Nitze-Akhromeyev group to continue their
efforts. Gorbachev, meanwhile, met privately with Vice President George Bush at the Soviet embassy, then presided over a
caviar and blini breakfast attended by Bush and five guests invited by the Vice President. It was not lost on rival Candidate
Bob Dole's campaign staff that three of the five were from the
key primary states of Iowa and New Hampshire. Dole Spokes-
woman Katie Boyle sniffed that she was "surprised Bush
didn't invite Gorbachev to Des Moines for a fund raiser."

The Vice President did not go quite that far but, by his
own account, he was responsible for Gorbachev's one sponta-
neous brush with the American people. As the two men were
riding to the White House in Gorbachev's limousine, Bush
told the Soviet leader, "It's too bad you don't have time to go
into a store or greet people." A moment later, Gorbachev suddenly barked to his driver, "Stop the car!" To the amazement
of several dozen passersby on Connecticut Avenue, the grin-

ning Soviet leader hopped out of the car, strode briskly over to the curb and began pressing the flesh like a polished Western politician. As delighted pedestrians scrambled to shake his hand—and security agents scanned the crowd nervously—Gorbachev said through an interpreter that he wanted his people to "come to a better understanding with the Americans."

"The guy is a p.r. genius," gushed one woman. "I'm still shaking," said another. "It was like the coming of the second Messiah or something." Duke Zeibert, whose famous power-lunch restaurant happened to be located at the site of Gorbachev's apparition, called down from his balcony for the Soviet leader to "Come on up and have lunch! We have borscht!" Bush, who seemed awkwardly out of place while Gorbachev worked the crowd, later asked the visitor why he had decided to stop. "He said that he does it a lot in the provinces," Bush recalled afterward, "and he likes it."

The interlude was the only time during the entire summit that Gorbachev departed from his rigid schedule of official talks, dinners and orchestrated discussion sessions to brush elbows with the hoi polloi. Many observers, in fact, were struck by his apparent lack of curiosity about the American people and their ways. When he did meet with hand-picked groups of Americans, he tended to lecture rather than listen and made no effort to disguise his distaste for pointed questions. Judging by his public performance during the summit, he seemed to regard communication as a one-way street. This was less true of his private meetings. Bush remarked that the Russian had a "Western way of communicating" marked by a "lively exchange" that "cut through a lot of the bluster."

Gorbachev's best personal rapport seemed to be with Reagan. The relationship between the two had improved steadily since their first meeting in Geneva in 1986, when they did not know each other at all. According to White House aides, the President had suggested at the outset of this, their third summit, that they refer to one another as "Ron" and "Mikhail" in their private sessions. Gorbachev may not have been entirely comfortable with such American-style familiarity, but he emphatically declared just before his departure: "I think we trust each other more."

"There is good chemistry between the two men," Nancy Reagan later told TIME's Hugh Sidey. "I think that each of them now has a pretty good understanding of the other one. They can talk candidly now and they do. They enjoy the one on one. I know Ronnie likes it, and Chairman Gorbachev likes it. They both understand there are big differences like Afghanistan and human rights. But they know where that point is beyond which they do not press each other. When they get there, they cool it."

The warm personal rapport was in evidence Thursday when Gorbachev's motorcade arrived at the South portico of the White House for a final working luncheon. The Soviet leader had been running late, and the flesh-pressing episode had made him even later. As the President greeted his guest, he remarked wryly, "I thought you'd gone home." Gorbachev laughed. The two men, both smiling amiably, took a brief stroll together through the White House park. Reagan used the occasion to press once more for a halt to Soviet military involvement in Afghanistan and Nicaragua. Gorbachev spoke vaguely of his interest in the Central American peace process, but made no specific commitments.

While the two leaders and their top aides were lunching in the Family Dining Room, the Nitze-Akhromeyev team was still closeted in the Roosevelt Room desperately trying to finish their work before the departure ceremony. Their goals: 1) to draft a joint communiqué text that would defer the SDI problem, and 2) to reach agreement on the "subceilings" that would be placed on different types of strategic missiles and bombers within the framework of a 50% reduction in each side's warheads. As the luncheon neared its end, Shultz, Defense Secretary Frank Carlucci and Lieut. General Colin Powell, the National Security Adviser, excused themselves and went to see what was holding up the arms control group. Stretching out their meal while waiting for the negotiators to finish, Gorbachev and Reagan lapsed into casual conversation. The Soviet explained that the little green spiral notebooks that he had often referred to during the talks were filled with thoughts he had jotted down during his 52-day absence from Moscow the previous summer. During that period, there had been speculation that Gorbachev might be ill, a chilling thought in light of his predecessors' health problems. He emerged from that long absence, however, with the nearly completed manuscript of his book, *Perestroika*.

As the lunch dragged on, the delay became uncomfortable. The military honor guards were already beginning to assemble on the South Lawn for the departure ceremony. White House Chief of Staff Howard Baker went to the usher's office and called Powell on the phone. Powell told him they still needed a little more time. "Do whatever needs to be done," Baker snapped. "But I've got an antsy President and a jumpy General Secretary on my hands, and I've got to end this lunch." Baker returned and suggested that they adjourn to the Red Room for coffee. While Baker shuttled back to the phone to check on the negotiations, the two leaders got to talking about being politicians. Reagan told Gorbachev that he had watched his curbside handshaking performance on TV, explaining that American politicians called that "working the crowds." Gorbachev laughed. Political leaders, he remarked, often learned more when traveling in the provinces than in their own capitals. Reagan nodded his agreement.

Finally, the arms-control group reached agreement and rejoined the leaders. Gorbachev was escorted to the Map Room to be briefed by Akhromeyev; Reagan retired to the Library, where Shultz and Powell explained the communiqué text to him. The Secretary of State did most of the talking, reporting that the Joint Chiefs had approved the language. Reagan looked up at Powell in silent inquisition. "It's fine, Mr. President," said the General. Reagan gave his approval. He then rejoined Gorbachev and accompanied him to the South Lawn for the farewell ceremony.

Bundled up in their dark overcoats, protected from a hard, cold rain by a canopy of black umbrellas wielded by security agents, both men looked tired and somber as they stood together on the dais. Remembering their grim faces following the collapse of the Reykjavík summit, some observers wondered if their talks had not reached a similar impasse this time. Reagan's words belied that notion.

Calling the summit a "clear success," he declared that the two leaders could "walk away from our meetings with a sense of accomplishment." Gorbachev replied that the visit had "on the whole justified our hopes." "Today," he summed up, "the Soviet Union and the United States are closer to the common goal of strengthening international security. But this goal is yet to be reached. There is still much work to be done, and we must get down to it without delay." When Gorbachev's concluding words had been translated by veteran Soviet Interpreter Victor Sukhodrev, the two leaders grinned for the first time during the brief ceremony and exchanged a cordial parting handshake.

If neither man referred to specific progress on strategic arms, it was because there had not been time to work any mention of the last-minute agreement into their prepared farewell speeches. Yet the final communiqué text, and the explanations of U.S. aides, soon made it clear that much had been accomplished. The Nitze-Akhromeyev team had refined instructions for the Soviet and U.S. negotiators in Geneva, who would seek to translate them into treaty language over the following months—ideally, in time for Reagan's planned visit to Moscow in the first half of 1988.

As originally agreed in Reykjavík, the plan called for a

50% reduction in overall nuclear warheads, down to 6,000 for each side. Of those, the combined number of intercontinental ballistic missiles plus submarine-launched ballistic missiles was to be limited to 4,900. No more than 1,540 warheads could be deployed on heavy multiwarhead missiles. The two sides also agreed to a limit of 1,600 delivery systems (missile launchers, bombers, submarines, etc.). Verification procedures remained to be worked out, although U.S. officials felt that their earlier breakthroughs on INF on-site inspections would take them a long way toward finding solutions. Said a jubilant Shultz: "You can literally see from this joint statement the shape of a START agreement."

Less precise, but no less important, was the way the two sides had agreed to handle the thorny Star Wars issue. The text they worked out was both tortured and vague, just what was needed to defer the dispute to another day. The negotiators in Geneva were instructed to "work out an agreement that would commit the sides to observe the ABM treaty, as signed in 1972, while conducting their research, development and testing as required, which are permitted by the ABM treaty, and not to withdraw from the ABM treaty for a specified period of time." Behind the convoluted language lay a compromise that allowed the two leaders to take opposed positions on SDI, at least for the time being. The Soviets had got an indefinite U.S. commitment not to pull out of the ABM treaty; the Reagan Administration had won the right to proceed with testing, "as required" by the needs of its Star Wars program, as long as those tests did not violate ABM. The crucial question of what kinds of tests were allowed under the ABM accord—the "broad" vs. the "narrow" interpretation—was not addressed at this time. In effect, said a senior summit participant, the two sides had "agreed to disagree."

That did not mean that Gorbachev was resigned to an eventual SDI deployment. He had merely given up on trying to get this President to accept any formula that would explicitly limit Star Wars testing. Yet he could see that Congress was applying its own budgetary constraints on the tests and that, given the preliminary state of the program at this point, no deployment was likely until well into the 1990s. Having won Reagan's commitment not to withdraw from the ABM treaty, Gorbachev seemed content to wait and deal with the next President on the question of what that treaty means. But as National Security Adviser Powell conceded in a letter published three weeks after the summit, the Soviets had reserved the right to pull out of any future strategic arms agreement if the U.S. violated Moscow's reading of the ABM treaty. Clearly, the Star Wars problem was not going to evaporate.

Gorbachev's final day in Washington did not end with his White House farewell. There was more salesmanship to be done. By 4 p.m. he was back at his embassy, conducting a meeting with 50 top U.S. banking and business leaders. This time, there was a special angle to his pitch: he was trying to convince these movers and shakers to invest in his country now that U.S.-Soviet political relations were on a "more predictable footing." Paradoxically, it was among these high-powered capitalists that the world's paramount Communist leader produced some of his most positive reactions. Jack Valenti, the Motion Picture Association president, jokingly told the Soviet leader he was so popular that he was "now running third in the Iowa primary." Gorbachev laughed and protested, "But I already have a job." Retorted Valenti: "In this country, we draft people."

The General Secretary next sped to the Soviet Union's brand new embassy complex at Mount Alto for a press conference attended by more than 400 U.S. and foreign reporters. Arriving 15 minutes late, he sat at a long table flanked by six senior members of his delegation, including Shevardnadze, Kremlin Propaganda Chief Alexander Yakovlev and Anatoli Dobrynin, the Central Committee Secretary in charge of foreign policy. Gorbachev then launched into a detailed 70-minute monologue summing up his talks with Reagan. The Soviet leader called the summit a "major event in world politics" and noted that there was a "deepening political dialogue" between himself and the President. "At the highest level of our two states," he proclaimed, "it has been recognized that they are now emerging from the long, drawn-out confrontation."

In discussing specific areas of the summit agenda, however, Gorbachev began to show flashes of testiness. Echoing his earlier words to Reagan on SDI, he observed sarcastically that "if the Americans have all that much money, let them squander it away. We will find an answer along other lines." On human rights, he struck an even more belligerent note. Claiming that only 220 people had been refused the right to emigrate because of their involvement in classified work, (Helsinki Watch puts the number of *refuseniks* at 11,000) he declared, "No matter what you say, no matter what you shout at us, we shall not let them go before their knowledge of these secrets has evaporated!" The General Secretary then unleashed a sharp attack on the press that recalled his earlier performance before the media executives. Chopping the air with his hands and jutting out his lower lip in defiance, he charged that the only thing journalists seemed interested in was grilling him on human rights, "as if we are agreeing to interviews not just to try to search for the truth, to prod each other to serious thinking, but to drive the politician into a corner. Is that dialogue? Is that an interview? That is not what the media is for." Pausing and folding his hands in front of him, he suddenly smiled and instructed the reporters, like an admonishing schoolmaster, to "think over this part of my talk."

The outburst, like his brusque and evasive answers to most of the questions that followed, highlighted the boundary between what he calls *glasnost* and the Western notion of press freedom. By once again castigating the media—the group he most needed to win over in order to get his message across—he revealed a serious flaw in an otherwise masterful public relations performance. Commenting on the press conference in the Washington *Post*, Tom Shales wrote that the General Secretary "wore out his welcome with a vengeance." That judgment seems excessive. But as the Gorbachevs' Ilyushin taxied down the runway Thursday night and roared off into the dark, rainy skies over Washington, it was inevitable that some of the early euphoria surrounding the visit should fall into perspective. Despite Raisa Gorbachev's professed admiration for Thomas Jefferson, it is unrealistic to hold a Soviet leader to the standards of Jeffersonian democracy. "The American people had better understand that they're still dealing with a Marxist-Leninist here," said a senior White House aide. "You strip away that outer layer, and he's still a Soviet." True, but a different kind of Soviet from any of his predecessors. "Compare the road we have traveled from Stalin to Gorbachev with the road you have traveled from Roosevelt to Reagan," said Writer Fyodor Burlatsky, a member of Moscow's summit delegation. "You have to agree that we have traveled the longer distance." He had a point.

Gorbachev's visit to Washington seemed to herald a new phase in the 40-year struggle between the U.S. and the U.S.S.R. Although the summit's meager substantive results hardly justified the hoopla, what really mattered—and captured the public imagination—were the images of personal accord and amity that pervaded the event. In diplomacy, especially in the age of television, the perception that tensions have been reduced tends to mean that tensions have in fact been reduced. What happened in Washington during the week of Dec. 7, 1987, is that the perceptions changed measurably—and for the better—on both sides. When it was all over, Reagan declared that the meeting had "lit the sky with hope for all people of good will." That was more than mere hyperbole. Something extraordinary was taking place: four decades of often truculent cold-war rhetoric were giving way to dispassionate discourse and high-level rapport. Neither side was for-

getting the vast ideological chasm that separated the superpowers, but they were learning to work around their
differences, to stake out common ground on which to build a
better understanding. For that, Gorbachev deserved his full
measure of credit.

The Washington summit was a major milestone in Gorbachev's career. The Soviet leader returned to Moscow with
his hand strengthened by diplomatic success. He could hold
up the INF treaty as proof that he knew how to deal advanta-
geously with the West's toughest anti-Communist. He could
claim that he had held Reagan to the ABM treaty. Most of all,
he could point to a public relations triumph that had reached
beyond Reagan's lame-duck presidency and into the permanent American psyche—an achievement that might lay the
groundwork for U.S.-Soviet cooperation well into the future.
To a Soviet population still haunted by memories of World
War II, and by four decades of superpower confrontation, that
was no small accomplishment.

The next task he faced was turning his newfound political capital to advantage at home, where he still faced daunting
challenges. On Jan. 1, 1988, just three weeks after the summit,
the new law on state enterprises took effect in the Soviet
Union. The measure put 60% of Soviet industry on a "self-financing" basis—and thousands of managers used to taking orders from Moscow-based bureaucrats were suddenly forced to
make business decisions on their own. A certain amount of
confusion and disruption would inevitably accompany this
process, and it was unclear whether the long-suffering Soviet
consumer would see any immediate benefit. Conceding that
his economic innovations still faced considerable opposition,
Gorbachev told a group of Soviet editors in January: "If we
take fright and stop the process we have begun, it would have
the most serious consequences, because we simply could not
raise our people to such a massive task a second time."

The summit increased Gorbachev's stature abroad—especially in Western and Eastern Europe, where reaction to the INF treaty signing was generally enthusiastic. During a stopover in East Berlin, where he briefed leaders from the other Warsaw Pact states, the Soviet leader was greeted by thousands of cheering East Germans as his motorcade entered the city. After exchanging the customary bear hugs with Gorbachev, the other East bloc leaders officially endorsed the treaty and called it a "step of historic dimension."

In the wake of his diplomatic triumph, Gorbachev launched a determined effort to solve his most painful foreign policy problem: Afghanistan. Although he had refused to set a firm withdrawal date in his talks with Reagan, the General Secretary may have concluded that the only way out of the costly stalemate was a unilateral pullout of Soviet troops. Within a month of Gorbachev's return from Washington, therefore, Foreign Minister Shevardnadze was in Kabul telling Afghan Leader Najibullah: "We would like the year 1988 to be the last year of the presence of Soviet troops in your country." *Pravda* later reported that the troops could begin coming home as soon as May 1. The details remained to be worked out, but the message was clear: Gorbachev wanted out. (Not coincidentally, perhaps, the name of the man who had launched the disastrous 1979 invasion, Leonid Brezhnev, was stripped from a Volga River city, a Moscow suburb and a Leningrad square the same week.)

There were also hopeful signs on human rights. The government in early January published a law aimed at curbing psychiatric abuses. Under the new statute, patients would be protected against arbitrary confinement in mental hospitals—a tactic frequently used in the past to silence dissidents—and given legal recourse against malpractice. If enforced, the new law would represent a major step toward ending one of the Soviet Union's most repugnant forms of political repression. Two weeks later, in another encouraging signal, Gorbachev met with members of an international peace and human rights group that included Physicist Andrei Sakharov. It was the first ever encounter between a Soviet leader and a prominent dissident.

Arms control remained the biggest challenge ahead. Here, in fact, was the key to all Gorbachev's reforms. Diverting money and brainpower from military spending to the domestic economy was a central theme of his *perestroika* drive. He and Reagan had just signed an INF agreement eliminating 4% of the superpowers' nuclear arsenals; now they were seriously talking about cutting the number of remaining warheads in half. Although the Star Wars dispute continued to hover over those negotiations like a black cloud over a picnic, there were realistic hopes that a strategic arms treaty could be wrapped up by the time Ronald Reagan arrived in Moscow in the late spring or summer to try out his own considerable charms on the Soviet people.

History would judge the success of those efforts, as it would assess the ultimate achievements or failures of both leaders. But Gorbachev had, in less than three years as General Secretary, captured the imagination of a West that for decades has been waiting for a Soviet leader who was not only reasonable but, for heaven's sake, halfway likable. Sure, he had his temper, his Dickensian view of U.S. society, his ideological stubbornness. And, of course, the Soviet Union was still an economic disaster area, a bureaucratic nightmare, a military menace and a human rights outrage. Perhaps most unsettling of all was the thought that the budding Gorbachev era might be merely a false dawn, and that the forces of privilege and shortsightedness would triumph in the end, as they did against Nikita Khrushchev in 1964.

In the early months of 1988, however, there was still plenty of latitude for optimism. At the least, it appeared unlikely that the former combine-harvester operator from Stavropol—a man molded by famine and war, promised a measure of hope after Stalin's demise and then abruptly disillusioned—would willingly drag his country back into the dark days of repression, economic hardship and international obloquy. Though his legacy would no doubt be years in the making, it was apparent that he had already given the Soviet Union, its allies and its enemies a gift they had not received from a Soviet leader in recent memory: a measure of hope.

Quotations from the General Secretary

On *Glasnost:*

We must not pretend that everything goes on smoothly . . . We all care for socialism and want to make it as attractive as possible, but if we go on glossing over, making things up, they get worse.

> –From a televised speech in Rumania, May 1987

Openness, criticism and self-criticism are simply mandatory for us . . . And if someone assumes that we only need this in order to subject the deficiencies of the past to criticism, he is badly mistaken. The most important thing is that openness, criticism and self-criticism and democracy are necessary in order for us to move forward and solve enormous problems. We will not solve these problems without the active participation of the people. That is what we need all this for.

> –From a speech to the Central Committee plenum, January 1987

Let's strictly observe the principle: everything which is not prohibited by law is allowed.

> –From Gorbachev's book *Perestroika,* 1987

On "Democratization":

We need democracy like air. If we do not realize this, and even if we realize it but do not take real steps in expanding and advancing it, and in involving the workers of the country in the process of restructuring, our policy will choke, and restructuring will suffocate, Comrades.

> –At the January 1987 plenum

We do not have an opposition party. How then can we control ourselves? Only through criticism and self-criticism. Most important, through *glasnost.* Democratism without *glasnost* does not exist. At the same time, democracy without limits is anarchy.

> –At a closed meeting of Soviet writers, June 1986

The working people have a part to play in everything. This is their country, this is their system, this is their society: they are in charge. The party organization and cadres are at the service of the people, and the party is entirely at the service of the people—not the other way around.

—From a speech in Murmansk, October 1987

On the Intelligentsia:

Politics needs to be nourished by the intellectual in each country because he is more likely to keep the human being at the center of his examination. Any other concentration is immoral. I read and reread Lenin, and in 1916 he wrote, "There must be a priority given to the general interest of humanity even above that of the proletariat."

—To American Playwright Arthur Miller, 1986

On Leadership:

The revolutionary is not he who uses revolutionary phrases, but rather he who knows how to plan ahead and rouse the people and the party to a lengthy and sustained struggle, noticing each step of progress and using it to gain a foothold for another, greater step.

—At the January 1987 plenum

We haven't walked away. Perhaps not all the decisions we make today are correct. Perhaps we err in some things. But we want to act and not sit with folded arms, letting the process pass us by.

—At the 1986 Soviet writers' meeting

On Soviet Economic Problems:

The economy is a mess. We are behind in every area. In 1969 in Stavropol we had a problem, what to do with all the meat and milk. Butter too—heaps of it. And now there is nothing. We have forgotten how to work. Not just that, but forgotten how to work in conditions of democracy.

—Ibid.

Sharp contrasts have emerged in our country . . . Our rockets find Haley's Comet with astonishing accuracy and fly to rendezvous with Venus, yet an obvious lag in the practical application of scientific achievements for economic needs and the vexing imperfections in unsophisticated household gadgets exist alongside this triumph of research and engineering.

-From a speech in Prague, April 1987

On *Perestroika:*

It happens sometimes that life, by and large, is a good house with a strong foundation and a reliable framework, but at the same time much in life does not satisfy us any longer and has fallen behind the increased requirements and needs. Minor repairs are not enough in this case. It takes a major overhaul.

-Ibid.

We should learn to spot, expose and neutralize the maneuvers of the opponents of *perestroika*—those who act to impede our advance and trip us up, who gloat over our difficulties and setbacks, who try to drag us back into the past. Nor should we succumb to the pressure of the overly zealous and impatient . . . it should be clear that one cannot leap over essential stages and try to accomplish everything at one go.

-From a speech at the 27th Party Congress, February 1986

Everyone must work harder. I emphasize, Comrades, everyone . . . Those who continue to advocate old technologies and old means must be corrected; if this is not possible, if some people display stubbornness or obstinacy and cannot be pulled out of the mire of yesterday's thinking, then we must part with such people, let them remain in the mire, while the country will go around them and continue to move forward.

-From a speech to workers in Khabarovsk, July 1986

A very profound and serious movement has begun, and a very profound and serious struggle lies ahead. Between the people who want these changes, who dream of these changes, and the leadership, there is a layer of officialdom that does not want changes and does not want to lose some rights associated with privileges . . . We have very many people who take advantage of their position. Nothing is exploited as much as official position.

—At the 1986 Soviet writers' meeting

I believe deeply in what we have begun. I believe deeply. And if I were told that we must stop the process of reconstruction ... I would never agree. I do not want to be associated with any other policy. Therefore for me there is no other way.

—During a visit to Estonia, 1987

Restructuring is not a stroll down a road that has been rolled smooth. It is a climb up a mountain, frequently along unused paths.

—At the January 1987 plenum

There is no reasonable alternative to a dynamic, revolutionary *perestroika*. Its alternative is continued stagnation ... The stakes are too high. Time dictates to us a revolutionary choice, and we have made it. We will not retreat from *perestroika* but will carry it through.

—From Perestroika

If we take fright and stop the processes we have begun, it would have the most serious consequences because we simply could not raise our people to such a massive task a second time ... To stop now would be disastrous. We must not permit it under any circumstances.

—To a group of Soviet editors, January 1988

On the World:

Our foreign policy today stems directly from our domestic policy to a larger extent than ever before. We say honestly for all to hear: we need a lasting peace to concentrate on the development of our society and to tackle the tasks of improving the life of the Soviet people.

—At a dinner in Moscow for British Prime Minister Margaret Thatcher, March 1987

The West is scrutinizing our position for signs of the Soviet Union's weakness. They claim that the Soviets have fallen hopelessly behind, that their system is not working and that the goal of socialism has proved altogether flawed. That is why, supposedly, any concession can now be wrenched from them if proper pressure is applied. It is a bad delusion.

-Ibid.

We are happy with our territory. We have enough, although none to spare.

-In an interview with Indian journalists, November 1986

The world today is one in which a struggle is under way between reason and madness, morality and savagery, life and death. We have determined our place in this struggle definitely and irreversibly. We are on the side of reason, morality and life. This is why we are for disarmament, most notably nuclear disarmament, and for creating a system of general security. This is the only possible way that mankind can regain immortality.

-Ibid.

Your President [Reagan] couldn't make peace if he wanted to. He's a prisoner of the military-industrial complex.

-To U.S. Industrialist Armand Hammer, 1986

Today the world's nations are interdependent, like mountain climbers on one rope. They can either climb together to the summit or fall together into the abyss.

-April 1987 Prague speech

The West is speaking of inequality and imbalance. Well, yes, there is a certain asymmetry in the armed forces of the two sides in Europe, due to historical, geographic and other factors. We are for redressing the imbalances existing in some of the elements, but not through a buildup by the trailing party, but through a build-down by the one that has broken away.

-Ibid.

Security is indivisible . . . The security of each nation should be coupled with the security for all members of the world community . . . Adversaries must become partners and start looking jointly for a way to achieve universal security.

—From *Perestroika*

On Other Socialist Countries:

We do not think we know the best answers to all questions put by life itself. We are far from urging others to indiscriminately follow our practices. Every socialist country is unique, and fraternal parties shape their policies proceeding from national specifics.

—April 1987 Prague speech

On Human Rights:

We hold it unacceptable to talk about human rights and freedoms while intending to hang up "chandeliers" of exotic weapons in outer space. The only ordinary element in that "exoticism" is the potential possibility of mankind's annihilation. The rest is dazzling wrapping.

—In a pamphlet entitled *Realities and Guarantees for a Secure World*, September 1987

I agree: the world cannot be considered secure if human rights are being violated. I will only add: it cannot be considered secure if a large part of this world lacks elementary conditions for a life worthy of man, if millions of people have a full "right" to go hungry, to have no roof over their heads and to be jobless and sick indefinitely . . . if, finally, the most basic human right, the right to life is disregarded.

—Ibid.

On Re-Examining Soviet History:

There should be no forgotten names and blank pages in Soviet history and literature.

—At a meeting of Soviet editors, February 1987

There is now much discussion about the role of Stalin in our history. His was an extremely contradictory personality. To remain faithful to historical truth we have to see both Stalin's incontestable contribution to the struggle for socialism, to the defense of its gains; the gross political errors and the abuses committed by him and by those around him, for which our people paid a heavy price and which had grave consequences for the life of our society.

—In a speech marking the 70th anniversary of the Bolshevik Revolution, November 1987

The guilt of Stalin and his immediate entourage before the party and the people for the wholesale repressive measures and acts of lawlessness is enormous and unforgivable. This is a lesson for all generations.

—Ibid.

On the Brezhnev Era:

Over the course of a number of years . . . the practical action of the party and state organs lagged behind the demands of the time and of life itself. Problems . . . grew faster than they were resolved. Inertia and paralysis of the forms and methods of management, a loss of dynamism in work, and the growth of bureaucratism—all this brought great harm to our cause.

—At the 27th Congress, February 1986

On Socialism and Equality:

On this point we want to be clear: socialism has nothing to do with equalizing. Socialism cannot ensure conditions of life and consumption in accordance with the principle, "From each according to his ability, to each according to his needs." This will be under Communism. Socialism has a different criterion for distributing social benefits: "From each according to his ability, to each according to his work."

—From *Perestroika*

On Gorbachev's Popularity:

When people speak about the popularity of Gorbachev they mean apparently not a concrete person but the policy which is pursued by the Soviet leadership . . . If we are consistent in implementing it, in both domestic and foreign policy, the authority will remain and increase. If not, no style, no personal charm will save us.

—Interview with the Italian Communist newspaper *L'Unita,* May 1987

A Chronology

1917. Bolshevik troops storm the Winter Palace in Petrograd (later Leningrad) on Nov. 7 and arrest members of the Provisional Government. Within days, Bolshevik Leader Vladimir Lenin issues decrees asking foreign governments for peace, abolishing private ownership of land and passing control of industry to workers' committees.

1918-20. Civil war and foreign intervention. Lenin invokes "War Communism," under which the government confiscates grain, prohibits private trade, nationalizes large sectors of the economy. By February 1920, Bolshevik forces retake control of the north Caucasus region around Stavropol, home of Gorbachev's forebears.

1921. Lenin introduces his New Economic Policy at the Tenth Party Congress, denationalizing some sectors of the economy, allowing agriculture to be largely market driven, and permitting small-scale private trading.

1922. Union of Soviet Socialist Republics officially founded.

1924. Lenin dies at age 54, and party leadership passes to a triumvirate that includes Joseph Stalin. The first constitution of the U.S.S.R. is enacted. Great Britain, France, Austria, China and Italy recognize the Soviet government.

1927. At the 15th Party Congress, Stalin outmaneuvers his rivals in the leadership, and the delegates make a definite commitment to rapid industrialization by approving the first Five-Year Plan, which calls for an increase in output of 150% during 1928-33. Leon Trotsky is exiled.

1929. The 16th Congress passes a resolution calling for a general purge of the party. Stalin officially signals the beginning of collectivization and declares that the party has moved toward a policy of "liquidating the kulaks [rich peasants] as a class."

1931. On March 2, Mikhail Sergeyevich Gorbachev is born in Privolnoye. By September, collectivization encompasses some 60% of peasant households.

1934. Leningrad Party Boss and Stalin Opponent Sergei Kirov is assassinated, thus beginning the great purges, which swing into high gear in 1936.

1939. The Nazi-Soviet pact is signed, and the party formally abandons the mass purges.

1941. On June 22, Nazi Germany invades the Soviet Union.

1942. German troops occupy large swatches of Soviet territory, including the city of Stavropol. Both the Siege of Leningrad and the Battle of Stalingrad begin.

1945. World War II ends, and Gorbachev's father Sergei returns to the Khleborob collective farm in Privolnoye to join his son, who has begun to work as a combine driver.

1949. The Chinese Communists are victorious in civil war, and the North Atlantic Treaty Organization is formed. In Stavropol, Mikhail Gorbachev is awarded the Red Banner of Labor for his diligent efforts on the collective farm.

1950. Gorbachev, 19, travels through the war-devastated countryside on his way to enroll in the law faculty at Moscow State University in September.

1952. Stalin, 73, convenes the first party congress in 13 years, and the Politburo is renamed the Presidium. At Moscow State University, Gorbachev is active in the Komsomol, the Young Communist League, and becomes a full member of the party.

1953. Stalin dies on March 6, and Khrushchev is elected First Secretary in September. Secret Police Chief Lavrenti Beria is arrested and executed during the summer.

1955. The Soviet Union is a founding member of the Warsaw Pact. Gorbachev and his wife Raisa graduate in June and return to Stavropol, where he is assigned to work in the regional Komsomol organization.

1956. Khrushchev's secret speech at the 20th Party Congress in February inaugurates a period of destalinization. Gorbachev is promoted to first secretary of the Stavropol city Komsomol. In the fall, Soviet troops crush a revolt in Hungary.

1957. Khrushchev has a successful year both at home and abroad. In July he defeats opponents in the antiparty group, and on Oct. 4 the Soviet Union launches the first satellite, Sputnik.

1958. Soviet Author Boris Pasternak is awarded, and later forced to decline, the Nobel Prize for Literature for his novel *Doctor Zhivago*. Gorbachev moves up in the regional Komsomol, eventually reaching the post of first secretary in 1960.

1961. China splits openly with the Soviet Union. East Germany erects a wall between the two halves of divided Berlin. In Moscow, Khrushchev intensifies the destalinization campaign in his speech at the 22nd Party Congress, the first one Gorbachev attends. The congress approves removing Stalin's body from the Lenin Mausoleum.

1962. The Cuban Missile Crisis shakes Khrushchev's standing in Moscow. Good political connections help Gorbachev advance in the Stavropol Krai (territory) party organization.

1964. Khrushchev is ousted in October, and Leonid Brezhnev replaces him as First Secretary. Gorbachev's mentor, Fyodor Kulakov, is elected to head the agriculture department of the Central Committee.

1966. At the 23rd Party Congress, the title of the top party official is changed back to General Secretary and the Presidium is renamed the Politburo. Gorbachev is made head of the Stavropol city party organization, and in the spring travels outside the Soviet Union for the first time, visiting East Germany. In the summer he takes an unofficial vacation trip through France.

1968. Warsaw Pact forces invade Czechoslovakia to crush a brief liberalization known as the Prague Spring. One year after receiving his degree from the Stavropol Agricultural Institute, Gorbachev joins the Stavropol Krai party committee as second in command.

1970. Gorbachev is elected first secretary of the Stavropol Krai party, and at the 24th Congress he is promoted to full membership in the Central Committee. One year later he is made a Deputy to the Supreme Soviet, the nation's parliament.

1972. President Richard Nixon travels to Moscow to sign the Strategic Arms Limitation treaty with General Secretary Leonid Brezhnev.

1975. The Helsinki Accords on human rights are signed in August. In December, Physicist and Dissident Andrei Sakharov receives the Nobel Peace Prize.

1977. Brezhnev assumes the additional title of President (head of state), and a new constitution is adopted. Success of the Ipatovsky harvesting method brings national attention to Gorbachev, and an interview with the Stavropol Krai party leader is published on the first page of *Pravda*.

1978. Politburo Member Kulakov dies, and Gorbachev is named to replace him as Central Committee secretary in charge of agriculture. Gorbachev and Raisa return to Moscow in the fall after 23 years in Stavropol.

1979. Soviet troops invade Afghanistan and install a Moscow-backed government. Gorbachev continues his meteoric rise by being named a nonvoting member of the Politburo in November.

1980. In January, Sakharov is exiled to the closed city of Gorky. In October, Gorbachev is promoted to full membership in the Politburo.

1982. Leonid Brezhnev's 18-year reign comes to an end with his death in November, and KGB Chief Yuri Andropov, a Gorbachev patron, is elected General Secretary.

1983. Soviet jets shoot down Korean Air Lines Flight 007 after it strays over Soviet territory. Gorbachev reportedly heads a crisis-management team that coordinates the response to international protests. He visits Canada in his capacity as party secretary in charge of agriculture.

1984. Andropov dies in February and is replaced by Konstantin Chernenko, a longtime Brezhnev retainer. Gorbachev becomes the unofficial No. 2 in the party leadership, overseeing ideology and culture and presiding over many Politburo meetings. Gorbachev, accompanied by Raisa, makes an official visit to Britain in December.

1985. Chernenko dies in March, and within hours Gorbachev is elected General Secretary. He begins campaigns against corruption and alcoholism, undertakes televised visits to workplaces and sets in motion sweeping personnel changes within the leadership. In November, Gorbachev meets President Ronald Reagan at the Geneva summit.

1986. Delegates at the 27th Party Congress approve Gorbachev's ambitious economic programs and elect allies of the General Secretary to key posts. In April, the world's worst civilian nuclear accident occurs at Chernobyl; the Soviets are slow to respond to international pressure for information. During the year, Gorbachev's policies of *glasnost* and *perestroika* become catchwords for internal liberalization in the arts, society and the economy. Gorbachev and Reagan meet again, in Reykjavík, Iceland. In December, Sakharov is released from exile.

1987. Gorbachev renews his call for political and economic reform at the Central Committee meeting in February. Some 140 political prisoners, including Dissident Iosif Begun and Psychiatrist Anatoli Koryagin, are released from exile or prison. A young West German named Matthias Rust flies his single-engine plane unmolested through hundreds of miles of Soviet airspace, landing near Red Square; Gorbachev uses the incident as occasion for a high-level shake-up of the military. Reagan and Gorbachev sign the INF agreement at the Washington summit in December and declare their intention to meet in 1988 in Moscow, possibly to initial a treaty limiting strategic arms.

Index

About the Authors

David Aikman, who traveled across the U.S. and five European countries to gather information for various parts of this book, and who wrote the chapters on Gorbachev's childhood and his years at Moscow State University, has been a TIME correspondent for 16 years. A specialist in Soviet and Chinese affairs, and in Communism generally, he has been the magazine's bureau chief in Beijing, Moscow, Jerusalem and Eastern Europe. Born in England in 1944, he was educated at Oxford University and the University of Washington, where he received a Ph.D. in Russian and Chinese history. Aikman is the author of *Pacific Rim: Area of Change, Area of Opportunity* (Little, Brown; 1986) and the editor of *Love China Today* (Tyndale House; 1978). He is currently writing a novel.

George Church, who wrote the chapter on Raisa Gorbachev, is a senior writer for TIME. Born in Union City, N.J., in 1931, he holds a bachelor's degree from Manhattan College, and attended the graduate school of communications at Syracuse University. He began his career in journalism as a copyboy for the New York *Times*. He worked for the *Wall Street Journal* as a reporter, Pittsburgh bureau manager and, eventually, news editor. Since joining TIME in 1969, he has written more than 80 cover stories, including the 1987 Man of the Year story on which this book is based.

Sally B. Donnelly, principal researcher for the project, is a reporter-researcher in TIME's World section. Born in Washington, D.C., in 1960, she graduated from Hollins College and earned a master's degree in Soviet politics from the London School of Economics. She also holds a certificate in Russian from the State Pedagogical Institute in Leningrad. She has specialized in Soviet affairs since coming to TIME in 1985.

James O. Jackson, who did the Moscow-based reporting for the book and wrote the chapters on Gorbachev's years in the Kremlin, has been the Moscow bureau chief of TIME since 1985. Before that he covered Prague for United Press International and spent five years in the Soviet Union for U.P.I. and the Chicago *Tribune*. He was also the *Tribune's* London bureau chief, deputy editorial-page editor and foreign editor. Born in Santa Fe, N. Mex., in 1939, he graduated in journalism from Northwestern University and was a Nieman Fellow at Harvard University, studying Soviet affairs. He is the author of a novel, *Dzerzhinsky Square* (St. Martin's; 1986).

John Kohan, who traveled to Stavropol and wrote the chapter on Gorbachev's years there, is a TIME correspondent based in Bonn. He was previously an associate editor in the magazine's World section, where he wrote cover stories on Soviet Leaders Yuri Andropov, Konstantin Chernenko and Mikhail Gorbachev. Born in Upper Darby, Pa., in 1952, he has studied at the University of Virginia, Leningrad State University and Columbia University, where he received a master's degree in Slavic languages and literature. A fluent Russian speaker, he has visited the Soviet Union many times as a participant in exchange programs and youth conferences and as a journalist.

Donald Morrison, who edited the book and wrote the chapter on a day in the life of Gorbachev, is the senior editor in charge of the TIME World section. In 20 years with the magazine, he has written and edited in virtually every department and was most recently a senior editor of TIME's international editions. Born in Alton, Ill., in 1946, he has a bachelor's degree from the University of Pennsylvania and was a Thouron Fellow at the London School of Economics, from which he received a master's degree in comparative government with emphasis on Soviet affairs.

Thomas A. Sancton, who wrote the chapter on Gorbachev's visit to the U.S., is an associate editor in TIME's World section. He has also been a Paris-based associate editor for the magazine's international editions. He is the author of major stories on Soviet and East European subjects, including the 1981 Man of the Year story on Poland's Lech Walesa and three cover stories about Gorbachev. Born in Jackson, Miss., in 1949, he holds a bachelor's degree from Harvard University, and as a Rhodes scholar at Oxford University, earned a doctorate in European history.

Strobe Talbott, who wrote the introduction, has been the Washington bureau chief of TIME since 1984. He was previously the magazine's diplomatic correspondent and has also covered the White House, the State Department and Eastern Europe. Born in Dayton, Ohio, in 1946, he was educated at Yale University and awarded a Rhodes scholarship to Oxford. He translated and edited two volumes of Nikita Khrushchev's memoirs, published by Little, Brown in 1970 and 1974. Talbott is the author of three books, *Endgame: The Inside Story of SALT II* (Harper & Row; 1979), *The Russians and Reagan* (Random House/Vintage; 1984) and *Deadly Gambits: The Reagan Administration and the Stalemate in Nuclear Arms Control* (Knopf; 1984). He is the coauthor, with Michael Mandelbaum, of *Reagan and Gorbachev* (Random House/Vintage; 1987). His latest book, on the career of Paul Nitze and the history of arms control, will be published by Knopf at the end of 1988.